THE REVELS PLAYS

Founder Editor, 1958-71: Clifford Leech
General Editors: F. David Hoeniger, E. A. J. Honigmann
and J. R. Mulryne

THE DUCHESS OF MALFI

THE
TRAGEDY

OF THE DVTCHESSE
Of Malfy.

As it was Presented priuatly, at the Black-Friers; and publiquely at the Globe, By the Kings Maiesties Seruants.

The perfect and exact Coppy, with diuerse *things Printed, that the length of the Play would* not beare in the Presentment.

VVritten by *John Webster.*

Flora.——— *Si quid——*
——— *Candidus Imperti si non his vtere mecum.*

Jo: yates .

LONDON:

Printed by NICHOLAS OKES, for IOHN
WATERSON, and are to be sold at the
signe of the Crowne, in *Paules*
Church-yard, 1623.

The Duchess of Malfi

JOHN WEBSTER

EDITED BY
JOHN RUSSELL BROWN

THE REVELS PLAYS

MANCHESTER
UNIVERSITY PRESS

Introduction, critical apparatus, etc,
© John Russell Brown 1974

This edition first published by Methuen & Co. 1964 and
reprinted 1969; reprinted in paper covers 1969,
1970, 1972, 1974, 1975
Reprinted by Manchester University Press 1976, 1977

Manchester University Press
Oxford Road, Manchester, M13 9PL
ISBN 0 7190 1608 8

North America
The Johns Hopkins University Press
Baltimore, Maryland 21218

Printed in Great Britain by
Unwin Brothers Limited
The Gresham Press, Old Woking, Surrey, England

To

PAUL HARMAN

GEOFFREY HUTCHINGS

and

ROSEMARY KERNAN

General Editor's Preface

The Revels Plays began to appear in 1958, and in the General Editor's Preface included in the first few volumes the plan of the series was briefly sketched. All those concerned in the undertaking recognized that no rigid pattern could be proposed in advance: to some extent the collective experience of the editors would affect the series as it developed, and the textual situation was by no means uniform among the plays that we hoped to include. The need for flexibility is still recognized, and each editor indicates in his introduction the procedures that have seemed best in relation to his particular play.

Nevertheless, we were fairly convinced that in some matters our policy would remain constant, and no major change in any of these respects has been made. The introduction to each volume includes a discussion of the provenance of the text, the play's stage-history and reputation, its significance as a contribution to dramatic literature, and its place within the work of its author. The text is based on a fresh examination of the early editions. Modern spelling is used, archaic forms being preserved only when rhyme or metre demands them or when a modernized form would not give the required sense or would obscure a play upon words. The procedure adopted in punctuation varies to some extent according to the degree of authority which an editor can attribute to the punctuation of the copy-text, but in every instance it is intended that the punctuation used in a Revels volume should not obscure a dramatic or rhetorical suggestiveness which may be discerned in the copy. Editorial stage-directions are enclosed in square brackets. The collation aims at making clear the grounds for an editor's choice wherever the original or a frequently accepted modern reading has been departed from. Annotations attempt to explain difficult passages and to provide such comments and illustrations of usage as the editor considers desirable.

When the series was planned, it was intended that each volume should include a glossary. At an early stage, however, it was realized that this would mean either an arbitrary distribution of material between the glossary and the annotations or a duplication of material. It has therefore become our practice to dispense with a glossary but to include an index to the annotations, which avoids duplication and facilitates reference.

Act-divisions are employed if they appear in the copy-text or if the structure of the play clearly points to a five-act division. In other instances, only scene-numbers are inserted. All act- and scene-indications which do not derive from the copy-text are given unobtrusively in square brackets. In no instance is an editorial indication of locality introduced into a scene-heading. When an editor finds it necessary to comment on the location of a scene, this is done in the annotations.

The series continues to use the innovation in line-numbering that was introduced in the first volume. Stage-directions which occur on lines separate from the text are given the number of the immediately preceding line followed by a decimal point and 1, 2, 3, etc. Thus 163.5 indicates the fifth line of a stage-direction following line 163 of the scene. At the beginning of a scene the lines of a stage-direction are numbered 0.1, 0.2, etc.

The Revels Plays have begun with the re-editing of a number of the best-known tragedies and comedies of the later Elizabethan and Jacobean years, and there are many such plays to which the techniques of modern editing need to be applied. It is hoped, however, that the series will be able to include certain lesser-known plays which remain in general neglect despite the lively interest that an acquaintance with them can arouse.

It has always been in the forefront of attention that the plays included should be such as deserve and indeed demand performance. The editors have therefore given a record (necessarily incomplete) of modern productions; in the annotations there is, moreover, occasional conjecture on the way in which a scene or a piece of stage-business was done on the original stage. Perhaps, too, the absence of indications of locality and of editorial scene-headings will suggest the advantage of achieving in a modern theatre some approach to the characteristic fluidity of scene and the neutrality of acting-space that Shakespeare's fellows knew.

CLIFFORD LEECH

Toronto, 1963

Contents

GENERAL EDITOR'S PREFACE   *page* vii

PREFACE   xiii

ABBREVIATIONS   xv

INTRODUCTION

    1. John Webster and the King's Men   xvii
    2. Sources   xxvii
    3. The Tragedy   xli
    4. Theatre Productions   lv
    5. The Text   lix

THE DUCHESS OF MALFI   1

APPENDICES

    I. Reprint from Painter's *Palace of Pleasure*   175
    II. The Music   210
    III. Webster's Imitation; an index   214

INDEX TO ANNOTATIONS   217

Frontispiece: The title page of the 1623 Quarto. Reproduced by courtesy of the Trustees of the British Museum.

Preface

This Revels Plays edition of *The Duchess of Malfi* is planned as a companion to *The White Devil* in the same series.

As a student of Webster I have been helped in many ways, by Professor F. P. Wilson, under whom I first started to work, by my colleagues, students, and friends at Birmingham and Stratford-upon-Avon, and by Dr Gunnar Boklund, Professor Fredson Bowers, Mr John Crow, Professor G. B. Howarth, Dr George Hunter, Professor F. W. Sternfeld, Professor R. K. Turner, Jr., and Mr Patrick Wymark. Three debts are specifically concerned with preparing this book: to Mr David Greer for the Appendix on the music; to my wife, Hilary, for much of the work on Appendix I and for help with the proofs; and to the General Editor of the Revels Plays, Professor Clifford Leech, for his forbearance and most generous and scrupulous criticism at all times. The pleasures of my studies have been greatly increased by this co-operation; I shall always be grateful.

The opportunity to direct a production of *The Duchess of Malfi* I owe to the Guild Theatre Group of Birmingham University: for this, as for many other opportunities of working in a theatre, I am most grateful to the Group and appreciative of its talents, enthusiasm, and capacity for taking pains.

JOHN RUSSELL BROWN

Birmingham, April 1963

Abbreviations

Abbott	E. A. Abbott, *A Shakespearian Grammar* (1879).
A.T.	W. Alexander, *The Alexandrean Tragedy* (1607).
Bentley	G. E. Bentley, *The Jacobean and Caroline Stage* (1941–56), 5 vols.
Boklund, *Duchess*	G. Boklund, *The Duchess of Malfi: Sources, Themes, Characters* (1962).
Dent	R. W. Dent, *John Webster's Borrowing* (1960).
Eliz. Stage	E. K. Chambers, *The Elizabethan Stage* (1923), 4 vols.
Dekker, *Dramatic Wks*	T. Dekker, *Dramatic Works*, ed. F. Bowers (1953–61), 4 vols.
Dekker, *Wks*	T. Dekker, *Non-Dramatic Works*, ed. A. B. Grosart (1884–6), 5 vols.
J.C.	W. Alexander, *Julius Caesar* (1607).
Jonson, *Wks*	*Ben Jonson*, ed. C. H. Herford and P. and Evelyn Simpson (1925–52), 11 vols.
Libr.	*The Library.*
Lucas	J. Webster, *Works*, ed. F. L. Lucas (1927), 4 vols.
Marston, *Wks*	J. Marston, *Plays*, ed. H. Harvey Wood (1934–9), 3 vols.
M.L.R.	*Modern Language Review.*
N. & Q.	*Notes and Queries.*
Nashe, *Wks*	T. Nashe, *Works*, ed. R. B. McKerrow (1904–10), 5 vols.
O.E.D.	*Oxford English Dictionary.*

PMLA	*Publications of the Modern Language Association of America.*
P.Q.	*Philological Quarterly.*
Pettie	S. Guazzo, *Civil Conversation*, tr. G. Pettie (ed., 1925).
R.E.S.	*The Review of English Studies.*
Revels, *W.D.*	John Webster, *The White Devil*, Revels Plays Edition (1960); ed. J. R. Brown.
S.B.	*Studies in Bibliography.*
Sh.S.	*Shakespeare Survey.*
Sidney, *Wks*	P. Sidney, *Works*, ed. A. Feuillerat (1912–26), 4 vols.
Tilley	M. P. Tilley, *A Dictionary of the Proverbs in England in the Sixteenth and Seventeenth Centuries* (1950).
T.L.S.	*The Times Literary Supplement.*
Wm. Shakespeare	E. K. Chambers, *William Shakespeare: a Study of Facts and Problems* (1930), 2 vols.

John Webster's plays are abbreviated as follows:

A.Q.L.	*Anything for a Quiet Life.*
A.V.	*Appius and Virginia.*
C.C.	*A Cure for a Cuckold.*
D.L.C.	*The Devil's Law Case.*
D.M.	*The Duchess of Malfi.*
N.Ho	*Northward Ho.*
W.D.	*The White Devil.*
W.Ho	*Westward Ho.*
Wyatt	*Sir Thomas Wyatt.*

For *The White Devil*, all references and quotations are from the Revels Plays edition, but for all Webster's other works (except *The Duchess*) quotations are from first editions and references to Lucas' edition or Bowers' Dekker.

Shakespeare's plays and poems are abbreviated as in C. T. Onions' *A Shakespeare Glossary* (ed. 1941); all quotations are from the Globe Shakespeare (ed. 1911), unless otherwise stated.

Introduction

Date

In 1612 *The White Devil* was published, 'as acted' by the Queen's Majesty's Men, and John Webster worked on a successor, *The Duchess of Malfi*. Several books published that year were used as sources for its dialogue, as Chapman's *Seven Penitential Psalms*, adapted from Petrarch, and Donne's *Second Anniversary, Of the Progress of the Soul*. Perhaps Webster was half-way through the main draft when Pierre Matthieu's *Life and Death of Henry IV*, translated by Edward Grimeston, and Thomas Adams' sermon, *The Gallant's Burden*, were published, for these two books were used as sources only in Act III and later. Adams' sermon was entered in the Stationers' Register, as a preliminary to publication, on 1 May, so the last Acts of *The Duchess* could not have been written earlier than some time that month. Probably Webster was working on Act III in late November or December of 1612, for he took time off from play-writing to provide an elegy for Prince Henry, who had died on 6 November, which has numerous echoes of *The Duchess*, especially of its third Act[1]; this *Monumental Column* (registered on 25 December 1612 and published the following year) draws on the same works by Donne, Chapman, and Matthieu.

The first performance of *The Duchess* must have been earlier than 16 December 1614, for William Ostler, who first acted Antonio, died on that day.[2] But it is likely that writing continued throughout 1613. There are unmistakable borrowings from Sidney's *Arcadia* from III. ii onwards, and this Elizabethan work was

[1] So Lucas, II. 2 and III. 286–90; for Webster's borrowings, see Dent, *passim*, and App. III.

[2] So C. W. Wallace, *The Times* (2 and 4 Oct. 1909).

reprinted, after a nine-year interval, in 1613. Some ideas for the madmen of IV. ii may have come from the masques performed for the marriage of James I's daughter, Elizabeth, to the Elector Palatine in February 1613.[1] And a reference to the 'transportation' of grain in the same scene would be particularly appropriate after the poor harvest that year.[2] There may even have been time to borrow from Sir Thomas Overbury's *Wife* (1614) and the accompanying Characters which were not entered in the Stationers' Register until 13 December 1613; but, although *The Duchess* has some close echoes[3] of this publication, they occur throughout and may have come from a reading of manuscript versions, or from Webster's influence on Overbury. Webster was to write new 'Characters' for an enlarged edition of 1615 which maintained the plan of the original volume. The most likely dates for the first performance of *The Duchess* are the spring or autumn of 1614, or perhaps the winter of 1613–14.

The First Performance

When *The Duchess of Malfi* was published in 1623, the title-page announced that it had been 'presented privately, at the Blackfriars, and publicly at the Globe, by the King's Majesty's Servants'. The change from the Queen's Men who had presented Webster's earlier tragedy represented a considerable gain in prestige. The King's Men were popular at Court, the Chamber of Accounts showing that they gave 109 performances there between the autumn of 1609 and the spring of 1616, when all the other companies together were responsible for only seventy-two.[4]

The membership of the King's Men when *The Duchess of Malfi* was performed is fairly well established, so that the list of 'Actors' Names' prefixed to the first edition can be interpreted with some precision. Of John Lowin, who leads as Bosola, James Wright has left a record which dates from after 1630: then he 'used to act, with mighty applause, Falstaff; Morose; Vulpone; and Mammon in the

---

[1] Cf. below, pp. xxxvi–xxxvii. See also p. xxxv for a possible debt in v. iii to a poem of 1612.

[2] See IV. ii. 56, note.   [3] See App. III, and annotations.

[4] See Malone Society, *Collections VI* (1962), pp. 48–68.

Alchemist; Melancius in the *Maid's Tragedy*'.[1] He also played the title rôle of *Henry VIII* (and, according to Downes' *Roscius Anglicanus*, 'had his Instructions from Mr. Shakespeare himself'), and in 1604 he had acted in Webster's Induction to *The Malcontent*. In a revival of *The Wild Goose Chase* in 1632, the part of 'Belleur . . . of a stout blunt humour' was said to have been 'most naturally acted by Mr. John Lowin'.[2] When *The Duchess* was first performed he was thirty-seven or eight years of age.

For Ferdinand, the cardinal, and Antonio, the list of actors gives two performers each, numbered 1 and 2, and, since it includes Ostler, the first cast is probably that of the first production. Richard Burbage, who created Ferdinand, was the foremost actor of his time. His repute is attested in many allusions and verses, and Jeronimo, Richard III, Othello, Hamlet, Lear, and Malevole (in *The Malcontent*) are his other known roles. His portrait at Dulwich College[3] suggests that he had the refinement and sensibility of a Hamlet, while his rôles of Lear and Othello imply vocal and physical strength as well. An Elegy of 1619 praises the 'just weight' of his delivery and his 'Inchaunting toung', and also gives grounds for believing that he could bring to Ferdinand's passion and madness an illusion of reality: he could act:

> . . . a sadd Louer, with so true an Eye
> That theer I would haue sworne, he meant to dye.[4]

He brought a mature art to Ferdinand—in fiction, the twin of a boy-actor's Duchess—for he was then at least forty years old.

Of Condell, the first Cardinal, Underwood the Delio, Tooley who appears opposite Forobosco, perhaps in error for Malateste,[5] and of Ostler, little is known except that Ostler was called 'the Roscius of these times' by John Davies in his *Scourge of Folly* (*c.* 1611), and that Tooley claimed in his will that Burbage had been his master. Except for Condell, these men were of a younger genera-

---

[1] *Historia Histrionica* (1699); quoted *Eliz. Stage*, IV. 371.

[2] For a full account of his possible rôles, see Bentley, II. 499–506.

[3] Reproduced in *Wm. Shakespeare*, I. 76.

[4] Quoted *Eliz. Stage*, II. 309; the full elegy is in E. Nungezer, *A Dictionary of Actors* (1929), pp. 74–6.

[5] See below, pp. lxvii–lxviii.

tion than Lowin or Burbage, Ostler and Underwood being members of the Chapel Company of boy-actors in 1601.

At least two of the cast named in the first edition can hardly have appeared in the first production. John Rice, the Pescaro, was only a boy in the company in 1610, when he played a nymph in a pageant. By 1611 he had left to join Lady Elizabeth's Men and there is no certain evidence that he rejoined his earlier company before 1619. In any event, an actor in his teens would have been too slight for the 'noble old fellow' Pescaro (v. i. 60) in a cast that included Burbage, Lowin, and Condell. Thomas Pollard, the Silvio, did not join the King's Men until within a year or two of 1615 when he was about twenty; so this actor, who was later to gain considerable success in comic rôles, was probably a young Silvio in some revival of The Duchess, and named in the printed cast for the sake of his later reputation.

Richard Sharp, the only actor assigned to the rôle of the Duchess, is known to have played young romantic leads from 1625 until his death in January 1632. If he was then in his twenties, he must have been about eleven or twelve when The Duchess was first performed, and possibly too young for such a large part. At that time Richard Robinson was the leading boy-actor of the company and would have been the obvious choice; perhaps his name was omitted for the part because he had already figured in the list as the actor who later took over the Cardinal from Condell. Numerous references to Robinson in female rôles have survived from 1611 to 1616, whereas the earliest to Sharp, if the cast list of The Duchess is discounted, dates from 1616. The talents of 'Dick Robinson' have been described by Ben Jonson in The Devil is an Ass (1616), telling the story of a masquerade in real-life as a lawyer's wife:

> to see him behaue it;
> And lay the law; and carue; and drinke vnto 'hem;
> And then talke baudy: and send frolicks! O!
>
> (II. viii. 71–3)

Robinson is named in the 1623 Folio of Shakespeare's works, among the 'Principall Actors in all these Playes'. Of Sharp little is known, although Professor Baldwin has argued that he was physically rather large, and apt for the proud and queenly heroines of Fletcher.[1]

While Sharp's assignment to the duchess probably refers to a revival close to the date of publication, John Thompson's to Julia must certainly do so. Not until 1621 did this boy-actor start to play a series of female rôles in Fletcher's plays, and he was still in skirts ten years later. Robert Pallant, 'the younger', who seems to have played both Cariola and the doctor,[2] was just nine years' old in September 1614,[3] so while he may have been an inexperienced Cariola in the first performance, he could not have played the doctor; perhaps he played both rôles in a revival when he was sixteen or seventeen.

In any reconstruction of the first performance of *The Duchess* the female parts will appear less interesting than the rôles played by Lowin and Burbage, about whom so much is known. But two members of early audiences have testified in their commendatory verses that the impersonal and transient art of a boy-actor had made the greatest effect; for Middleton and Rowley, the enactment of the duchess herself was the pathetic and eloquent centre of the play, and proof of Webster's genius.

Although most readers of this introduction will be familiar with models and pictures of 'Shakespeare's Globe', research has established few facts about the 'public' theatre at which *The Duchess* was performed.[4] It seems to have been a traditional building, reminiscent of inn yards and bear-baiting arenas, and basically similar to the Curtain or Red Bull where *The White Devil* had been produced. But it was larger, and, especially after rebuilding in 1613, finer and more elaborately equipped. Above two thousand spectators could be accommodated on three or four sides of the stage; some sat in the

---

[1] T. W. Baldwin, *The Organization and Personnel of the Shakespeare Company* (1927).

[2] See below, p. lxviii, and note 1.   [3] Cf. Bentley, II. 520.

[4] J. C. Adams, *The Globe Playhouse* (1942), and I. Smith, *Shakespeare's Globe Playhouse* (1956), are highly speculative despite their detailed measurements and drawings; C. W. Hodges, *The Globe Restored* (1953), is, frankly, an artist's attempt to go beyond the known facts. A. M. Nagler, *Shakespeare's Stage* (1958), is a succinct discussion of both the Globe and Blackfriars which carefully distinguishes between certainty and conjecture.

'lords' rooms' and galleries, and many stood in the upper galleries and in the open yard. Professor J. C. Adams has calculated that the stage was forty-three feet wide and twenty-nine deep, and certainly there was plenty of space for processions, crowd scenes, 'shows', and battles. Yet the encircling audience could also give an effect of concentration or intensity, as described by Webster himself in the *Character* of 'An Excellent Actor' (1615):

> sit in a full Theater, and you will thinke you see so many lines drawne from the circumference of so many eares whiles the *Actor* is the *Center*.

Its stage had an upper terrace or balcony, a curtained recess or enclosure, at least two doors opening from the tiring-house, one on each side, and one or more trap-doors in the main stage. An actor could be lowered mechanically from the 'heavens', or 'roof', that covered most of the acting area.

The Blackfriars 'private' theatre differed from the Globe in important ways. It was constructed in an enclosed hall, measuring only sixty-six by forty-four feet. A full audience probably numbered six or seven hundred, all of whom were seated in the pit or galleries, with a few on the stage itself. This stage seems to have been a smaller version of the Globe's, but it was lit by torches and candles. The auditorium could be darkened by covering its windows.[1]

The King's Men had first used the Blackfriars in 1609 and they may have tried to develop a 'new kind of play for the new theatre and audience'.[2] Certainly there are several indications that *The Duchess of Malfi* was written with its special opportunities in mind. Although the presence-chamber scenes and the dumb show of III. iv are similar to elaborate episodes in *The White Devil*, there are passages of action and dialogue which are more intimate, still, or quiet than anything in the earlier play, and more appropriate to a small enclosed auditorium in which spectators were comfortably seated. Silence is used several times to intensify pathos or terror.[3]

---

[1] An excellent, brief account of this theatre is W. A. Armstrong, *Elizabethan Private Theatres* (Society for Theatre Research, 1958).

[2] G. E. Bentley, *Sh.S.*, 1 (1948), 40 and ff.   [3] See below, p. lv.

Still more noticeable is the five-act form into which the narrative has been shaped. *The White Devil* has a continuous movement so that the single natural pause is between Acts IV and V. But *The Duchess* has important time-gaps between each Act, and Webster has been particularly criticized for giving only a slight indication in the text of the several years that pass between Acts II and III. The choice of this new form can be explained, and Webster's stage-craft vindicated, if the play had been designed primarily for the Blackfriars where it was a regular custom to play music between the acts.[1] *The Duchess* was not forcibly made to fit this practice; rather it depends upon it and the resultant interludes.[2] Modern productions that do not mark four intervals in some analogous manner are usually faulted for obscurity of action or characterization.[3] And thirdly, Webster seems to require a lighting device that would have been impossible at the Globe. Of course night-scenes were common at the open-air theatres where darkness could be implied by words, acting or the carrying of torches and lanterns, but the incident of the dead man's hand, following the line 'Take hence the lights' in IV. i of *The Duchess*, has a shock effect that depends on a partially darkened stage. If the duchess had to kiss a dead man's hand 'affectionately' (l. 45) in full daylight and, more than that, remain silent throughout Ferdinand's lingering speech that follows, the boy-actor would have been hard pressed to maintain any illusion of life-like playing, no matter how 'unrealistic' his style. And his effort would have brought little reward of emotional response, no sudden horror for the audience on 'Hah! lights! O, horrible!', and little pathos when Ferdinand's 'Let her have lights enough' is followed by the duchess' broken and now understanding words, 'What witchcraft doth he practise . . .' What would be difficult, clumsy, and grotesque at the Globe, could be thrilling and sensitive in the darkened auditorium of the Blackfriars. Ben Jonson's *Catiline*, first produced by the King's Men in 1611, has a stage-direction '*A dark-nesse comes ouer the place*' (I. i. 312–14); the text implies that this effect was gradual, but six lines later '*A fiery light appeares*'. Jonson

---

[1] Cf. J. Isaacs, *Production and Stage-Management at the Blackfriars Theatre* (1933), p. 13.

[2] See below, pp. xlii–xliii and liv–lv.   [3] See below, p. lix.

and Webster may have been at one in exploiting some simple opportunities of the Blackfriars.[1]

Subsequent Events

After *The Duchess*, Webster probably wrote a play which is now lost, called *The Guise*, and in 1616 or 1617 *The Devil's Law Case*, a tragi-comedy of citizens, lawyers, and young noblemen. Then followed a Lord Mayor's Pageant and several plays in collaboration with Ford, Rowley, Dekker, Middleton, and, perhaps, Massinger and Heywood. But the close of his career, like its beginning, is hard to trace among the uncertainties of collaboration and plays which are lost or have never been highly regarded. He probably died some time in the early sixteen-thirties.[2]

But the two tragedies had already secured Webster's reputation. He was satirized in Fitzjeffrey's 'Notes from Black-Fryers' in 1618,[3] praised in commendatory verses published with *The Duchess*, and associated with Fletcher as a 'learned' poet in Heywood's *Hierarchy of the Blessed Angels* (1634). An *Elegy on Randolph's Finger*, written in the early 1630s by William Heminges, son of Shakespeare's fellow actor, pictures 'the Malfy dutches' drawn 'sadly on her way' with a great following of mourners, while verses on 'Mr. Webster's most excellent Tragedy, called The White Devill', published by Samuel Sheppard in his *Epigrams* (1651), rates it above all the tragedies of Euripides and Sophocles. In 1631 *The White Devil* was reprinted with a title-page proclaiming that it had been 'diuers times Acted, by the Queenes Maiesties seruants, at the Phoenix, in Drury Lane'; this company had been formed in 1625 or the following year. A second edition of *The Duchess of Malfi* did not appear until 1640, but this tragedy was also revived within Webster's lifetime.

Probably there were at least two revivals before its publication in 1623. The first record is a description of a performance by Orazio Busino, an Italian visitor to London[4]; this is dated 7 February 1618

---

[1] See also the lighting-effect in *The Second Maiden's Tragedy*, also performed by the King's Men in 1611; p. xxxv, below.

[2] See Revels, *W.D.*, pp. xxiii–xxv.

[3] Reprinted, Revels, *W.D.*, p. xxiv.

[4] In his *Anglopotrida*; quoted in *Eliz. Stage*, III. 511, and Lucas, II. 172.

but may refer to an earlier occasion. As a Jacobean account of Webster's play it is disappointing; either Busino misunderstood and misrepresented what he saw, or he invented from hearsay. Perhaps he had seen an adaptation or a revision of the text that was later published, but even then some inaccuracy is implied when he runs together the deaths of Julia and the Duchess. A later revival is indicated by the list of Actors' Names in the first edition. Here Joseph Taylor replaces Burbage as Ferdinand, and this actor did not join the King's Men until after Burbage's death on 13 March 1619. The assignment of John Thompson to Julia suggests a date a little after 1619, for other records of this boy-actor begin in 1621. After publication the play was again revived, being performed before the King on 26 December 1630 in the new Cockpit Theatre at Whitehall.[1]

Several scholars have argued that the printed version of *The Duchess* contains passages added for an early revival. Their theses are made both plausible and uncertain by Webster's habit of incorporating lines from his commonplace book. So, when Antonio says:

> Last, for his brother, there, the cardinal—
> They that do flatter him most say oracles
> Hang at his lips. . . .   (I. i. 183–5)

Rupert Brooke could argue that this was a late addition, for Antonio had already given a finished verbal portrait of the cardinal and had passed on to depict Ferdinand.[2] But now we know that this detail is one of several borrowings from Hall's *Characters* (1608), and is only a little more obviously an embellishment than several others from the same source.[3] The fact that a passage can be detached from its context is no indication in this play of a later addition; Webster's final draft of 1613 or 1614 may have occasionally resembled a mosaic. When suspected lines seem to imply a date of composition later than 1614, the argument is obviously stronger. There are two instances of this, the first at the very beginning: 'How do you like the French court?—I admire it . . .' At one time it was confidently asserted that Antonio's lengthy reply must refer to Louis XIII's *coup d'état* on 24 April 1617, in which Concino Concini, Maréchal

---

[1] Cf. Folger MS., 2068.8; quoted Bentley, I. 27–8.
[2] Cf. *John Webster* (1916), p. 247.   [3] See App. III.

d'Ancre, was murdered in order to free the palace from an 'infamous' sycophant and adventurer. The affair made a great impression in England, as Professor Stoll and Mr Lucas have shown, but there is no need to think that Webster referred to it. The whole passage is borrowed from Sir Thomas Elyot's *Image of Governance* of 1541, or some other early book, and a further passage in the same scene (ll. 398–403), which is so closely integrated that it could hardly be an addition to the original version, was taken from the same source. Moreover, some reference to France must always have stood at the beginning of the play, for without this account of Antonio's visit abroad two later references (i. i. 140–2 and ii. i. 118–25) would have been markedly obscure. Like many writers, including Montaigne, Bacon, Sidney, and Justus Lipsius,[1] Webster was plainly concerned with the probity of the courtiers years before the Concini affair; his development of Flamineo and Bosola from the slightest suggestions in his sources testifies to this, and so does his treatment of Antonio, as well as some lines in his elegy on Prince Henry, beginning:

> Those men that followed him were not by friends:
> Or letters prefer'd to him: he made choice
> In action, not in complementall voice. . . .   (ll. 99–101)

The disputed passage has sufficient reference to the following entries of Bosola and the cardinal, and to the general interest of the play, without a topical reference to events in France. There is no need to believe that the lines were written after Webster first sent his manuscript to the players. The second disputed passage is near the end of the play:

> I do glory
> That thou, which stood'st like a huge pyramid
> Begun upon a large and ample base,
> Shalt end in a little point, a kind of nothing.   (v. v. 76–9)

This, it has been said, is borrowed from Part ii of *Don Quixote*, which was published in Spanish in 1615, and translated into French in 1618 and into English in 1620.[2] But Professor Dent has argued

---

[1] Cf. J. R. Brown, *P.Q.*, xxxi (1952), 358–62.
[2] So T. M. Todd, *M.L.R.*, li (1956), 321–3.

that Cervantes and Webster could easily have shared a common source[1] and, indeed, the similarities may well have been coincidental: the pyramids were commonly cited as examples of man's pride,[2] and a comparison between their diminishing size and a loss of strength before death was made elsewhere by Webster in 1615, the year when Part II of *Don Quixote* was published: a virtuous widow 'stands like an ancient Piramid', he wrote, 'which the lesse it growes to mans eye, the nearer it reaches to heauen'.[3] Again there is no proof that Webster added to his text for one of the early revivals of *The Duchess*.

2. SOURCES

Painter's 'Palace of Pleasure'

The story of the Duchess of Malfi was told by Matteo Bandello as his twenty-sixth *novella*: this is a clear, circumstantial account, by an author who may have been the Delio who tried to help Antonio shortly before his assassination in Milan in October 1513.[4] The Italian account was then translated and augmented to four times its length by Belleforest in his second volume of *Histoires Tragiques* (1565). Now the tale was embellished with long speeches and made an occasion for recommending traditional moral attitudes, and in this form William Painter rendered it in English, with only minor alterations of emphasis, for the second volume of his *Palace of Pleasure* (1567). It was this version that Webster used. Here, and not in Bandello, were hints of Ferdinand's fury and Cariola's protesting death, and here was the name Castruccio. *The Duchess* may possibly have two or three echoes of the wording of the Italian, but more than forty of Painter's phrases,[5] and many of these are unquestionable.

Webster accepted the main outline of Painter's story, but modi-

---

[1] See Dent, p. 264.

[2] See, for example, Pliny, *Natural History* (tr. 1601), XXXVI. xii.

[3] *Characters*, 'A Virtuous Widow'.

[4] Bandello called himself Delio in his sonnets; see Lucas, II. 11. The fullest discussion of the various versions is in Boklund, *Duchess*.

[5] For echoes of Bandello, see Boklund, *Duchess*, pp. 39–40; for echoes of Painter see the footnotes to App. I, a reprint from *The Palace*.

fied, reshaped, and elaborated it to sustain a wider interest and lead to a wider conclusion. The most obvious change is the recasting of several agents of the duchess' brothers as one person, Bosola. This at once simplified the narrative and complicated the characterization. By name, Bosola is the 'bloudy beast' who killed Antonio, but he may also be the '*Neapolitan* captaine' who avoided meeting Antonio so that he might not 'be constrained' to fulfil his charge and kill him, and so 'offende his Conscience' and 'grieue the same all the dayes of his life'; he is the 'Gaoler' who advised the duchess to 'consider vpon' her conscience immediately before she was killed by 'two Ruffians', one of whom he also represents; he is leader of the 'horsemen' who captured the duchess and deceived her with promises of safety; and he takes the place of unnamed 'espials' whom the brothers sent into her household after the birth of the second child. Webster seems to have been unafraid of the psychological problems occasioned by joining these many rôles, but gave his Bosola the marks of an ambitious malcontent and scope for commenting on corruptions in society, inventing a new character for Castruccio and developing the midwife as 'an Old Lady' to provide more victims for his lash. He also made Bosola instrumental in the deaths of both brothers immediately before his own at the end of the play, and brought him into the very first scene as a dependant on the cardinal and a spy on the duchess before her marriage. This last modification involves Webster's other major change, the introduction of both brothers in the duchess' court before her wooing and marriage, and their prominence throughout the action. Their opposition to her marriage is thus presented before the lovers meet, and their reactions are in the forefront of the drama from the start. They hear of the first child in the second Act, and this also shows the cardinal with his mistress, Julia, a character wholly Webster's invention and the wife of his Castruchio. In Painter's tale Antonio leaves his wife after they have noticed spies in their household, and she follows when she is pregnant for the third time; but Webster delayed both escapes. His third Act begins after the third birth and brings Ferdinand to Malfi once more, to break into his sister's bed-chamber and, with a strange mixture of fury, pain, and restraint, to avoid an encounter with Antonio who had just been in his wife's company; it is Ferdinand's intervention which causes Webster's Antonio to flee, and Bosola is re-introduced to encourage the duchess to follow. The meeting of husband and wife in Ancona, the occasion in Painter for an affecting speech in which the duchess tells her servants of the marriage, is not shown in the play, but the cardinal is given new prominence in this Act, in dumb show, divesting himself of clerical garments to take charge of an army and helping to banish the fugitives from Ancona. In the fourth Act, Webster prolonged the suffering of the duchess with various horrors and brought Ferdinand to the prison before and after her death. In the last Act he brought both the cardinal and Ferdinand to Milan, so that much of its action is concerned with their cunning and madness, and with their deaths: all this being without suggestion from the source.

Further changes seem directed toward two main ends. First, Webster widened the setting in which the tragedy is viewed by developing Delio to be a *confidant* and support for Antonio and by introducing his wooing of Julia in Act II and Julia's of Bosola in Act v. And to the same effect the courts of the brothers and the duchess are enlarged by Malateste as a 'sugar-candy' soldier and prospective husband, and by the sketchy characters of Silvio, Grisolan, Roderigo, court officers, a comic doctor, and the honest old soldier, the Marquis of Pescara. Further changes seem intended to ensure that the duchess is seen as clearly as possible to influence the action after her death. Webster's Antonio has something of the melancholy and ill-founded optimism of Painter's, but in addition he has been given the scene near his wife's tomb where he sees her face and hears her voice in an echo; Bosola also thinks he sees her as an apparition (v. ii. 345–6). In the last moments, Delio presents the son of Antonio and the duchess that he may be established in 'his mother's right'; this is in direct contradiction to the source, which does not mention the son after his flight from the horsemen with Antonio, but rather emphasizes that the Duke of Malfi, the duchess' son by her earlier marriage, was left without rival to his title or possessions. In creating a wider setting and giving continuous prominence to Bosola, Ferdinand, and the Cardinal, as well as to the lovers, Webster re-formed the action into five movements which are nicely judged to sustain the full range of interest.

Webster's moral judgements and his characterization have greater finesse than those of his source, and this change is pervasive. But Belleforest's version, as retold by Painter, may well have stimulated and in part directed the dramatization. Webster was given a double view of both Antonio and the duchess. In the source, the husband is 'valiant', 'well estemed amongs the best' and 'beloued' for his good graces, but also a 'poore and simple gentleman' who climbed higher than his 'force' permitted and allowed himself to 'be haled fondly forth with desire of brutal sensualitie'. Painter's duchess is a 'fine and subtile dame' who showed herself a 'foolish woman' in taking 'a husband, more to glut hir libidinous appetite, than for other occasion'; before her death, she calls herself 'innocent' and asks pardon of God for her unknown sin; she dies with dignity. The brothers survive in the source, but the narrator condemns them at last for their cruel and remorseless revenge. As the footnotes to Appendix I of this edition show fully for the first time, Webster echoed the phrasing of some of Painter's judgements: it is probable that these attitudes, in their contradictions and in their assured tone, found some place in the subtle web of motivation and moral concern of *The Duchess of Malfi*.

The White Devil

An important source of *The Duchess* was the earlier *White Devil*. Webster had a persistent and brooding mind, and for him creation often involved repetition[1]; he worked in series, like a painter who re-aligns the elements of one composition in his next to suggest less obvious inter-relations, new astringencies, or sudden simplifications of form. Within Webster's plays, scenes echo each other, and his two great tragedies, both set at court and with a central heroine, are in important ways two versions of a single subject.

The Duchess has verbal echoes, as 'the cardinal Bears himself much too cruel', 'Banish'd Ancona!' (at the beginning of a scene like the startling 'Banish'd' of *The White Devil*), 'let my son fly the courts of princes', and repeated references to the 'mist of death'.[2]

---

[1] Cf. Revels, *W.D.*, pp. xxxvii f. and l–lvii.
[2] *D.M.*, III. iv. 26–7; III. v. 1; v. iv. 72; and v. v. 94, etc.

But more than this, whole incidents seem to be based on the management of earlier ones: for example, the use of commentators upon the action, notably at the beginning of I. i, in Bosola's part of II. i and II. ii, and in III. iii; the dumb show of III. iv, bringing a public occasion to the drama like the election of the Pope in *The White Devil*; the apparitions seen by Antonio and Bosola in Act V, like the ghosts of Isabella and Brachiano; the entry of a new generation after the final slaughters. These repetitions sometimes affect characterization, for the impotent Castruchio offsets Antonio and the cardinal, as Camillo contrasted with Bracciano, and Bosola accepts Julia's courtship as Francisco did Zanche's. Bosola is clearly related to Flamineo in his ambition and satirical humour, and the Arragonian cardinal to Cardinal Monticelso. The onlookers' belief that the cardinal feigns his cries for help when Bosola is killing him brings a strange humour to the end of the play like that derived from Flamineo's game with the false pistols. At least once *The Duchess* picks up a detail and develops it so strongly that we are led to re-value its occurrence in the earlier play: this is Lodovico's passing jest 'We have brought you a masque', spoken to the doomed Vittoria and Flamineo, which, in view of the masque of madmen, Bosola's disguises, and the formal presentation of '*coffin, cords and a bell*', may suggest that the conspirators' disguise was meant to introduce a formal, ritualistic element. Perhaps the most pervasive debt to *The White Devil* is the structure of the last Act: both plays depart from their narrative source to widen and complicate the conclusion.

Viewed as a reworking of the subject-matter of its sister tragedy, *The Duchess* shows three highly significant changes. One is the provision of objects for Bosola's satire which are independent of the main action; he does not often mock the duchess' love as Flamineo does his sister's and her lover's. A second again concerns Bosola: Flamineo had felt 'a strange thing' within himself which he could only call 'compassion', and similarly, when Bosola has murdered the duchess and has been rejected by Ferdinand, he feels a new 'pity' (IV. ii. 347) and weeps; but, where Flamineo's discovery did not affect the development of the action and provided only one strand in his characterization, Bosola's is an important crisis. Climactically placed at the end of an Act, Bosola's compassion leads to penitence and an attempt to make a 'worthier' life; and it actuates a sequence of events which are a 'main' cause of the final catastrophe. The third major change is in the presentation of the death of the duchess. It was Webster's 'trade to fashion death-beds' and make 'horror look lovely', as he jestingly said of Edward, the Black Prince[1]; and, as on a battlefield, deaths usually crowd together or yield to other business so that each victim holds the stage briefly. In *The White Devil*, Vittoria shared her death-scene with Flamineo, and even Zanche; but the duchess is the centre of a long sequence of incidents. After Ferdinand has gone, Bosola is her only possible rival, and, in the second prison scene, he is disguised until after her death; her last exchanges are with anonymous executioners, and Bosola is silent. For the duchess, Webster's presentation of death is more sustained and more concentrated than ever before. By reducing the individual interest of other characters and lengthening the presentation of torture and death through two scenes, he has simplified the dramatic focus without loss of subtlety or complexity, and has enlarged the emotional and intellectual impressions of the duchess' last moments. No other character in Webster's plays holds the stage so continuously; no other single incident so dominates a whole play. The death of Vittoria is at the latest possible moment; that of the duchess in the fourth Act so that its consequences can be shown in every scene that follows.

All the major changes in echoing the earlier play are bound up with the different character and story of Webster's new heroine: to those who know *The White Devil*, they reveal the effects of these new elements upon a familiar world, and upon a familiar view of that world.

Narratives

From earlier speculation and research concerning Webster's narrative sources, Dr Gunnar Boklund has winnowed some grains, and has gleaned more on his own account. He records this investigation in *The Duchess of Malfi: Sources, Themes, Characters* (1962). So we know that from Bandello's original *novella* Webster may

---

[1] *Monumental Column*, ll. 84–6.

have taken a phrase or two (for I. i. 477 and II. v. 33–6); but we have no proof that Webster knew Italian and a fairly strong suspicion that he did not. In a translation of Simon Goulart's *Admirable and Memorable Histories* (1607), he may have read that the cardinal advised Bosola to hire a dozen *bravi* to kill Antonio (cf. v. ii. 313–14); this is the book he drew on for an account of Ferdinand's lycanthropia in the same scene (cf. v. ii. 5–19, and note). The military career of the cardinal, probably suggested by a comparison to Pope Julius II at the end of Painter's tale (App. I, p. 208), may have been elaborated by reference to Guicciardini's well-known *History of Italy*, translated by Fenton in 1579 and reprinted in 1599, especially its accounts of Julius and of Cardinal San Severin.[1]

Of tales concerning other characters or times, Webster made some little use. Professor Mario Praz has suggested that Ferdinand's trick with the severed hand (IV. i) may derive ultimately from Herodotus' account of a thief escaping in the dark by leaving a dead man's hand in the captor's grasp; Webster could have read this in Bandello, in the *novella* immediately preceding that of the duchess, or in B. Riche's English translation of *The Famous History of Herodotus* (1584).[2] Again, if he could read Italian or some translation was available, Webster may have taken some hints from a *novella* about Oronte's love for the King of Persia's daughter, Orbecche, which was told in Cinthio's *Ecatommiti*; here was a secret marriage followed by flight, imprisonment, and deaths, in which the husband, supposing he is reconciled, returns to the king's palace, the wife is shown his dead body and those of their children, one of the boys groans as he returns to life for a moment (cf. IV. ii. 347–53), and the king twice assures his daughter that she is forgiven only to make his ultimate revenge more terrible (cf. IV. i. 31–3). Dr Boklund believes that this is a source for Act IV, rather than Lope de Vega's play, *El Mayordomo de la Duquesa de Amalfi*, which has similar, but less numerous, parallels and can offer in addition only the device of making Antonio's departure appear the consequence of a fault, here fornication not peculation as in *The*

---

[1] See Boklund, *Duchess*, pp. 33 and 47–9.
[2] Cf. *T.L.S.* (18 June 1954) and Boklund, *Duchess*, pp. 28–9.

Duchess. While none of these debts is certain, Webster undoubt-edly borrowed many phrases from Sidney's *Arcadia*[1] and some from its account of how Queen Cecropia imprisoned and tortured the sisters, Pamela and Philoclea: Webster therefore read this epi-sode and it would not be surprising if he took some suggestions for his play's action. Cecropia terrifies the two princesses by noise and darkness; she forces Philoclea to watch the execution of a lady who is apparently her sister and shows Pamela Philoclea's head appar-ently severed from her body; and she watches her victims as they are broken by these horrors and wish to die, Pamela refusing to eat (cf. IV. i. 76). Queen Erona's majesty in adversity in Book II, Chap-ter xxix of *Arcadia* provided Webster with several phrases that he used so consistently of the duchess in prison that this episode should also be considered a narrative source as well as a mine of rich 'sentences'.

Webster seems to have searched farthest for incidents that would extend the torture and death of the duchess, which is a brief episode in Painter, and that would bring Ferdinand into these scenes.

Plays and Masques

In the preface to *The White Devil* Webster wished that he might be 'read by the light' of Chapman, Jonson, Beaumont, Fletcher, Shakespeare, Dekker, and Heywood, and so indicated something of his debt to other dramatists. Professor Bogard's *The Tragic Satire of John Webster* (1955) traces the influence of Chapman and Marston, and the Revels Plays edition of *The White Devil* has a brief account of Webster's imitation of a wide range of plays, both well-known and neglected today (pp. xxxviii–xlii). In *The Duchess*, reflections of Chapman, Jonson, Fletcher, Marston, and Shake-speare may often be caught by someone familiar with the plays of the period. Some verbal echoes are indexed in Appendix III to this edition, and others are noticed in the annotations.[2] But, in the main, this is a general debt, of theatrical technique, language, character-ization, form, and subject-matter.

Two groups of borrowings, however, require separate notice. One lies behind the echo-scene (v. iii). The device itself was com-

---

[1] See App. III.   [2] See, especially, at III. ii. 141 and V. v. 0.1.

mon—Dekker's *Old Fortunatus*, Jonson's *Cynthia's Revels*, and the
anonymous *2 Return from Parnassus* have some of the better echo-
scenes—and R. Scot's *Discovery of Witchcraft* (1584), xv. xli, had
noted, like Delio (ll. 8–9), that an echo can be supposed 'a spirit that
answereth'. The manner in which the scene allows the duchess to
return from death may have been taken from George Wither's
Prince Henry's Obsequies, published in 1612; in this poem, on the
same occasion as Webster's *Monumental Column*, there is a 'supposed interlocution' in which a personified 'Great Britain' first
hears the deceased prince speaking in an Echo, but then '*The Spirit
leaues his Eccho and speakes on*' (E1). The odd thing about Webster's echo is that Antonio thinks she is also visible:

> — Shall I never see her more ?
> —   *Never see her more.*
> — I mark'd not one repetition of the echo
>   But that: and on the sudden, a clear light
>   Presented me a face folded in sorrow.   (ll. 42–5)

This could be Antonio's 'fancy, merely' as Delio points out, but,
read with the entry-direction of the first edition, Antonio's words
seem to imply a lighting-effect that reveals the duchess herself
within a grave; the words '*Eccho, (from the Dutchess Graue.)*' would
be a strange and unnecessary way of indicating that the voice came,
simply, from anywhere off-stage. Among the multiple sources for
Webster's echo-scene was probably *The Second Maiden's Tragedy*,
performed by the King's Men in 1611, in which a stage-direction
reads:

> *On a sodayne in a kinde of Noyse like a Wynde, the dores clattering,
> the Toombstone flies open, and a great light appeares in the midst of
> the Toombe; His Lady as went owt, standing iust before hym all in
> white. . . .*   (Malone Society Reprint (1909), ll. 1926–31)

Perhaps Webster saw this piece of machinery among the properties
of the King's Men and so the whole scene was born.[1]

[1] The lack of a stage-direction to describe the device is not surprising;
the printer's copy had little more than bare entry-directions (see pp. lxiv–
lxviii, below), so that '*from the Dutchesse Graue*' is in itself a remarkable
elaboration. The scene could be cut for performance at the Globe (see
title-page); its loss would not confuse the narrative, for Antonio's intentions have been stated at the end of v. i. Indeed this echo scene may have

The other group of borrowings lies behind Act IV, Scene ii, the second prison-scene. Miss Inga-Stina Ekeblad has shown (*R.E.S.*, n.s., IX (1958), 253–67) how the eight madmen, with their song, dialogue, and concluding dance, form an antimasque—a grotesque episode which, from 1608–9 onwards, customarily preceded the main dances of a court masque and anticipated, distorted or opposed its principal themes. In masques performed at Princess Elizabeth's wedding, in February 1613, individualized comic characters were first used; and those in Campion's *Lords' Masque* and Beaumont's *Masque of the Inner Temple and Gray's Inn* were described on entry, one by one, like Webster's madmen. By using this well-known form, Webster ensured that his audience would receive the song of howling and death, the bawdy, devil-ridden, and competitive dialogue and the fantastic dance as expressions of the duchess' situation as well as instruments of Ferdinand's cruelty; they would know that, somehow, she had to accept or control this lewd, egocentric, and doomed world. The dance would be the climax of the episode, a concerted expression of uncontrolled 'wildness' (cf. l. 41).[1] The audience would also expect the masque proper to follow. Bosola's disguises as 'tomb-maker' and 'common bellman' carry this expectation forward, and soon he delivers a 'present' of '*coffin, cords and a bell*' in a 'presence-chamber' (l. 171), accompanying this with a formal speech. So far Webster continued within the masque form, and he accentuated the correspondence by making Bosola's dirge echo such an epithalamium as Jonson provided in his *Hymenaei*.[2] The conjunction of death and love was common and traditional in the literature of Webster's day, but its presentation in the idiom of a court masque was a fairly recent elaboration; in the last Act of Marston's *Malcontent* (1604) Maria makes her intentions explicit:

---

been added at a late stage of composition, for if Delio's speech (ll. 51–5) were placed at the end of the earlier scene its oblique reference to the Cardinal ('his blood') would, perhaps, be more effective.

[1] Miss Ekeblad argued that the dance was a 'charivari', a folk-custom for baiting quick marriages of widows, or unequal matches. But it is doubtful if the folk tradition persisted in this way; in masques, disorderly antimasques graced weddings of absolute propriety.

[2] See notes to IV. ii. 179, 190, and 194–5.

Ile mourne no more, come girt my browes with floures,
Revell and daunce; soule now thy wish thou hast,
Die like a Bride, poore heart thou shalt die chast.

and in 'mourning habit' Aurelia quotes a couplet anticipatory of Bosola's dirge:

Life is a frost of colde felicitie,
And death the thaw of all our vanity,

and then Mercury announces his masque in the 'presence-chamber', inviting all to:

. . . make this presence their Elizium:
To passe away this high triumphall night,
With song and daunces, courts more soft delight.

The death of the Duchess of Malfi is her brother's celebration for her marriage, a counterpart to howling madness, a royal occasion, a formal and necessary meeting, a mingling of sensuality, love, religion, and art, all this as well as a manifestation of cruelty, courage, and suffering. Webster's various sources helped him to make this episode reflect upon the whole play, and upon a wide view of life.

Sentences

The Duchess of Malfi, like Webster's other works, is studded with phrases culled from other authors; here are the words of William Alexander, Chapman, Donne, of Florio translating Montaigne and Grimeston translating Matthieu, of Guevara, Joseph Hall, Jonson, Marston, Nashe, Overbury, Pettie translating Guazzo, Sidney, Whetstone, and others; here, too, are many proverbial sayings. Webster did not use these phrases as fixed counters, but retuned, reapplied, recast them for his own purposes. Some of his subtlest dramatic modulations or hesitations, some of his most lyrical or resonant poetry, are made out of stiff phrases taken from prose read, or half-read, with a commonplace book at his side.

The researches of many scholars—in particular of Professor R. W. Dent, who collected his own work and that of others in *John Webster's Borrowing* (1960)—have been drawn upon to furnish the annotations to this edition with as many of these verbal sources as possible[1]: to read each phrase as Webster found it and then observe what has become of it in the dramatic context is an illuminating entry to an understanding of Webster's dramatic style.[2] Appendix III to this edition indexes the borrowings by authors.

Webster's England

Webster chose an old story and in the telling introduced many old-fashioned maxims. And he added fantasy, with strange horrors and strange coincidences. But *The Duchess* was also a contemporary play, reflecting the actual society of its first audiences. Webster's England must be counted among its sources.

The story had been retold in an Elizabethan book Webster had certainly read,[3] George Whetstone's *Heptameron of Civil Discourses* (1582), and there the cardinal is condemned as a tyrant for revenging 'the base choice of his Sister': it argues that 'the example of these Marriages are usual'. In Webster's day there were famous instances: the 'lady of the Strachey' had married a Yeoman, the Duchess of Suffolk her Master of the Horse. In Overbury's *Characters* it is said that the 'inheritance' of a serving-man is 'the chamber-maid, but often [he] purchaseth his master's daughter, by reason of opportunity, or for want of a better'. Unequal matches were talked about with keen interest, for the sale of honours during James' reign, mentioned several times in *The Duchess*, and the new wealth of the city, a theme of *The Devil's Law Case*, had affected men's notions of greatness and were beginning to challenge the structure of society. The duchess was also a widow, and, while Webster could describe a 'vertuous Widdow' who never remarries, he followed this with the character 'an ordinarie Widdow' who 'Is like the Herald's Hearse-cloath; shee serves to many funerals, with a very little altering the colour'; so the match of Webster's duchess also revealed a general conflict between old rules and convenient practices which had become more than usually prominent in this

---

[1] Besides the various modern editions of Webster, see especially C. Crawford, *Collectanea*, II ser. (Stratford-upon-Avon, 1907), 1–63, Marcia L. Anderson, *S.P.*, xxxvi (1939), 192–205, and G. K. Hunter, *N. & Q.*, new ser., iv (1957), 53–5.

[2] See Revels, *W.D.*, xxxv–xxxviii, for a brief discussion.

[3] Cf. App. III.

expansionist, empirical age—in this instance the Church's advice against remarriage, opposed to the obvious advantages of a second husband.[1] She was 'royal' too (cf. II. v. 22) and this lent current interest: when *The Duchess* was performed for the first time, Lady Arabella Stuart lay imprisoned in the Tower for marrying Lord William Seymour, a man who might strengthen her claim to James' throne. The story of the tragedy was a syndrome for contemporary issues.

It was set in the courts of princes. This did not mean the fancy-dress roundabout of modern stage-settings, but the centre of a country: dynastic, social, intellectual, and, not least, administrative. Gabriel Harvey had called the 'prynces Court, ye only mart of preferment, & honour. A Goulfe of gaine'[2]: it was there that ambition, power, knowledge, experience, sexual attraction, personality counted. A few years later than *The Duchess*, Nicholas Breton wrote a pamphlet, *The Court and Country* (1618), which gave the traditional comparison in up-to-date terms:

> What should a Courtier be alwaies iealous of ? *Insinuating spirits, intruding wits, alluring eyes, and illuding tongues.* What is the life of a Courtier ? *The labour of pleasure, the aspiring to greatness, the ease of nature, and the commaund of reason.*   (C3ᵛ)

Bosola's private conferences with Ferdinand in I. i and III. i ('place and riches oft are bribes of shame. . . I never gave pension but to flatterers'), Antonio's reception of the duchess' wooing ('Ambition, madam, is a great man's madness . . .'), and the sparring of Bosola and Antonio in II. i ('you would not seem to appear to the world puffed up with your preferment . . .') are only a few of the incidents in the play which present a 'slice' of court-life as it was known in Webster's day: a petty court representing the court of England. 'Intelligencers' were common in London, Donne's Fourth Satire delineating a mean member of the species. The servant of a 'great man' could wield almost the same power as his master: it was said of Sir Thomas Overbury, when he was Carr's secretary, that 'Over-

---

[1] Some forward-looking clerics compromised; cf. F. W. Wadsworth, *P.Q.*, xxxv (1956), 394–407.

[2] *Gabriel Harvey's Marginalia*, ed. G. C. Moore Smith (Stratford-upon-Avon, 1913), p. 142.

bury governed Carr, and Carr governed the King'. The opening
lines of *The Duchess* inveighing against sycophants and 'dissolute
and infamous persons' in a prince's court might have been spoken
of Whitehall: in 1613 Overbury died in prison, slowly poisoned (as
it was later proved) by Carr's new wife, because he had opposed her
divorce; the Commons' Journal tells of angry complaints about
the king's favourites and pensioners, and about 'Misinforma-
tions', immediately before the dissolution of parliament in June
1614.[1]

Letters, documents, treatises, and pamphlets of James' reign
could illustrate abundantly the court setting of the play. One published after the Overbury trial may serve as an example; it describes an ambitious man:

> if hee rise from obscurity, (as many haue done) hee laboureth to be
> skilfull in those things, which are most pleasing to the greater sort,
> and tollerable among the Commons: His study is for prayse, and
> not for Vertue: His lookes like *Mausolus* Toumbe, faire and comely
> without, but within, nothing but rotten bones, and corrupt prac-
> tises: his apparell increaseth with his Fortune, and as worldly
> affaires direct him, so suteth hee both fashions and affections; in
> his study he affecteth singularity, and is proud in beeing Author of
> a new Stratagem: if hee chance to come into the eye of the World,
> hee then creepes into the fauour of some great Personage, in feeding
> whose humors (to relieue his wants) he makes intrusion into som
> heritage, and matcheth not according to his birth, but to the in-
> crease of his fortune, and by that meanes, by hooke or crooke, he
> attaineth to some place in the Court. Then begins hee with guifts
> to win hearts, by fained humility to auoyd hatred, by offices of
> friendship to bind his equals, by cunning insinuations to worke
> his Superiors, by which meanes he is held to be worthily a
> Statesman. Beeing growne to this step higher, the authority likes
> him not without the stile, wherein if any crosse him, looke for poy-
> son in his cup, or conspiracy in his walkes, yea so pestilent is his
> nature, that (like fire raked vp in embers) he neuer sheweth but to
> consume, both himselfe and others... Hee giues entertainment to
> witches and charmers, and consorts him-selfe with nouell mongers,
> and strange inuenters of banquets to set lust on fire, and that can
> deuise confections to besot youth with luxury, that for an ireful
> man can worke strange reuenges, for a fearefull a strong tower to

[1] Cf. G. Davies, *Early Stuarts* (1937), pp. 16–17, and *Commons' Journal*,
i. 497–501.

keepe him in: to be excellent at poysons, to kill lingringly, like the *Italian*. . .[1]

A popular pamphlet on the news of Webster's world can evoke the world of *The Duchess of Malfi*.

3. THE TRAGEDY

I hold it, in these kind of Poems with that of Horace: Sapientia prima, stultitia caruisse; *to bee free from those vices, which proceed from ignorance; of which I take it, this Play will ingeniously acquit it selfe.*

Webster's introduction to *The Devil's Law Case* will serve for his earlier tragedy. *The Duchess* is skilfully and meticulously contrived; like a Pygmalion's image, it has been almost killed by being cherished too much.

Structure

Artfully the characters have been made to reflect upon each other. Julia with the cardinal and Delio in Act II and with Bosola in Act V, where she is the 'great woman of pleasure' who would court a man 'in the street', invites comparison with the duchess who also loves in private and woos for herself. Julia then dies with a resolution which denies second thoughts, a contrast to Antonio, Ferdinand, Bosola, closer to the cardinal; and these contrasts are pointed by dying speeches. If Julia were omitted from the play, none of the main characters except the cardinal would be affected; and the narrative would be clearer and the final Act tightened and more forceful. Her part might be dismissed as an 'ignorant' afterthought. But the author's invention was still unflagging; rather, Julia is an 'ingenious' reflection and elaboration of central concerns of the tragedy.

When we scrutinize the full picture carefully, we can discern the construction-lines that Webster used to organize its troublous and extravagant details. One of the two brothers seems wholly ruled by his intelligence; the other directly contrasted to him by giving way to his passions. Two ambitious men of ordinary stock succeed at

---

[1] *The Just Downfall of Ambition, Adultery, and Murder* (1616?), A3^v–B1.

court, Antonio on account of his 'virtue' (I. i. 439–40), Bosola
through his 'corruption' (I. i. 286–7). Later both are revalued,
Antonio's 'ambition' becoming 'fearful' (II. iv. 80–1) so that he is
uncertain of 'any safety' he can 'shape himself' (V. i. 14), and
Bosola's forcing him to hide in other 'shapes' than his own (IV. i.
134–6). At last Antonio sees the 'quest of greatness' as a child's
game with a bubble, and Bosola, supposing that men yield 'no
echo', urges 'worthy minds. . . To suffer death, or shame for what
is just'. Cariola dies wildly, in contrast to the duchess. Pescara is
considerate, in contrast to Malateste, Roderigo, Grisolan. The
madmen are 'loosed', while the duchess is 'chain'd' (IV. ii. 59–60).
Antonio 'sounds' his own danger and escapes, while the duchess
looks for 'virtue' and bends herself 'to all sways of the oppressor's
will' (III. v. 91–2; 120–1 and 140 ff.). Whole scenes are linked together, behind the dialogue, as if in a diagram. So the first presence-
chamber scene, with the duchess at ease among her brothers and
her court, is reflected in the second, where she is alone and then has
to rush from the stage, calling for lights; in Act III she has dreamed
of wearing her 'coronet of state' and then receives an embassage
outside her palace, in open country; and in Act IV she has her fourth
and 'last presence-chamber' (IV. ii. 171), as the coffin is brought
before her. In the final moments of the tragedy, long after her
death, there is a further reflection, identified by the central position
of her unnamed son and the silent homage of everyone on the
stage; it is partly evaluated in Delio's words:

> Nature doth nothing so *great*, for *great men*,
> As when she's pleas'd to make them *lords of truth*:
> Integrity of life is fame's best friend,
> Which nobly, beyond death, shall *crown* the end.

The words 'great', 'lords', and 'crown' are not used carelessly, and,
if the acknowledgement of the 'mother's right' in her child must be
condemned as false to history and primogeniture, it can be 'ingeniously acquitted' as necessary for the completion of a significant
dramatic design.

We may speak, as Webster did in the preface already quoted, of
the 'ingenious structure of the scene'. His handling of Act-intervals
shows the aptness of the phrase. At the end of Act I, for example,

Antonio leads his 'fortune by the hand' to his marriage bed, and
then Cariola speaks of the 'spirits' of greatness and woman, and of
a 'fearful madness'. In the following scene, with the new Act nine
months later, the foolish Castruchio is trying to appear an 'eminent
fellow' and wants to know if the people will judge him to be one;
he is told to 'couple' with an 'Old Lady' who paints to hide her face.
Bosola says that they both pay for the 'sin' of their youth, and both
misjudge:

> Man stands amaz'd to see his deformity
> In any other creature but himself.

They have nothing to say to his insults, and he dismisses them,
having 'other work on foot':

> I observe our duchess
> Is sick o' days, she pukes. . .

The narrative of the previous scene has been dropped for a time,
and all its particular concerns. But the new scene keeps its concluding sentiments in the memory of the audience, for comparison
and contrast, bringing obvious folly and ambition, and natural behaviour (cf. l. 47), into the complex composition. This is not a
direct comment by the author; the audience is left to discover the
resemblances and differences for itself. It is like an antimasque, but
one that follows rather than precedes its main action.

Webster's ingenious structure is accentuated verbally. This
aspect of his art has often been noticed[1]: various animals, birds and
diseases, powdered hair, '*Quietus Est*', anchorites, cannon, horse-
dung, poison, ruins, tombs, mines, eclipses, a glass-house, geometry, tythes, coal, and many other matters are mentioned in one
scene and then in others, so helping to bind the composition together and suggesting ironies and revaluations. A chain of references to witchcraft illustrates this technique. In Act I, Ferdinand
associates it with death, poison, and sexual attraction:

> be not cunning:
> For they whose faces do belie their hearts

---

[1] See, especially, H. T. Price, 'The Function of Imagery in Webster',
PMLA, lxx (1955), 717–39, reprinted in *Eliz. Drama*, ed. R. J. Kaufmann
(1961), and C. W. Davies, 'The Structure of *The Duchess of Malfi*', *English*,
xii (1958), 89–93.

> Are witches, ere they arrive at twenty years—
> Ay: and give the devil suck.   (I. i. 308–11)

In Act II, Bosola says a lady's closet would be suspected 'for a shop
of witchcraft . . .' (II. i. 35 ff.), and then, later, the cardinal tells
Ferdinand that his rage carries him:

> As men convey'd by witches through the air,
> On violent whirlwinds.   (II. v. 50–1)

In the next scene there is a lengthy, yet energetic, digression as
Ferdinand argues that witchcraft cannot force a man to love, and
then, finally, 'The witchcraft lies in her rank blood'. It has become
a synonym for the power of sex: Ferdinand's rage seems motivated
by it and he is fascinated by it; women are said to minister to it;
Ferdinand says it is in the veins of the duchess. In the next scene,
Ferdinand almost brands his sister as a witch and then rushes from
the stage:

> *Duchess.*   I have youth,
>   And a little beauty.
> *Ferdinand.*   So you have some virgins
>   That are witches:—I will never see thee more.
>   (III. ii. 139–41)

When he hears that Antonio is the father of her children he says
nothing at first; it is Delio who comments: 'In such a deformed
silence, witches whisper Their charms' (III. iii. 58–9). When he
visits his sister in the darkened prison she supposes that he has
practised 'witchcraft' in leaving a dead man's hand in her grasp
(IV. i. 54–5). In the last Act, the idea recurs with Julia who asks how
Bosola has put a 'love-powder' in her drink to make her 'fall in love
with such a face' (V. ii. 154–8). Ferdinand now speaks of innocence,
justice, patience, 'beasts for sacrifice', hell, death, silence, warfare,
'The devil', and pain; after his sister's death he forgets witchcraft.

  More general concepts, like madness, blood, death, silence,
noise, virtue, nature, darkness, and light, similarly recur throughout the play. As much could be said of most tragedies, but Webster
seems to have been particularly aware of the reiterations. So Ferdinand will only see his sister in the 'dark'; and after her death his
'eyes dazzle' at the sight of her, and he leaves to 'hunt the badger

..., a deed of darkness'. For Bosola, the duchess returns momentarily from 'darkness' to reveal his own conscience as a 'black register'. Ferdinand now howls like a wolf at midnight; he has 'cruel sore eyes'; he knows that slaughter 'must be done i' th' dark', and that the 'day' may be lost. The cardinal knows, too, that the death of his sister must be hidden within his breast, as in a 'dark and obscure' grave. Antonio sees the duchess for a moment in a 'clear light', and Bosola, while recognizing another existence, sees his own world as a 'shadow, or deep pit of darkness'. Finally, Delio remembers that the 'sun shines' and the impression of eminent men can melt like the imprint of someone who had fallen in a frost: any brightness they had given was like a stain in snow. The reiterations are frequent but inconstant, varying restlessly and, sometimes, uneasily: they do not suggest the fulfilment of an ample pattern, but a prolonged engagement with both 'form and matter', an attempt to record all repercussions and to question all established positions.

Language

Webster's verbal artifice is incessant; nowhere else is his work so nearly over-cherished. During a performance the audience must either be held by strong, intelligent speech and so follow—or try to follow—the quick turns and deep allusions, or else it will lose contact and be left to understand intermittently.

The range of Webster's vocabulary and imagery is obvious. To this he added a subtlety derived from curious lore (see, for example, the note on 'hyena' at II. v. 38-9), and from mythology and emblematic traditions (see, for example, on IV. i. 68-9). He introduced elaborate similitudes that compare the devil to a 'rusty watch', or the duchess to a mouse. He used enumerations, apostrophes, antitheses, rhetorical questions, and many other figures of speech. As he loaded his dialogue with *sententiae* from other writers, so he 'wrote up' consistently: and the audience (and the actor beforehand) must strain to follow.

Yet this is not literary decoration. Besides accenting the structure of the play, the verbal elaboration is intervolved with each dramatic moment. (Webster is the rare dramatist who is obviously literary without ceasing to be wholly dramatic; once they have mastered it, actors delight in his language.) His puns illustrate this. Often words seem chosen for the sake of a quibble: 'dead wall', 'swing', 'executed', 'quicksilver'. Some seem always to awaken word-play, like 'blood' (life-blood, lineage, passion) or 'will' and 'wilful'. But these tricks cannot be neglected without greatly simplifying or even falsifying the drama: they suggest a double level of consciousness in the speaker. *Doubles entendres* are concentrated at special points: in the public scenes between the duchess and Antonio to show their sexual instincts secretly or unthinkingly controlling their words (see several notes within I. i. 361–414, II. i. 108–45, and III. ii. 183–209), and, more remarkably, in Ferdinand's speeches almost every time he is on stage before his sister's death, giving even to some of his lightest talk a half-hidden sexual urgency. In a tragedy of love, such effects are crucial.

When Webster's dialogue is considered dramatically its theatrical life is evident, but it is no less difficult or ambitious. There are sudden surprises, giving an impression of reserves of excitement or power: 'You are my sister', 'Look you, the stars shine still'. Simple words suggest large realizations: 'You have parted with it now', 'Cover her face . . .'; or sudden irony, as in Bosola's 'I am very sorry' as the duchess is taken in labour, or Ferdinand's 'How is't, worthy Antonio?' when he considers him his sister's bawd; or a new simplicity or trust: 'Do not think of them', 'This good one that you speak of, is my husband'. There are rapid transitions, from 'We'll only lie, and talk together . . . keep us chaste', to the acceptance of 'O, let me shroud my blushes in your bosom . . .', from Ferdinand's sustained denunciation of Antonio to his curt judgement on his sister, and then to a slow self-pity:

> And thou hast ta'en that massy sheet of lead
> That hid thy husband's bones, and folded it
> About my heart.

Alternate speakers can be so far apart from each other as 'I am Duchess of Malfi still' from Bosola's reasonable answer, 'That makes thy sleeps so broken', and his following couplet.

The line of the dialogue—if we may liken speech in drama to drawing in a painting—the line is light and discontinuous, rapid or deliberate at will but neither persistently. The longer speeches usually accumulate power by numerous touches or seem to release it in a moment after a passage of uncertainty: the line has no regular, constructed development. Only in couplets and sententious utterances is it firm and straight; only occasionally, as in the stories of Reputation and the Salmon and the Dogfish (III. ii. and III. v) or Bosola's 'meditation' and dirge (II. i and IV. ii), does it have a prolonged regularity. These variations have been called 'unnatural' and unnecessary,[1] but in performance they prove their worth in strengthening, by momentarily simplifying, the composition: they are necessary 'fixes', or 'holds'. Nor are they isolated moments, but related to a tendency towards sententious speech in almost all the characters. The light and discontinuous line and the occasional, momentary regularity create a style wholly appropriate to a drama of interplay between passion and conscious thought, contrasts of appearance and truth, and interrelationships of characters who often try to live for themselves alone. Webster wished to show a fragmentary and disordered world and at the same time to suggest that some men conceived of a 'fix'd order' and a fame that outlasts death.

Viewpoint

Although Webster chose a simple, affecting story, his dramatization has perplexed and divided opinion. 'The most serious error that critics of Webster have committed', says Professor Ribner in his *Jacobean Tragedy* (1962), 'has been to regard him as a dramatist lacking in moral vision' (p. 99). But a concern with such matters has not brought agreement. According to Ribner, Antonio's death proves 'the nobility of his endurance' (p. 121), and according to Professor Ornstein, in *The Moral Vision of Jacobean Tragedy* (1960), his death is 'contemptible' (p. 144). Una Ellis-Fermor thought that the cardinal 'redeems himself at the last' (*Jacobean Drama* (1936), p. 180), but Dr Gunnar Boklund sees him revealed then as a 'coward', without 'even the redeeming feature of bravado' (pp. 133–4). To some critics the courtship of Antonio by the duchess

---

[1] See, for example, J. R. Mulryne's sensitive treatment of the style in *Stratford-upon-Avon Studies, I: Jacobean Theatre* (1960), pp. 214–25.

is 'a charming idyll' (Ribner, p. 116), but others say that 'the more
we consider the Duchess, the more hints of guilt seem to appear'
(C. Leech, *John Webster* (1951), p. 75). Bosola is said to be more a
chorus than a character; or, on the other hand, to show a development from illusion to self-knowledge. Ferdinand's madness is 'con-
vincing' and 'unconvincing'; his motivation 'sexual', 'emblematic',
'routine', 'muddled'. Whether critics look for a 'moral vision' or
consistent characterization, they do not often agree. Not all would
subscribe to Professor Leech's temperate judgement:

> in *The Duchess* we are pulled successively in different directions,
> and on the completion of our reading are likely to feel we have the
> task of constructing a whole of which Webster has given us the
> separate parts.[1]

Some believe that the play would always 'ingeniously acquit
itself'.[2]

This disagreement should be expected. The main source offers
conflicting judgements. The action is subtly planned. The dialogue
is delicate and vexed. The play was intended for skilled performance in an intimate theatre, before a sophisticated audience. And
we know that Webster worked arduously and persistently, and
sought intractable issues: at the centre of his earlier tragedy was the
dazzling incongruity of the 'White Devil'.[3] From the beginning of
The Duchess the audience is taught to look for contradictions, and
to expect subtle resolutions:

> if 't chance
> Some curs'd example poison 't near the head. . .
>
> Some such flashes superficially hang on him, for form; but
> observe his inward character. . .
>
> What appears in him mirth, is merely outside; . . .
>
> . . . will seem to sleep o' th' bench
> Only to entrap offenders in their answers; . . .

---

[1] 'An Addendum on Webster's Duchess', *P.Q.*, xxxvii (1958), 253–6.

[2] In *Webster: The Duchess of Malfi* (1963), Professor Leech has recon-
sidered the 'inconsistencies': 'A vacillation in the attitude to the Duchess
may appear to be induced in the play . . .; but in this compound of attitudes
I now think we have Webster's chief claim to major status in this play'
(p. 49).

[3] On characterization, see Revels, *W.D.*, pp. l–lvii.

> As I have seen some
> Feed in a lord's dish, half asleep, not seeming
> To listen to any talk; and yet these rogues
> Have cut his throat in a dream. . .
>
> Your darkest actions—nay, your privat'st thoughts—
> Will come to light.   (I. i. 13–316)

The cardinal at one moment turns Bosola away and then, in private, recommends his preferment. Antonio is the duchess' steward who is sent a brief message by his mistress, and then her beloved. Contradictions span the whole play: Ferdinand tells his sister that it is a sin to remarry, and in Act IV calls her innocent; she doubts and then affirms a renewal of love in 'another world'; the cardinal seems 'fearless' and then falls helplessly, like a young hare.

What 'principle of unity' is there in this view of men and actions? First, an 'atmosphere', developing in the course of the tragedy: a dark sensationalism and menace, contrasted with softness, intrigue, madness, moral sayings. Around 1920 this was Webster's chief appeal; for Rupert Brooke, F. L. Lucas, and T. S. Eliot:

> He knew that thought clings round dead limbs
> Tightening its lusts and luxuries.
>   (T. S. Eliot, 'Whispers of Immortality')

Since then critics have searched rigorously for a unified 'moral vision', and have divided opinion; and this division points to the play's other unity. So does the play's style and structure. It is a unity of empirical, responsible, sceptical, unsurprised, and deeply perceptive concern for the characters and society portrayed.

This view sounds like a product of the 1960s, but it was also Jacobean. Webster's concern with 'secretest thoughts' is echoed in Bacon's essay 'Of Friendship', published in 1612: 'There be some whose lives are, as if they perpetually played upon a stage, disguised to all others, open only to themselves. But perpetual dissimulation is painful. . .' Webster was interested in pretence and self-deceit, changes and reversals of rôles, as modern writers are, and as Jonson was in *Volpone*, *The Alchemist*, or *Epicœne*, and Shakespeare in Iago, and as John Ford would be some twenty years afterwards. He did not question moral laws methodically like Donne in *Biathanatos* or Montaigne in 'An Apology of Raymond Sebond', but, with them and many others, he was sceptical of particular examples: regretfully his duchess contrasts man's restrictions to the freedom of 'birds that live in the fields'.

The originality of Webster's viewpoint is shown partly by his understanding acceptance of strange fantasies in thought and behaviour: in *The Devil's Law Case*, Jolenta is made conscious of this:

> Oh my phantasticall sorrow!—Cannot I now
> Be miserable enough, vnlesse I weare
> A pyde fooles coat ? Nay worse, for when our passions
> Such giddy and vncertaine changes breed,
> We are neuer well, till we are mad indeed.   (III. iii. 208–12)

It is also found in the moments of gentleness and clear thought which he gave to his giddy and dismal world, or in his sense of reality which made him place the last moments of his duchess— which, to Bosola, seemed like 'Heaven' opening—in the fourth Act, although he knew 'the last Act' should be the 'best i' th Play' (*D.L.C.*, II. iii. 129); he saw the painful and inept attempts to accommodate such a death and recognized them as part of that death and necessary to the unity of his tragedy.

Characters

The main characters 'live' as if they played on a stage and tried, sometimes consciously, sometimes unconsciously, various disguises. Love, guilt, and disaster seem to direct them, fatefully, towards an hour when each must unmask. But there is no assurance that they end truthfully. Perhaps they immediately snatch another seemingly protective dissimulation and are never exposed to the audience's view. In performance the precise moment of truth, or moment in which truth is possible, will depend on the interpretations, personalities, and physiques of the actors: what must be ensured, if the tragedy is to be fully presented, is that the whole cast recognizes Webster's means of presenting his characters so that they 'live', so that the audience is made aware of their depths of consciousness and subconsciousness. The contradictions must be welcomed and a secret co-ordination maintained throughout each rôle.

Bosola is obviously complex. An observer might believe that 'he rails at those things which he wants' (I. i. 25); but that is half the truth. Despite the energy of his railing and his service for Ferdinand, there is almost nothing he wants: his 'garb' of melancholy sits naturally upon him after his preferment, as before. He has served in the galleys 'for a notorious murder' and has become an isolated man. He takes as much, and as little, pleasure in describing his own corruption as the vices of anyone else. Nor does he only rail: he mocks Antonio but then praises him, and mocks him again and praises him again. His one constant development is a growth of pity and admiration for the duchess. This begins as irony in the second act, leads him to disguise himself with a vizor and then as a tombmaker and as the common bellman who seeks to save souls, and then as a presenter of a masque to celebrate love and death; and finally pity leads him, after he has been rejected by Ferdinand, to tears and repentance and the attempt to find some deed 'worth his dejection'. He has found something he needs; but he has not changed. He still dissimulates instinctively and murders; although the duchess 'haunts' him, his world is still 'gloomy' and 'fearful'. He knows what worthy men should do and that his 'is another voyage', to death; he dies, as he had lived, alone.

Bosola believed at one time that he wished to see Antonio 'Above all sights i' th' world', and yet he killed him on meeting: so far had Bosola been from controlling his actions and so far had Antonio failed to impress himself as the husband of the duchess. The brave horseman and upright steward fails to find words to answer his mistress' suit; he describes her movingly when they are separated at court, but when she declares her love he speaks of himself. He fails to confront Ferdinand when he seems to threaten his wife's life, and rather suspects Cariola of treachery. He knows that 'Man, like to cassia, is prov'd best, being bruis'd' (III. v. 75), and 'proves' himself by kissing 'colder' than 'holy anchorite', sounding his own danger, and riding off. He returns, attracted to the nets that are laid for him by hope of 'safety'; his wife's sorrow is clearly in his mind, but at the end he revalues life as a meaningless 'quest for greatness'. This may be truth after dissimulation, for it echoes the wooing scene when he recognized a 'saucy and ambitious devil' dancing in the ring which the duchess put upon his finger. Wishing that his son should 'fly the courts of princes' may be his deepest response. Bosola may have been right: drawn to danger by ambition, beauty, and the excitement of mastering his horse, Antonio may have been, at a deeper level, 'drawn to fear' (III. v. 52–4).

The cardinal is proud, reserved, resourceful: the obvious contradictions in his rôle—moralist and lecher; prelate and soldier—seem fully under his control. But he is 'weary' as well as active; and his imagination can hold him in terror by the side of his fish-ponds or in speculation about the fire of hell. He had seemed fearless, but then gives way to panic. When Bosola sees this, he believes the cardinal's 'greatness was only outward' (v. v. 42–4). But adversity reveals more resources: 'Help me, I am your brother', and, when this cry is ignored, a concern with justice and payment.

Too much and too little attention has been given to Ferdinand's incestuous excitement. Too little because the critics have often missed his sexual puns and the sudden flashes of his speech, and the series of allusions to witchcraft. Usually his sexual imagery, the irrationality of his rage (in II. v), his 'Damn her! that body of hers . . .' in response to the suggestion that she should have a penitential garment 'next to her delicate skin' (IV. i. 119–31), and his concluding, 'My sister! O! my sister! there's the cause on't', have been considered the main indications of this motivation.[1] And sometimes it has been dismissed as irrelevant to the tragedy, or insufficiently worked into its development. But it is precisely when these hints are considered within the play as a whole that Webster's intentions become clear: a hidden motivation for Ferdinand is in keeping with the general mode of characterization. It is like the characterization of other plays, too: the incestuous hints between Cesario and his sister in *Fair Maid of the Inn*, I. i, which verbally echo *The Duchess*, III. ii,[2] Clare's strange behaviour in *A Cure for a Cuckold* which is not explained until IV. ii when she confesses her hidden desire for Bonvile (a scene which again echoes *The Duchess*), and Jolenta's strange confession in *The Devil's Law Case* of being

[1] The most thorough account is McD. Emslie, 'Motives in Malfi', *Essays in Criticism*, ix (1959), 391–405, which discusses some of the puns.
[2] See III. ii. 116–18, note.

'bewitched' to be plighted to Ercole (I. ii. 253–60) which is not resolved until the last scene when she silently accepts this man whom she *thought* she did not love.

Too much attention has been paid to Ferdinand's hidden desire, in that it has been allowed to obscure his inward pain and deep sense of guilt. His response to news of his sister's child is not all rage, sexual fantasy, and frustration. There are tears (cf. II. v. 27) and, after his resolve to 'seem the thing I am not', the simple words, revaluing the whole scene:

> I could kill her now,
> In you, or in myself, for I do think
> It is some sin in us, heaven doth revenge
> By her. (ll. 63–6)

It is this, and not his fury, which makes the cardinal ask, 'Are you stark mad?' Immediately his sexual fantasy is released again and then, surprisingly, he resolves not to stir until he knows who 'leaps' his sister. The next scene, at Malfi, when Ferdinand is said to bear himself 'right dangerously', shows him again holding back, and he acknowledges all the 'quicksands' of the world within himself. In his sister's bed-chamber he tells her to 'die', but then to 'pursue her wishes'; he refuses to see her lover because he is 'now persuaded' it would 'damn' them both; he tells a tale of Reputation and like an 'apparition' flees from his sister's 'beauty' vowing never to see her again. Ferdinand is motivated by pain and guilt, although this is only once explicit in words, as well as by pride and desire. After he has tortured the duchess with madmen and ordered her death, his acknowledgement of her innocence, his attempt to cover up the 'main cause' for seeking her death, the value he puts on 'pardon' for Bosola, his refusal to see him again, and his incipient madness in a cry for darkness, all speak pain and guilt. So does his lunacy, raging like a wolf and studying patience, seeking solitariness and condemning the world for 'flattery and lechery'. So does his whispering about the 'quiet death' of strangulation, and his last entry calling for a fight and assuring others that bodily pain is insignificant: 'The pain's nothing: pain many times is taken away with the apprehension of greater' (v. v. 59–60). His last speech acknowledges his sister as the 'cause' of his fall, and speaks, too, of the enduring diamond and of laceration by one's own dust. Once Webster's means of presenting the inward nature of his characters is recognized, Ferdinand's motivation is revealed as the strongest and most unequivocal in the play: perhaps it had to be so, because of its subconscious origin and force.

The duchess herself has been copiously praised: her intelligence and sensuality, and the tender and outward movement of her imagination; her discretion and rashness; her pride, simplicity, and submission to 'heaven's scourge-stick'. The encomiums are easy and warrantable: and also inconsistent. Moreover, it can be argued that Webster approved, or that he disapproved, of her neglect of rule, her lies and 'jesting with religion', her base, secret, and second marriage: there is no clear judgement in the play, only that Bosola and Ferdinand at last declare her to be innocent. But for the audience, as for these characters, the contradictions are lost to sight in recognition of a certain and absolute effect. Here, perhaps, is a typical Websterian conceit. From majesty that woos and virtue that may 'seem the thing it is not' (I. i. 442 and 448), there is a development, through adversity, to a majesty in suffering and a natural virtue. In 'obedience' (IV. ii. 169–70), kneeling, and a desire for sleep in death—in submission—the duchess reveals her strength and power over others. At first the irreconcilable demands of greatness and womanhood showed, to Cariola's eyes, a 'fearful madness': now the madness is all around her and she herself appears to be deeply at peace. She is still the same woman—proud, instinctive, passionate, intelligent—but stripped of her obvious greatness she has been 'proved' great: she has lost everything and nothing. It is very difficult to describe her characterization: hesitantly, for it sounds callow, we might argue that the Duchess of Malfi had to submit in order to rule. But certainly the main effect of the tragedy is the terror, pity, and admiration aroused by her death.

Effect

Many details have to be held in the mind in order to discuss Webster's characters. And, indeed, there is a careful ingenuity in every element of the writing—all except one, which is not verbal: the large and sweeping impression of the play in performance.

In the first three Acts, crowded court scenes alternate with private scenes. The focus moves incessantly, illuminating briefly a whole court, groups, couples, individuals; no one person holds the stage for long. The birth of the first child in Act II is attended by alarms and followed by a still darkness. In Act III the flight from Malfi leads the duchess and her husband to the open country where they separate and the duchess becomes a prisoner. In Act IV, the prison provides the one consistent setting and a steady dramatic focus: it is dark, and alternately frighteningly still and frighteningly wild. The duchess dies separated from everyone she loves or knows. Then the last Act is a mixture of slow cunning and sudden moves. Entries seem timed by some manipulating fate: there is a sharp decisiveness ('O, my fate moves swift!'), an elaborate involvement ('you'll find it impossible To fly your fate'), and a contrivance ('Such a mistake as I have often seen In a play'). In a tragedy where appearances and judgements change like quicksilver, and the plot has many by-paths and hesitations, and some irreducible contradictions (the neglect of the son of the first marriage and, perhaps, Bosola's long failure to find the duchess' husband), the simple eloquence of the shape of the action is especially impressive. The dramatist's silent handling seems to have something like a 'meaning': a suggestion that the duchess had to die, and her impermanent world to be destroyed.

And, briefly, in the last silent homage to the son of the duchess, there is a hint that men may, perhaps, wish for some renewal and order.

4. THEATRE PRODUCTIONS

At the Restoration, *The Duchess* was one of the pre-war plays allotted to Davenant and there are records of performances in 1662, 1668, and, at court, in 1686. From the Quarto edition of 1678, 'As it is now acted at the Duke's Theatre', we know that Betterton played Bosola, Mrs Betterton the duchess, and Harris Ferdinand. In 1662, Pepys judged the play 'well performed, but Betterton and Ianthe [Mary Saunderson, later Mrs Betterton] to admiration', and John Downes noted in *Roscius Anglicanus*:

This Play was so exceeding Excellently Acted in all Parts; chiefly, Duke Ferdinand and Bosola: It fill'd the House 8 Days Successively, it proving one of the Best of Stock Tragedies.

There was a revival, under the new title, *The Unfortunate Duchess of Malfy, or the Unnatural Brothers: a tragedy*, at the Haymarket on 22 July 1707. Cast and text were printed in the quarto of that year: Mrs Porter was the duchess, Verbruggen Ferdinand, and Mills Bosola. The cuts reduced playing-time (the pilgrim scene, III. iv, is gone; the Reputation and Salmon stories marked for omission), and tidied up the narrative (III. iii. 69–71, the lines referring to the son of the first marriage, were omitted). There was some rephrasing to regularize the metre, modernize the vocabulary, or remove obscurities, and sometimes to make the play more respectable; so 'lecher' becomes 'lover' at III. ii. 100, for example, and 'I pour it in your bosom' at III. i. 52 is omitted. But the text is useful, being the first to provide adequate stage-directions.

In 1735, *The Fatal Secret* by Lewis Theobald was published. This was an adaptation of *The Duchess* that had been performed at the Theatre Royal: the duchess and Antonio are reunited at the end together with a twelve-year-old son; the scene is Malfi throughout and the action starts after the marriage; Julia is omitted.[1]

In the nineteenth century, *The Duchess* was usually performed in a version by R. H. Horne. He had made it as regular and respectable as possible; there is no Julia, and the duchess, now called Marina, is strangled off-stage. It became a star-vehicle for actresses: Miss Isabella Glyn at Sadler's Wells in 1850 and many subsequent tours; Mrs Emma Waller at the Broadway, New York in 1858, and subsequent tours; Miss Mariott at Sadler's Wells in 1864; and Miss Glyn in a new production under her 'immediate Direction', at the Standard, Shoreditch, in 1868. *The Lady's Newspaper* of 23 November 1850 commented:

Miss Glynne's performance of the duchess is one of the most striking achievements of that rising actress. The scenes, intrinsically coarse, in which she makes love to her steward, were admirably softened by the playful spirit of coquetry which she

[1] The fullest account is in C. Leech, *John Webster* (1951), pp. 19–25.

infused into them. The soft passages of sorrow stole with mournful effect upon the naturally mirthful temperament, and, when her wrongs aroused her alike to a sense of pain and dignity, her denunciations were terrific. . .

Mrs Waller was famous for her impersonation of Meg Merrilies, and the duchess was billed for a tour in 1876 as:

A part in which Mrs. Waller has always created a profound Sensation, and is the only lady in this country who attempts the portrayal of this grand and difficult character.

The only other rôle, in this group of revivals, to be particularly noted was Bosola as portrayed by George Bennett at Sadler's Wells. Westland Marston recorded in *Our Recent Actors*, ii (1888), that it

was one of his most impressive characters. In the appalling scene with the Duchess, where, as an old man, he prepares her for her approaching murder, there was something in his servile appearance, in his deep, sepulchral tones, slow movements, and watchful, deliberate revelation of the coming horror, that seemed as if he himself had had such near commerce with Death as to be the fit representative of his terrors to the living.   (p. 61)

At the end of the century, in October 1892, the Independent Theatre Society gave two performances in a new version by William Poel, directed by Poel at the Opéra Comique. Irving lent costumes and scenery. There was no Julia, but a 'Dance of Death'. Sidney Barraclough was Ferdinand, Murray Carson was Bosola, and Mary Rorke the duchess.

In the present century there have been more productions and a greater reliance on Webster's text, although always cut:

1919 Lyric, Hammersmith. (Two performances)	*Duchess*, Cathleen Nesbitt; *Ferd.*, R. Farquharson; *Bos.*, W. Rea. *Julia* was restored, played by Edith Evans. Directed by Allan Wade.
1935 Embassy, Swiss Cottage.	*Duchess*, Joyce Bland; *Ferd.*, John Laurie; *Bos.* R. Graham. There was no Julia. Directed by John Fernald.
1937 Gate, Dublin.	*Duchess*, Jean Anderson; *Ferd.*, Norman Scase; *Bos.*, B. Gifford. Directed by Peter Powell.

1945	Haymarket, London.	*Duchess*, Peggy Ashcroft; *Ferd.*, John Gielgud; *Bos.*, Cecil Trouncer. Directed by George Rylands.
1946	Ethel Barrymore, New York.	*Duchess*, Elisabeth Bergner; *Ferd.*, D. Eccles; *Bos.*, Canada Lee. Adapted by W. H. Auden; directed by G. Rylands; music by Benjamin Britten.
1957	Phoenix, New York.	*Duchess*, Jacqueline Brookes; *Ferd.*, J. Wiseman; *Bos.*, P. Roberts. Directed by Jack Landau.
1960	Shakespeare Memorial Theatre, and Aldwych, London.	*Duchess*, Peggy Ashcroft; *Ferd.*, E. Porter; *Bos.*, P. Wymark. Directed by D. McWhinnie.

At first directors were shy of the horrors. The critic of *The Times* in 1919 excused the audience's 'tittering . . . towards the close' and the next production of 1935 played safe: 'horror was absent altogether. The masque of madmen was turned into a sort of ballet' (*Daily Telegraph*); 'The dead-hand scene is produced in a pleasant amber light and the pallor of human flesh is hidden by a glove' (*New Statesman*); the director 'cannot put Elizabethan ferocity into the hearts of his actors' (*Times*). Peggy Ashcroft has twice played the duchess, and now Ferdinand and Bosola have returned to Restoration prominence. Even in the tame 1935 production, 'John Laurie's . . . epileptic frenzy' as Ferdinand was 'genuinely terrible and his ranting [had] a ghastly perverse sincerity'. In this part the chief laurels are Gielgud's: fifteen years after his performance, Mr Tynan remembered the 'thrill of finality' he gave to 'I will never see thee more' (*Observer*, 18 Dec. 1960) and Mr Hobson his 'torment of spirit that still excites the imagination' (*Sunday Times*, 18 Dec. 1960). Gielgud had accepted the indications of incestuous desire; and they seemed so up-to-date that he was praised for an originality that is partly Webster's. William Rea's Bosola of 1919 exploited the character's isolation, playing him 'with an air of melancholy reverie and aloofness which gave him immense distinction' (*Times*). Cecil Trouncer, in 1945, risked consistency to give a full interpretation: in *The Sunday Times*, James Agate called it 'a grand exhibition. I am not persuaded that the actor knew quite what to do with this mixture of Enobarbus and Thersites; to watch him do it was nevertheless a rich experience'. *The Times* called his 'vital study, of . . . a murderer of fortune prematurely aged in the galleys', the 'supreme attraction of the revival'.

The constant problem has been the shape and effect of the play as a whole. The fifth Act has often been called 'irredeemable'. According to *The Hartford Courant* (10 Jan. 1946), Auden's adaptation was chiefly confined to Acts IV and V, but:

> Early in the play an interpolated passage . . . establishes the Duke's concern for his sister as born of affection, if perhaps a little incestuous, while the Duke's original confession that he merely sought to secure her estates is saddled on the Cardinal.

But still Rosamund Gilder, in *Theatre Arts* (Dec. 1946), called the production laboured, lacking 'intensity and lurid beauty'. Productions have often been praised for isolated 'moments': *Theatre Arts* said that the play at the Phoenix was 'curiously episodic, and the episodes are somehow not cumulative'; and Mr Hobson said that the Aldwych *Duchess* had 'no drive, no force, no continuity', as if the director had decided that 'it is in single lines that the genius of Webster lies'. The rôles of the duchess, Bosola, and Ferdinand have been variously and effectively realized in performance, but the structure of the play has yet to be vindicated. This may not be Webster's fault. The records suggest that no production has been interested in manifestations of guilt, judgement, and responsibility, or in the workings of fate or the presentation of society. At the Aldwych, the Five-Act structure was ignored; there was no presence-chamber; and among the lines cut were Bosola's concluding:

> Let worthy minds ne'er stagger in distrust
> To suffer death, or shame for what is just.

While such neglect is possible, the tragedy cannot be said to have had a fair chance in the theatre.

5. THE TEXT

The Quarto of 1623

The Duchess of Malfi was first published in a quarto dated 1623, and this edition was obviously authoritative. It was furnished with commendatory verses by three dramatists, a list of actors who had

played in the original production and in a revival, and a dedication
by Webster himself to a nobleman who had family connections
with the King's Men. Unlike any other play from the same printer
or publisher between 1615 and 1625, its title-page was given a
motto, which was in Latin and ascribed to Horace. This quotation
in its full form would have been pretentious ('If you know wiser
precepts than these of mine, kindly tell me; if you do not, practise
these with me'), and being shortened is obscure as well. Undoubtedly it was placed there by the author, rather than publisher,
printer, or some other. And above this exhortation the title-page
advertised 'The perfect and exact Coppy, with diuerse things
Printed, that the length of the Play would not beare in the Presentment'. A discriminating purchaser would also have noted that the
volume was thicker than usual—only three dramatic quartos first
printed between 1615 and 1625 come within a dozen of the 104
pages of *The Duchess*—and turning over its leaves he would have
found clear divisions into acts and scenes, and character-names
assembled together at the head of each scene in the manner approved for learned drama. He might have been assured that this
was 'the book of the play' that the King's Men had performed, in a
complete, authentic, and formal version.

By studying six copies of this quarto (and photographs of twelve
more) and by comparing other works by Webster and other plays
from the same printing-house, a bibliographer can now confirm
this general impression and attempt a more precise judgement.[1]

Printing and Correcting

It is now known that two compositors set the book in Nicholas
Okes' shop, dividing the work thus:

Compositor A A1–4^v, B3–C2^v, D3–E2^v, F3–G2^v, H3–I2^v,
               K3–L2^v, M3–N2^v

Compositor B B1–2^v, C3–D2^v, E3–F2^v, G3–H2^v, I3–K2^v,
               L3–M2^v, N3–4

This means that, excluding prefatory matter on sheet A, the first

---

[1] For fuller information about the 1623 quarto and for evidence in support of statements in this textual introduction, see J. R. Brown, 'The Printing of John Webster's Plays, I, II and III', *S.B.*, vi (1954), 117–40; viii
(1956), 113–27; and xv (1962), 57–69.

four pages of each gathering of eight were set by one man, and the second four by the other; and that A and B alternated regularly. Press-correction cannot have been thorough or regular, for some nonsense words and obvious errors have been left, especially in sheets D, E, and K. Compositor A was the less efficient. He was more apt to substitute one short word for another or to set one or two wrong letters in a word; and he alone made obvious errors or omissions in the speech-prefixes. He was slightly more prone to omit short words, but A and B were equally liable to omit single letters from the ends of words. So much the obvious errors can betray, and variations in punctuation—on A's pages there are two, three, or, at the beginning, four times the number of colons found on B's—suggest that one or both compositors altered the punctuation of their copy. But, in comparison with errors and variations in other quarto plays of the time, these blemishes are slight, and we may judge that the compositors worked from a very clear copy and provided a clean text—or, possibly, in view of Webster's idiosyncratic writing elsewhere, an over-clear and over-clean text.

Indeed, it was set so regularly that it is difficult to trace the work of the two compositors in other books from Okes' shop. Their preferred spellings are most evident in Samuel Daniel's *Cleopatra* and *Queen's Arcadia*, two plays reprinted by Okes in 1623, the year of *The Duchess* quarto. A few pages of *Cleopatra*, reprinted from an edition of 1601, may be assigned to them individually with some confidence.[1] Here Compositor A was responsible for some errors similar to his obvious ones in *The Duchess*, and we can see that he introduced minor changes in the punctuation, making it heavier at the end of a line, adding or omitting commas, substituting a comma for a colon. However, the two Daniel plays show that both workmen were generally faithful to the elision of their copy and surpassed others who had reprinted these plays in scrupulously retaining peculiarities like the indentations marking Daniel's verse-paragraphs. They followed (and sometimes regularized) their copy's use of italics for proper names, but occasionally modified its capitalization. Changes like *beene* to *bin*, *trueth* to *truth*, *of* to *off*,

---

[1] The evidence for A is clearest on Ss1–3, 4ᵛ, 8ᵛ, and Tt1–2ᵛ, 3ᵛ–4, and for B on Ss5ᵛ–6, 8.

occur sporadically throughout the plays. Thus a study of these
reprints confirms the differentiations between the two compositors
of *The Duchess* and, in many respects, shows them to be con-
servative and careful workmen.

However, a study of the press-work of *The Duchess* complicates
this view, proving that both compositors introduced changes in
punctuation and the arrangement of the text to suit their own con-
venience. Nicholas Okes had only one printing press in 1623[1] and
limited quantities of type, so his compositors, working simul-
taneously on *The Duchess*, did not set the pages in the order in
which they are read, but the inner-forme pages before the outer-
forme. Each sheet was probably set in this order: 1^v and 2 with
3^v and 4; and then, 1 and 2^v with 3 and 4^v. This means that, if the
pages of a gathering are numbered 1 to 8, one compositor would set
pages 2 and 3 before 1 and 4, while the other set 6 and 7 before 5
and 8. They used two skeleton formes (the 'furniture' for holding
the type in the press and including running titles) so that the pages
of the inner forme of each sheet could be machined while those of
its outer forme were still being set. (This procedure reduced the
demands on the type, for there would be fewer pages waiting for
machining at any one time; as soon as the first four of any gathering
were ready, machining could start. Setting in the order of reading,
on the other hand, would mean that machining could not start until
7 out of 8 were set, and then another complete forme of 4 pages
would be ready almost at once.) In order to work in this way the
printer's copy had to be 'cast off', that is, marked so that compositors knew in advance of composition the amount of text to be
accommodated on each page; only so could they know how much
to leave for page number 1 when starting to set a new gathering
with page number 2, and so on. And here alterations to their copy
became almost inevitable, for manuscript copy could be cast off
accurately only by taking great care and, as work proceeded, there
would be many miscalculations. On the first pages set in each sheet
or gathering these could be rectified easily by printing more or less
than was marked off, but errors on subsequent pages (especially 1,

[1] Cf. W. A. Jackson, *Records of the Court of the Stationers' Company*
(1957), p. 158.

2ᵛ, 3, and 4ᵛ) forced compositors to compress or extend the text to fit the text-space of the page assigned to it in the casting-off. For these purposes compositors would save a line of type by printing a half verse-line at the end of a speech with the preceding line as if all were one line, or they would gain an extra line by splitting one verse-line and printing it as two separate lines. Adjustments of these kinds were made in *The Duchess* and, excepting the few occasions where two or three words were misplaced without altering the number of lines of text, all the obvious mislineations (those which both Lucas and McIlwraith correct in their editions) can be accounted for in this way. And possible mislineations are often better judged when considered, in conjunction with the obvious ones, as similar accommodations of the cast-off copy to the available text-space.

Simultaneous composition by formes did not wholly prevent type-shortage: sometimes italic type was used for roman, and *vice versa*; and, more important editorially, there are indications that the compositors were occasionally forced to depart from their copy because colons, semi-colons, hyphens, and brackets were in short supply. The bibliographer cannot trace changes of punctuation so precisely as those of verse-lining, but at least he knows where they are most likely to occur.[1]

A comparison of eighteen copies of the quarto has disclosed the presence of variant readings on ten formes,[2] and so proved that some attempt at press-correction must have been made after a number of sheets had been printed off. Seven of the ten formes have three variants or less, and all these correct obvious errors and imply no more authority than a corrector's sense of what is fitting; most are obviously right, as 'remembre' to 'remember' on I2 (IV. i. 74), but three, 'did' and 'pleadon' to 'died' and 'pardon' on B2 (I. i.

---

[1] E.g. colons seem to have been in short supply on L1, 2, and 4ᵛ; hyphens on K3 and 4ᵛ, L1, 1ᵛ, and 2, and M2ᵛ; brackets on K3 and 4ᵛ, L3, 4, and 4ᵛ, and M1 and 2ᵛ.

[2] Forty-five are listed in *S.B.*, viii (1956), 117–19. Almost certainly other changes were made at this stage of press-correction, as re-spacing or re-placement of damaged type; but these would not be noticed by a reader and are unlikely to affect the received text. Proof-sheets from Okes' shop are discussed in *S.B.*, xi (1958), and xiv (1961).

57–8) and 'too' to 'go' on M4 (v. iii. 28), may give a plausible rather than a correct reading. The first sign that the corrector consulted the copy or some other authority is the addition of a stage-direction on the inner forme of Sheet F (III. ii. 71); and here the change from 'approbation' to 'apprehention' (III. ii. 41) and the correction of two proper names may also be so authorized. The next variant forme, G outer, is in three states, implying two phases of correction, and again in the second of these some kind of authority must have been invoked: here spellings are altered rather than corrected, as 'doombe' to 'doome' and '*Bermoothes*' to '*Bermootha*'s' (III. ii. 238 and 266), while the change from 'Pewterers' to 'Painters' on G4ᵛ (III. iii. 20) is the first that cannot have been suggested by an obvious error in the proof-sheet, for both readings make good sense; and this one is unlikely to have been made after reference to the copy, for if that had read 'Painters' it is hard to see how 'Pewterers' could have been set originally. Variants in Sheet H indicate the probable authority for these corrections. Here '*order*' was changed to '*habit*' and '*Hymne*' to '*Ditty*', the heading 'The Hymne' was excised and a note 'The Author disclaims this Ditty to be his' was added, all on H1ᵛ and 2 (III. iv. 7.1–11). None of these modifications corrects an obvious error, none would appear necessary to a printer or his workman, and none could have been made after reference to the copy. They prove that Webster himself was helping with proof-correction at this stage, and that he might have done so for the two preceding sheets. A new stage-direction on H4 (III. v. 95), the supply of a 'sir' and two indefinite articles on H2 and 4 (III. iv. 30 and III. v. 94 and 111), and the addition of '*in dumbe-shew*' on H1ᵛ (III. iv. 7.5) may also have been Webster's alterations, for these likewise do not correct obvious errors. Webster had visited the press to help correct *The White Devil*,[1] and variants show that he gave the same attention to one, two or, perhaps, three formes of *The Duchess*.

With this play, however, his last-minute alterations were probably more extensive than press-variants alone suggest. Besides entries at the head of scenes, a dumb-show, and simple exits, there are only sixteen stage-directions in the whole book: two were additions during press-correction and there is evidence for believing

[1] Cf. Revels, *W.D.*, p. lxviii.

that at least six of the others were not in the printer's copy but were added at the last minute. Three of these occur on, or contiguous to, pages where new speeches are set in line with the conclusion of earlier ones, thus reversing a rule followed on all preceding sheets and saving sufficient space for adding the directions (IV. i. 55.1–2, IV. ii. 60.2 and 114.1–2); another is on a page with thirty-eight instead of the normal thirty-seven lines of type, and this is the only direction to have a single line of type to itself (III. ii. 141.1); another is out of alignment with the rest of the type on the page (IV. i. 43.1) and another uses an italic *B* where these were not available for the text itself (IV. ii. 166–8). All these irregularities would be accounted for if the six directions had been added after the original typesetting. They occur in the work of both compositors and after Sheet F where Webster's presence in the printing-shop has first been suspected. The six directions therefore, like the two among the variants, may have been added on Webster's instructions after the text had been set up from the printer's copy, but before any sheets had been printed off. Possibly all the others were added in this way, for none occurs in the formes showing authorial press-variants; only '*he kneeles*' on C3ᵛ (I. i. 415) would be an oddity, occurring three sheets before any more obvious sign of Webster's changes to the type as set from the printer's copy.

The Printer's Copy

The copy from which the compositors of *The Duchess of Malfi* worked was specially prepared for readers. No manuscript intended for use in a theatre would have the character-names together at the head of each scene, rather than where they enter individually; and very few would be so inadequately furnished with stage-directions. These features of *The Duchess* and the clarity and regularity of its text imply that its copy was a good, professional transcript.

It was probably prepared by Ralph Crane, an expert scrivener associated with the King's Men from before 1621: the arrangement of entries, some spellings and devices of presentation, the elided forms and punctuation, all indicate his hand. The unusual arrangement of almost all the prose in unjustified lines, with a capital letter at the beginning of each, is probably due to Crane's frequent practice of beginning both verse and prose lines with lower-case letters so that the two kinds of dialogue are not readily distinguished.[1]

Crane can be relied on for careful work, but the 'perfect and exact coppy' advertised on the title-page of the quarto must have been far from the author's manuscript in stage-directions, arrangement, orthography, elision, and punctuation. Besides re-arranging entries and pruning stage-directions, the scribe probably regularized character-names and speech-prefixes (*The White Devil* has several variations in these) and generally tidied up the text in accordance with his own notions of propriety. A comparison of Crane's transcripts of *A Game at Chess* with those made by the author or copied faithfully from his papers[2] shows how he rephrased the stage-directions and substituted *you would* for *you'de*, *they are* for *they're*, *I am* for *Ime*, and so forth, and *hath* and *doth* for *has* and *does*. He also introduced capitals for emphasis and provided fuller and more careful punctuation—though he would modify his practice for special purposes, as in the light punctuation for the formal address of the Prince of Orange in *Barnavelt* (ll. 1823 ff.). Moreover, while all Crane's manuscripts are of fine workmanship, they are sometimes ambiguous in minor details: in three of them ' ?' is not distinguished from '!'; L, M, N, W, and Y are not always different from l, m, n, w, and y; occasionally word-divisions are not clear, as in 'gentle woman' or 'gentlewoman'. Errors corrected by modern editors of his transcripts show that Crane was sometimes responsible for small inaccuracies: the most prevalent of these are the wrong number of minim strokes in words containing a sequence of them, misplaced apostrophes in abbreviations, and omissions or errors involving the final letter of a word, especially when this was an 'e'. Such modifications and practices must be taken into account when assessing the quality of the quarto text of *The Duchess*.

The general authority of the text will, of course, depend on the kind of manuscript from which Crane prepared the printer's copy. But of this the regularizing efficiency of the transcription has left no clear evidence. The inclusion of a song which the author 'dis-

---

[1] In *D.M.*, verse lines begin with lower-case letters at I. i. 233 and 235.
[2] Cf. *A Game at Chess*, ed. R. C. Bald (1929).

claimed' to be his (III. iv) suggests that the scribe was working from a theatrical manuscript with additions to the author's text; but the song fits its context precisely and may thus have been taken by Webster from some source, or commissioned by him from a writer who was primarily a musician. The direction at the head of v. iii, '*Antonio, Delio, Eccho, (from the Dutchesse Graue.*)' is readily explained as a rephrasing of a note in the author's fair copy, for a prompter would hardly use these words to remind himself that the actor of the Duchess was to speak the Echo; but author's directions were sometimes retained in theatrical manuscripts, and here the scribe may have adapted one of two notes in the manuscript from which he was working. The claim on the title-page that the text includes '*diuerse things . . . that the length of the Play would not beare in the Presentment*' again suggests an author's copy; but cuts were usually marked in prompt-books so that the full text could still be read. More important is the naming of 'Forobosco' as played by '*N. Towley*' in the list of actors prefacing the text; this character does not appear in the play itself, beyond a passing reference to him as keeping the key of the park gate (II. ii. 31), so it might be argued that a scene was omitted after the first performance and that the copy must be dependent on a prompt-book in which the cut was marked. Yet on further consideration even this argument is insecure. The list of actors was probably drawn up by another hand than that responsible for the printer's copy, and may therefore have different authority. Only here are there variations in the names of characters, 'the Marquesse of Pescara' instead of 'Pescara' and 'The Cardinals Mⁱˢ' instead of 'Julia'; Roderigo, Grisolan, Castruchio, and the Old Lady are all omitted. Possibly the list was written out by Webster from memory ten years after the first performance, and he included Forobosco because he had once intended to give him some significance; so this name would be like one of the 'ghost characters' in *The White Devil* which are known only from stage-directions. Or perhaps there were two versions of *The Duchess*, the play described by Orazio Busino[1] being the version, including a Forobosco scene, which is now lost. Or again, '*N. Towley*' might have been intended to appear opposite 'Malateste' on the next line,

[1] See above, pp. xxiv–xxv.

to whom no actor is assigned; this error would be similar to the obvious one of placing 'R. Pallant' opposite 'Cariola' and the 'Court Officers' instead of 'The Doctor' and 'Cariola'.[1] The closest definition of the authority of the quarto text is that it was printed from a transcript in which no clear signs of its origins survived; the most reassuring fact is that its publication was under the aegis of Webster himself.

Censorship

In *The Duchess of Malfi* the word 'god' occurs only twice, in references to Pluto (III. ii. 243–6), and the word 'heaven' or 'heavens' thirty times. A table setting out the number of occurrences shows a marked contrast to *The White Devil* and suggests that the text has been purged of profanities[2]:

	White Devil	Duchess
God	16	0
god	1	2
Abbreviations for God (as in ''Ud's death')	7	0
Lord (for 'God')	3	0
heaven, heavens	11	30

Yet numerical counts give an exaggerated impression. Fourteen times 'heaven' (or 'heavens') in *The Duchess* refers to the skies or the world of heaven and could not have replaced an original 'God'. Moreover, twice in *The White Devil* 'heaven' is clearly used of God as Fate or Destiny (v. ii. 20 and v. vi. 196) and at least five more occurrences of 'heaven' in *The Duchess* have this connotation. Obviously Webster directed attention to the 'heavens o'er our heads' more frequently in the second than in the first of these tragedies, and this new emphasis may go far to account for the numerical contrasts. The strange fact is rather the complete absence of oaths involving 'God'; it is this which makes it almost certain that the play has been censored.

---

[1] Commas following the latter pair may indicate that the compositor intended to place the bracket correctly; 'Officers' is followed by a full stop (like 'Malateste', *'Children'*, and *'Pilgrime'*, all of which are without an actor's name).

[2] See G. P. V. Akrigg, *N. & Q.*, cxcv (1950), 231–3.

At one time scholars believed that a text which had been altered in this way must be derived from an acting version, but now Alice Walker and W. W. Greg have argued that plays in the Shakespeare Folio of 1623 (the year of *The Duchess* quarto) were purged of profanities only for appearance in print.[1] *The Duchess* was probably censored for the same reason. Crane might have been responsible for this, or Okes or one of his workmen. But since Webster was concerned with the publication of his play and visited the press on at least one occasion, he may have undertaken the task himself; such an action would be in accordance with his sustained interest in detail.

This Edition

Three quarto editions of *The Duchess of Malfi* followed the first, in 1640, 1678, and 1708.[2] They were all straight reprints, correcting some obvious errors, introducing some new ones, and occasionally simplifying difficult passages. The present text is that of the first quarto (which I shall call Q). I have, however, emended the text where desirable, modernized its spelling, altered its punctuation, and cleared away irregularities and obscurities introduced by Okes' compositors.

All emendations (other than the correction of technical slips, such as turned letters, and obvious errors where there is no doubt of the required reading) are noted in the collation, together with those substantive readings from later editions which, in my opinion, might be correct or are of special textual interest. I have normally followed each reading collated with only its first known authority. Words quoted in the collation from this text are in the type in which they occur in the text. Other readings are quoted in their original spelling but in the same type as the relevant quotation from this text; where more than one authority is given for such a reading, the spelling is that of the first authority quoted. Although I believe that Q represents a censored text, I have not tried to re-introduce oaths involving God's name; I judged it impossible to

---

[1] *Textual Problems* (1953), p. 31, and *Sh. First Folio* (1955), pp. 149–52.
[2] Some copies of the 1640 quarto were issued with a new title-page (n.d.), c. 1664.

know the precise oath used or to detect all places where the text has been purged.

Act- and scene-divisions are reproduced from Q without the customary indication of the location of the action: this is discussed, in terms of Jacobean and modern staging, in the annotations. I have replaced Q's collective entries at the head of each scene with directions at the appropriate places for individual entries, but the form of Q's entry is always recorded in the collation. I have retained all the stage-directions of the copy-text and have supplied new ones which are the briefest that can make action clear to a reader; all additions, including each entry after an earlier exit in the same scene, are printed within square brackets. The collation records the authority for additions or changes to Q's directions and Act- and scene-divisions, but I have standardized the manner of marking exits without notification of changes from Q, unless there is some ambiguity (as at III. ii. 322).

Because Crane sometimes used italics and capitals at his own discretion, and because the compositors sometimes regularized the one and modified the other, I have followed normal modern practice in these respects, collating changes only where the sense is affected or where Q's italics indicate quotation or song. I have, however, made an exception for sententious statements which are clearly marked as such in Q. Unlike those who set *The White Devil*, both compositors of *The Duchess* marked *sententiae* throughout the play, B with quotation marks (and once italic type and insetting as well) and A with italic type (occasionally inset) or with quotation marks. Moreover, a press-variant shows that one such notation was added during press-correction (III. v. 75), thus indicating a concern for such detail in the printing-shop; and being on the inner forme of Sheet H, this may have been introduced by Webster himself. I have used italic type without insetting in order to mark these passages, noting Q's arrangement in the collation.[1]

Newly acquired knowledge about the setting of Q from cast-off copy has been used to judge suspected mislineation, and I have

[1] I have also followed the use of roman type for salient words in the generally italicized dedication; the usage here is not paralleled in the text of the play and may represent that of Webster's autograph dedication.

also borne in mind Webster's undoubted employment, in this play and *The White Devil*,[1] of incomplete verse-lines and short passages of prose for dramatic effects. However, the proper arrangement of some passages remains uncertain (as at II. iv. 51–5 and 72–4, and III. ii. 33, 61, 160, 235, and 246–7) and so I have made it a rule to collate all modifications of Q's verse-lining and to record Q's precise arrangements wherever there is some doubt whether a speech, or part of a speech, which I have printed as prose should be so, or whether a new paragraph should be marked in a prose speech. I have printed the beginning of each new speech on a new line, judging that Q's variations from this rule in a few sheets were introduced to save text-space. Where the end of one speech and the beginning of the next clearly make up one verse-line I have indicated this by insetting the second half-line. Where two arrangements seemed possible (as at v. ii. 101–2) I have taken dramatic effectiveness into account as well as the metre. Where the proper arrangement remained in doubt (as at I. i. 311–12) I have printed both consecutive half-lines without insetting. Modifications of Q's placing of the first lines of speeches are not recorded in the collation.

The only departures from modern spelling in this text are a few archaic forms where a rhyme or a primary sense would be lost by the modern form; in such cases, and where an archaic form *might* be preferred, the collation records the authority for the text's spelling and notes one or more alternative spellings. All contractions have been expanded, changes being collated only where the correct form is debatable. Where the metre clearly demands elision within a word, Q has been modified if necessary—this rule is particularly expedient in view of Crane's known habits as a transcriber—and the usual modern elided form has been used here and when following Q. These changes are not recorded. But where the metre suggests elision involving more than one word, Q's form has usually been retained and any change is collated. In prose Q's elisions are not retained except between words or where emphasis in speaking seems to be affected (as in 'o'erladen' instead of 'overladen' at I. i. 50). Changes in elision in prose are not collated.

The original punctuation of the play—the pointing of the lines

---

[1] See, for example, I. i. 496 and IV. i. 108, and Revels *W.D.*, pp. lxx–lxxi.

suggested by Webster's fair copy—can never be recovered. This text has therefore been repunctuated throughout, using the lively pointing of the first quarto of *The White Devil* as a guide as well as Q's punctuation and what is known of the influences that affected it. The collation does not record changes from Q's punctuation unless they affect the sense or clearly modify dramatic emphasis in delivery.

For collating the 1640 quarto I have used the copy in the British Museum with the press-mark 644 f. 73. The following is a list of editions collated and of symbols used to refer to them:

Q	First Quarto of 1623; variant readings due to proof-correction during printing are distinguished by 'Q^a' for the uncorrected state, 'Q^b' and 'Q^c' for successive corrected states.
Q2	Second Quarto of 1640.
Q3	Third Quarto of 1678.
Q4	Fourth Quarto of 1708.
Scott	Walter Scott, *Ancient British Drama* (1810), III.
Dyce i	A. Dyce, *The Works of John Webster* (1830), I.
Dyce ii	A. Dyce, *The Works of John Webster* (1857).
Haz	W. Hazlitt, *The Dramatic Works of John Webster* (1857), II.
Kel	J. S. Keltie, *The Works of the British Dramatists* (Edinburgh, 1870).
Samp	M. W. Sampson, *The White Devil and The Duchess of Malfi* (Boston and London, 1904).
Thorn	A. H. Thorndike, *Webster & Tourneur* (New York, 1922).
Luc i	F. L. Lucas, *The Complete Works of John Webster* (1927), II.
Har	G. B. Harrison, *Selected Plays of Webster and Ford* (1933).
McIl	A. K. McIlwraith, *Five Stuart Tragedies* (1953).
Luc ii	F. L. Lucas, *The Duchess of Malfi* (1958).

THE DUCHESS OF MALFI

[DEDICATION]

To the Right Honourable, George Harding, Baron Berkeley
of Berkeley Castle, and Knight of the Order of the Bath to the
Illustrious Prince Charles.

My Noble Lord,

That I may present my excuse why, being a stranger to your   5
lordship, I offer this poem to your patronage, I plead this
warrant: men who never saw the sea, yet desire to behold that
regiment of waters, choose some eminent river to guide them
thither, and make that, as it were, their conduct or *postilion*; by
the like ingenious means has your *fame* arrived at my know-   10
ledge, receiving it from some of worth who both in *contempla-*
tion and *practice* owe to your *Honour* their clearest service. I do
not altogether look up at your *title*, the ancientest *nobility* being
but a *relic* of time past, and the truest *honour* indeed being for a
man to confer *honour* on himself, which your *learning* strives to   15
propagate and shall make you arrive at the *dignity* of a great

4–31.] *italicized* Q.   9, etc. *postilion, fame, etc.*] *roman* Q.

1. *George Harding*] Son of Sir Thomas Berkeley by Elizabeth Carey
(daughter of George, Lord Hunsdon), he was born 7 Oct. 1601. In 1619 he
was entered as canon-commoner at Christ Church, Oxford. He travelled
widely and died in 1658. While still at Oxford he received the dedication
of Burton's *Anatomy* (1621); and gave the author the living of Seagrave,
Leics., in 1630. Some years after Webster's dedication he received those of
Massinger's *Renegado* (1630) and Shirley's *Young Admiral* (1637).

7–9. *men . . . thither*] found in Erasmus, *Adagia* (from Plautus, *Poenulus*,
III. iii): 'Viam qui nescit, qua deveniat ad mare, / Eum oportet amnem
quaerere comitem sibi.' See also Tilley R137: 'Follow the river and you'll get
to the sea'.

9. *conduct*] conductor, escort.

postilion] guide, forerunner; a word introduced into English at the end
of the 16th century, and still restricted to these meanings (cf. *O.E.D.*).

11–12. *some . . . service*] perhaps the King's Men, who as the Chamber-
lain's Men had 'served' Lord Hunsdon (see l. 1, note above); *clearest* =
unqualified, most entire.

13. *look up*] The sense of 'feel respect' is first recorded by *O.E.D.* in
Bacon, *New Atlantis* (1626).

13–14. *ancientest . . . past*] Cf. *D.L.C.*, I. i. 40–1: 'Gentrie . . . [is] nought
else / But a superstitous relique of time past': both passages echo Overbury's *The Wife* (1614), xx. 3.

example. I am confident this work is not unworthy your
Honour's perusal; for by such *poems* as this, *poets* have kissed
the hands of *great princes* and drawn their gentle eyes to look
down upon their sheets of paper when the *poets* themselves 20
were bound up in their winding sheets. The like courtesy
from your *Lordship* shall make you live in your grave and
laurel spring out of it, when the ignorant scorners of the *Muses*
(that like worms in *libraries* seem to live only to destroy *learning*) shall wither, neglected and forgotten. This work and my- 25
self I humbly present to your approved censure, it being the
utmost of my wishes to have your Honourable self my weighty
and perspicuous comment: which grace so done me, shall ever
be acknowledged

By your Lordship's   30
in all duty and observance,
John Webster.

32. *John Webster*] roman Q.

18–20. *by . . . paper*] Cf. Dedication, *D.L.C.*: 'I present this humbly . . .
knowing the greatest of Caesars, haue cheerefully entertain'd lesse Poems
then this', which Dent paralleled in Warner's dedication of *The Con-
tinuance of Albion's England* (1606).
    28. *perspicuous*] perhaps 'discerning' rather than, more properly, 'lucid'.

[COMMENDATORY VERSES]

In the just worth of that well-deserver, Mr. John Webster, and upon this masterpiece of tragedy.

In this thou imitat'st one rich, and wise,
That sees his good deeds done before he dies;
As he by works, thou by this work of fame,　　　5
Hast well provided for thy living name.
To trust to others' honourings is worth's crime—
Thy monument is rais'd in thy life-time;
And 'tis most just; for every worthy man
Is his own marble, and his merit can　　　10
Cut him to any figure and express
More art than Death's cathedral palaces,
Where royal ashes keep their court. Thy note
Be ever plainness, 'tis the richest coat:
Thy epitaph only the title be—　　　15
Write, 'Duchess', that will fetch a tear for thee,
For who e'er saw this duchess live, and die,
That could get off under a bleeding eye?

In Tragœdiam.

Ut lux ex tenebris ictu percussa Tonantis,　　　20
Illa, ruina malis, claris fit vita poetis.

Thomas Middletonus,
Poeta & Chron. Londinensis.

VERSES] Ford was later to commend plays by Massinger, Shirley, and Broome, but Middleton and Rowley never performed this service for another play.
19–21.] 'To Tragedy: As light from darkness springs at the Thunderer's stroke, / So she brings ruin to the wicked and life to the poet.'
22. *Middletonus*] Thomas Middleton collaborated with Webster during their earlier days (cf. Revels *W.D.*, pp. xvii–xviii) and either imitated him or again collaborated with him in *A.Q.L.*, performed by the King's Men in 1621 (cf. Lucas, iv. 66–8 and Bentley, iv. 859–61). He frequently collaborated with Rowley, here his fellow commender, in the years around 1620. He was appointed City Chronologer, 6 Sept. 1620.

To his friend, Mr. John Webster, upon his *Duchess of Malfi*.

> I never saw thy duchess till the day　　　　25
> That she was lively body'd in thy play;
> Howe'er she answer'd her low-rated love,
> Her brothers' anger did so fatal prove,
> Yet my opinion is, she might speak more,
> But never, in her life, so well before.　　　30
>
> 　　　　　　　　　*Wil. Rowley.*

To the reader of the author, and his *Duchess of Malfi*.

> Crown him a poet, whom nor Rome, nor Greece,
> Transcend in all theirs, for a masterpiece:
> In which, whiles words and matter change, and men　　35
> Act one another, he, from whose clear pen
> They all took life, to memory hath lent
> A lasting fame, to raise his monument.
>
> 　　　　　　　　　*John Ford.*

---

27. *answer'd*] justified.
28. *Her . . . prove*] i.e., 'Which her . . .'.
31. Rowley] actor and dramatist (*c.* 1585–1625/6): he collaborated with Webster once or twice in 1624–5 (cf. Revels *W.D.*, p. xxv).
35–6. *whiles . . . another*] i.e., 'while literature has its fashions and the theatre lasts'; *words and matter* was a common phrase, opposing the style and substance of writing.
37. *all*] i.e., words, substance, and character.
39.] John Ford (1586–?1639) may have commenced dramatist, like Webster, under Dekker's tutelage (so Bentley): he collaborated with Webster (and Dekker and Rowley) in the lost *Late Murder in Whitechapel* (1624).

The Actors' Names
[as given in the first edition].

Bosola, *J. Lowin.*
Ferdinand, 1. *R. Burbidge.* 2. *J. Taylor.*
Cardinal, 1. *H. Cundaile.* 2. *R. Robinson.*
Antonio, 1. *W. Ostler.* 2. *R. Benfield.*
Delio, *J. Underwood.*   5
Forobosco, *N. Towley.*
Malateste.
The Marquis of Pescara, *J. Rice.*
Silvio, *T. Pollard.*
The several madmen, *N. Towley, J. Underwood, etc.*   10
The Duchess, *R. Sharpe.*
The Cardinal's Mistress, *J. Tomson.*
The Doctor, ⎫
Cariola,   ⎬ *R. Pallant.*
        ⎭
Court Officers.   15
Three young children.
Two Pilgrims.

1–17.] *before dedication, A2ᵛ, Q.*   13–14.] *bracket so Luc ii; bracket opposite* Cariola *and* Court Officers *Q.*

Actors' Names] *The Duchess* is the earliest English play to be published with a list of actors assigned to individual rôles; this innovation was not copied until 1629, in plays by the courtier Carlell, and Massinger and Shirley. For the casting, see Intro., pp. xviii–xxi.

Dramatis personae were often printed before plays. Here Bosola has been given unprecedented prominence at the head of the list; characters were usually placed in order of rank and status. Webster may have been responsible for this (cf. Intro., p. lxvii), thus expressing his view of the play's dramatic structure.

6. *Forobosco*] Cf. Intro., p. lxvii.

[DRAMATIS PERSONAE

FERDINAND, *Duke of Calabria, twin brother to the Duchess.*
The Cardinal, *their brother.*
DANIEL DE BOSOLA, *returned from imprisonment in the galleys*
following service for the Cardinal; later the Provisor of
Horse to the Duchess, and in the pay of Ferdinand. 5
ANTONIO BOLOGNA, *Steward of the Household to the Duchess;*
later her husband.
DELIO, *his friend; a courtier.*
CASTRUCHIO, *an old lord; husband of Julia.*
Marquis of PESCARA, *a soldier.* 10
Count MALATESTE, *a courtier at Rome.*
SILVIO, *a courtier at Malfi and Rome.*
RODERIGO ⎱
GRISOLAN ⎰ *courtiers at Malfi.*
Doctor. 15

The Duchess of Malfi, *a young widow; later wife of Antonio;*
sister to the Cardinal and twin sister to Ferdinand.
CARIOLA, *her waiting-woman.*
JULIA, *wife of Castruchio and mistress of the Cardinal.*
Old Lady, *a midwife.* 20

Two Pilgrims.
Eight Madmen, *being an Astrologer, Lawyer, Priest, Doctor,*
English Tailor, Gentleman Usher, Farmer, and Broker.
Court Officers; Servants; Guards; Executioners; Attendants;
Churchmen. 25
Ladies-in-Waiting.

SCENE: *Malfi, Rome, Loretto, the countryside near Ancona,*
and Milan.]

Dramatis Personae . . .] so this ed.

7

The Duchess of Malfi

Act I

Enter ANTONIO *and* DELIO.

Delio. You are welcome to your country, dear Antonio—
　　　　You have been long in France, and you return
Precise　　A very formal Frenchman in your habit. dress.
　　　　How do you like the French court ?
Ant.　　　　　　　　　　　　I admire it—
　　　　In seeking to reduce both state and people　　　　　5

I. i. 0.1.] *Q4; Antonio, and Delio, Bosola, Cardinall Q.*

Actus . . . Prima] Ralph Crane (cf. Intro., pp. lxv f.) followed a common practice in using Latin for marking Act- and scene-divisions. But he may have represented his author's wishes here, for *D.L.C.* (a literary, rather than theatrical, text) also has Latin divisions. The first ed. of *W.D.* has no divisions.

2. *long in France*] Cf. Painter; App. I, p. 177.
3. *formal*] precise, punctilious.
habit] dress.
5–15.] probably from Elyot, *Image of Governance* (1541), viii : Mammen, mother of Alexander Severus, 'with good reson perswaded to hym, that he coulde neuer wel stablyshe his astate Imperyall, but onely by reducynge of the senate and people into their prystinate order, whyche coulde neuer be brought to passe, except that fyrste his own palaice were cleane purged of personages corrupted with vices, . . . consydering that the princis palaice is lyke a common fountayne or sprynge to his citie or countrey, wherby the people by the cleannes therof longe preserued in honestie, or by the impurenes therof, are with sundry vyces corrupted. And vntylle the fountain be purged, there can neuer be any sure hope of remedy. / Wherefore Alexander immediatly after that he had receiued of the senate and people the name of Augustus, . . . fyrste he dyscharged all minysters, . . . banyshing also out of his palaice, al such as he mought by any meanes knowe, to be persones infamed, semblably flatterers, . . .' The passage can be paralleled in many Renaissance books on policy, but Webster is indebted to Elyot at

To a fix'd order, their judicious king
Begins at home: quits first his royal palace
Of flatt'ring sycophants, of dissolute
And infamous persons—which he sweetly terms
His Master's masterpiece, the work of heaven—   10
Consid'ring duly, that a prince's court
Is like a common fountain, whence should flow
Pure silver drops in general: but if 't chance
Some curs'd example poison 't near the head,
Death, and diseases through the whole land spread.   15
And what is't makes this blessed government,
But a most provident Council, who dare freely
Inform him the corruption of the times ?
Though some o'th' court hold it presumption   *Cowt–scowrge.*
To instruct princes what they ought to do,   20
It is a noble duty to inform them
What they ought to foresee:—

Enter BOSOLA.

                    Here comes Bosola,
The only court-gall:—yet I observe his railing
Is not for simple love of piety;

15.] *italicized this ed.;* "Death . . . *Q.*   22. S.D.] *so this ed.; at l.* 0.1 *Q;*
after l. 28 ('. . . *Bosola, Cardinal*') *Q*4.

I. i. 398–403. For the dramatic and topical importance of this speech, see
Intro., pp. xxv–xxvi and xxxix–xli.

5. *state*] ruling body, grand council; cf. Elyot's 'senate and people'.

13. *in general*] everywhere.

16–22. *And . . . foresee*] Dent compared Painter, *Palace*, II (1567), xiii,
p. 87: the Senate addresses Trajan, 'sith you wrote unto us the maner and
order what we ought to do: reason it is that we write to you againe what you
ought to foresee . . . Princes oftentimes be negligent of many things, not for
that they will not foresee the same, but rather for want of one that dare tel
them what they ought to doe.'

23. *court-gall*] court-scourge. Primarily, *gall* = 'sore, produced by
chafing', and hence 'harasser, tormenter'. But *gall* also = 'bile' and,
hence, 'asperity, bitterness of spirit', and something of this is implied by
'rail' of ll. 23 and 25. Shakespeare often associated *gall* = 'bile' with railing;
cf. *Troil.*, I. iii. 193: 'whose gall coins slanders like a mint'.

Indeed he rails at those things which he wants,   25
Would be as lecherous, covetous, or proud,
Bloody, or envious, as any man,
If he had means to be so:—

Enter Cardinal.

Here's the cardinal.

Bos. I do haunt you still.
Card.   So.
Bos.   I have done you
Better service than to be slighted thus:—   30
Miserable age, where only the reward
Of doing well, is the doing of it.

Card. You enforce your merit too much.

Bos. I fell into the galleys in your service, where for two
years together, I wore two towels instead of a shirt, with   35
a knot on the shoulder, after the fashion of a Roman
mantle:— slighted thus? I will thrive some way: black-
birds fatten best in hard weather; why not I, in these
dog-days?

28. S.D.] *so this ed; at l. 0.1 Q; at end of line ('. . . Bosola, Cardinal') Q4.*
29–32. I have . . .] *so Q; as prose Dyce i.*

25–8. *he rails . . . so*] from *A.T.,* V. ii. 2932–4: 'We what we wish for
most, seeme to mislike: / And oft of others doe the course disproue, / Whilst
we want nought but meanes to doe the like.'

27. *envious*] perhaps 'malicious' (a common meaning).

29. *haunt*] follow after; or, perhaps, 'search for' (cf. *W.D.,* II. i. 175,
note).

31–2.] probably taken from Florio (there derived from Seneca and
Cicero), II. xvi: 'The reward of wel doing, is the doing, & the fruit of our
duty, is our dutie'; the idea was proverbial, as 'Virtue is its own reward'
(Tilley V81). Cf. Bosola's last couplet, V. v. 103–4.

35–7. *I . . . mantle*] Cf. *1H4,* IV. ii. 44–51. Sarcastically, Bosola gives a
mock dignity to poverty.

37–8. *black- . . . weather*] Dent compared Hall, *Epistles* (1611), VI. vii:
'growne wealthy with warre, like those Fowles which fatten with hard
weather . . .' The particularization of '*black*-birds' may be Webster's
independent colouring to show Bosola's cast of mind.

39. *dog-days*] days during the Heliacal rising of the Dog-star, renowned
as the hottest and most unwholesome time of the year; usually reckoned as
the forty days following 11 August.

Card. Would you could become honest. 40

Bos. With all your divinity, do but direct me the way to it—
[*Exit* Cardinal.] I have known many travel far for it, and
yet return as arrant knaves as they went forth, because
they carried themselves always along with them;—Are
you gone ? Some fellows, they say, are possessed with the 45
devil, but this great fellow were able to possess the greatest devil, and make him worse.

Ant. He hath denied thee some suit ?

Bos. He, and his brother, are like plum-trees, that grow
crooked over standing pools; they are rich, and o'erladen 50
with fruit, but none but crows, pies, and caterpillars feed
on them: could I be one of their flattering panders, I
would hang on their ears like a horse-leech till I were full,
and then drop off:— I pray leave me.

Who would rely upon these miserable dependences, in 55
expectation to be advanced tomorrow ? what creature
ever fed worse than hoping Tantalus ? nor ever died any

---

42. S.D.] *so this ed.; after* them, *l. 44* Dyce i.   54. and] *Q2;* an *Q.*
55–62.] *4, out of 6, lines justified as prose (exceptionally) in Q.*   55. depen-
dences] *Q;* dependencies *Dyce i.*   57. died] *Q^b;* did *Q^a.*

---

42. S.D.] An early exit seems preferable: so the cardinal does not appear
to wait on Bosola's words, and Bosola's tendency towards soliloquy, or
'contemplation' (cf. II. i. 76), is established at the outset. 'Are you gone ?',
a few lines later, implies that the cardinal has already left the stage and that
Bosola has not watched him for some time.

42–4. *I . . . them*] Cf. Florio, I. xxxviii: 'It was told Socrates, that one was
no whit amended by his travell: I beleeve it well (saide he) for he carried
himselfe with him.'

49–52. *like . . . them*] a common simile, usually of fig trees growing on
steep mountains; Dent found one example with fig trees 'growing ouer
deepe Waters, full of Fruite, but the Iayes eate them: Ruffians, Harlots,
vicious Companions enioy those Graces, that might honour God', in T.
Adams, *Gallant's Burden* (1612), F2.

standing = stagnant; cf. Tilley P465: 'Standing pools gather filth'.

crows, pies, and *caterpillars* were frequently used of inhuman men:
feeding on carrion; wily (magpies); and rapacious.

53. *horse-leech*] i.e., blood-sucker; cf. *W.D.*, v. vi. 166.

56–7. *what . . . Tantalus*] from Whetstone, *Heptameron* (1582), I2^v:
'. . . no man dyneth worse, then hoping Tantalus'.

Tantalus was a proverbial figure of the hoping and disappointed man;

man more fearfully than he that hoped for a pardon.
There are rewards for hawks, and dogs, when they have
done us service; but for a soldier, that hazards his limbs in   60
a battle, nothing but a kind of geometry is his last supportation.

Delio. Geometry?

Bos. Ay, to hang in a fair pair of slings, take his latter swing in
the world upon an honourable pair of crutches, from hos-   65

---

58. pardon] Q^b; pleadon Q^a.   59. dogs,] $Q2$; dogges, and Q; dogs, and
horses, *conj. Luc i;* dogs, and whores, *conj. this ed.*

---

the Eng. vb 'tantalize' is derived from his name. He was said to have been
punished in Hades by perpetual thirst and by being placed in the middle of
a lake of water which receded whenever he tried to drink; fruit hung above
him which always eluded his grasp; and a huge rock over his head was
always threatening to fall.

59. *dogs,*] Q's 'dogges, and' may be due to the erroneous repetition of
the preceding 'and'. But *service* is not particularly appropriate to either
dogs or *hawks*, and an omission may be suspected. But more evidence must
be considered. First, 'dogges, and' is at the end of a line of text in Q and
followed by a space sufficient for three to five pieces of type; this is remarkable in that the three previous lines and the one following have been 'justified' to run to the full width of the text-space, as usual in setting prose but
unique in this book (see Intro., pp. lxv f.). Some type may have dropped
out, or been removed as an obvious error, before printing.

Lucas suggested that 'horses' had dropped out, and then warned that
reward as a technical term of the chase is suitable only to *dogs* and *hawks*.
Dent, however, supported this conjecture by quoting Florio who compared man's treatment of men with his treatment of horses and then of
dogs and *hawks*: 'The men that serve vs, doe it better cheape, and for a less
curious and favourable entreating, than we use vnto birds, vnto horses, and
vnto dogges. . . We share the fruites of our prey with our dogges and
hawkes, as a meede of their paine and reward for their industry' (II. xii).

Further evidence is Webster's use of *reward* elsewhere: at II. ii. 15–17,
Bosola speaks of 'reward' for women's 'entertainment'; and in *W.D.*
Vittoria, having blamed Bracciano for treating her as a whore, makes
her last reproach, 'Your dog or hawk should be *rewarded* better / Than
I have been' (IV. ii. 107–19, 136, 145, and 190–1). If a word is missing
in association with *reward*, *hawks*, and *dogs*, it may well be 'whores'. The
following *service*, *limbs*, and *supportation* also have associations fitting to
'whores'.

61. *geometry*] 'Hang by geometry' was a proverbial phrase; see Tilley
G82.

64. *swing*] quibblingly: (1) 'forcible movement', as on crutches, and (2)
'fling' ('to *take* one's *swing*' was to indulge oneself, as with mod. 'fling').

pital to hospital—fare ye well sir. And yet do not you
scorn us, for places in the court are but like beds in the
hospital, where this man's head lies at that man's foot, and
so lower, and lower.　　　　　　　　　　　　　　[*Exit.*]

Delio. I knew this fellow seven years in the galleys　　　70
　　　For a notorious murder, and 'twas thought
　　　The cardinal suborn'd it: he was releas'd
　　　By the French general, Gaston de Foix,
　　　When he recover'd Naples.

Ant.　　　　　　　　　　　　　'Tis great pity
　　　He should be thus neglected—I have heard　　　75
　　　He's very valiant: this foul melancholy
　　　Will poison all his goodness, for—I'll tell you—
　　　If too immoderate sleep be truly said
　　　To be an inward rust unto the soul,
　　　It then doth follow want of action　　　80
　　　Breeds all black malcontents, and their close rearing,
　　　Like moths in cloth, do hurt for want of wearing.

---

69. *Exit*] *Q4*.　　　73. Foix] *Q2* (Foyx)*; Foux Q*.

---

73. *Foix*] Webster probably wrote thus, and not 'Foux' as in Q, for the
name derives from Painter (see App. I, p. 177); extant MSS. by Crane
occasionally have too many minims in a word. Foix was too young to have
had a part in the 'recovery' of Naples in 1501.

76. *melancholy*] This was both a mental disease (thought to be due to an
excess of 'black bile'; cf. T. Bright's *Treatise of Melancholy*, 1586) and an
affectation. In Renaissance Italy, partly on the authority of Marsilio Ficino,
the disease was regarded as the infirmity of great minds, and so it became
fashionable to affect it; 'malcontents', disappointed by their fortunes or
opposed to an established regime, were especially given to this pose. In the
1580s the fashion spread to England (cf. Z. S. Fink, 'Jaques and the Malcontent Traveller', *P.Q.*, xiv (1935), 237–52). Ferdinand assumes that Bosola only affects melancholy, as a 'garb' (l. 278).

Malcontents were 'usually black-suited and dishevelled, unsociable,
asperous, morosely meditative, taciturn yet prone to occasional railing'
(L. Babb, *Elizabethan Malady* (1957), p. 75).

78–82.] Cf. *W.D.*, v. vi. 274, and T. Coghan, *Haven of Health* (1584),
Hh1ᵛ: 'immoderate sleepe maketh the bodie slowe, and vnapt to honest
exercises, and subiect to manie diseases, and the witte dull and vnable
either to conceiue or to retaine'.

82. *do*] Strictly 'close wearing' is its subject, but this verb is in the
plural influenced by 'malcontents' and 'moths'; cf. Abbott §412.

Enter SILVIO, CASTRUCHIO, JULIA, RODERIGO, *and* GRISOLAN.

Delio. The presence 'gins to fill—you promis'd me
           To make me the partaker of the natures
           Of some of your great courtiers.

Ant.   The Lord Cardinal's   85
           And other strangers', that are now in court?
           I shall:—

                    Enter FERDINAND.

               Here comes the great Calabrian duke.

Ferd. Who took the ring oftenest?
Sil. Antonio Bologna, my lord.
Ferd. Our sister duchess' great master of her household?   90
           Give him the jewel:—When shall we leave this sportive
           action, and fall to action indeed?

82.1.] *Samp; Scena II.* | *Antonio, Delio, Ferdinand, Cardinall, Dutchesse,*
Castruchio, Siluio, Rodocico, Grisolan, Bosola, Iulia, Cariola Q; Exeunt. |
Scena II. | *Enter Antonio, Delio, Ferdinand, Castruchio, Sylvio Q4; not in*
Dyce ii.   87. S.D.] *so this ed.; at l. 82.1 Q, Q4; at end of line Dyce ii.*
Ferdinand] *Q; Ferdinand, Castruccio, Silvio, Roderigo, Grisolan and*
Attendants Dyce ii; Ferdinand, with Attendants conj. this ed.

   82.1.] To avoid confusion of references, it is useful to follow other
modern editions, rather than Q, and print Act I as a single continuous
scene. But Antonio and Delio may well leave the stage after l. 82 to enter
again in the wake of the state entry to the 'presence'; this is the customary
arrangement for Camillo and Archidamus between I. i and I. ii of *Winter's
Tale* (cf. *S.B.*, vi (1954), 131–2).
   83. *presence*] presence-chamber.
   88. *ring*] Riding at the *ring*, to carry it away on a lance, was a common
form of jousting.
   Webster may have intended Ferdinand to speak with (unintentional)
irony: (1) his abrupt manner of speech on his first, elaborate entry gives
unusual emphasis to the phrase; (2) Antonio 'takes the *ring*' at the end of
this act (ll. 404–15) and in prison Ferdinand gives the duchess a 'ring' (IV.
i. 44–51); and, perhaps, the cord which strangles her is a further echo, for
Cariola's is called her 'wedding ring' (IV. ii. 249); and (3) *ring* may have an
(unintentional) undertone that is sexual; it was a common word in sexual
jokes (see, e.g., *Mer.V.*, v. i. 304–7) and is here followed by 'jewel' (also
common in bawdy) which in *W.D.*, I. ii. 221–8 Webster used for a series of
suggestive puns (and cf. *D.L.C.*, II. i. 296); sexual undertones may be continued in '*fall* to action' (l. 92) and are certainly present by ll. 105 (see note)
and 112–14.

Cast. Methinks, my lord, you should not desire to go to war
    in person.

Ferd. Now for some gravity!—why, my lord?   95

Cast. It is fitting a soldier arise to be a prince, but not neces-
    sary a prince descend to be a captain.

Ferd. No?

Cast. No, my lord, he were far better do it by a deputy.

Ferd. Why should he not as well sleep, or eat, by a deputy?   100
    This might take idle, offensive, and base office from him,
    whereas the other deprives him of honour.

Cast. Believe my experience: that realm is never long in
    quiet, where the ruler is a soldier.

Ferd. Thou told'st me thy wife could not endure fighting.   105

Cast. True, my lord.

Ferd. And of a jest she broke, of a captain she met full of
    wounds:—I have forgot it.

Cast. She told him, my lord, he was a pitiful fellow, to lie,
    like the children of Ishmael, all in tents.   110

Ferd. Why, there's a wit were able to undo all the chirur-
    geons o' the city, for although gallants should quarrel,
    and had drawn their weapons, and were ready to go to it,
    yet her persuasions would make them put up.

Cast. That she would, my lord—   115

93–104.] Cf. *W.D.*, II. i. 116–23, and note. Webster is probably indebted
here (as at ll. 16–22 above) to Painter, *Palace*, II (1567), xiii, p. 84: 'Truly
it liketh me wel, that from the degree of Captains men be aduanced to be
Emperors, but I thinke it not good, that Emperours do descend to be
Captains, considering that the realme shal neuer be in quiet, when the
Prince is to great a warrior' (so Dent).

   105. *fighting*] with a *double entendre*: the implication is that Castruchio's
'realm', or marriage, is 'unquiet'.

   110. *tents*] (1) ordinary sense, (2) 'surgical dressings', and, possibly,
(3) 'intentions' (cf. *O.E.D.*, *sb.* 2). The third meaning is clearer in Middleton, *More Dissemblers* (?1615), II. iii, where Aurelia complains of a soldier's
talk immediately before making the same jest: 'All his discourse [is] out of
the Book of Surgery, / Cere-cloth and salve, and lies you all in tents, / Like
your camp-vic'lers.'

   111–12. *chirurgeons*] surgeons.

   112–14. *although . . .*] with *doubles entendres*, especially on *drawn their
weapons* and *put up*.

Ferd. How do you like my Spanish jennet?

Rod. He is all fire.

Ferd. I am of Pliny's opinion, I think he was begot by the
wind; he runs as if he were ballasted with quicksilver.

Sil. True, my lord, he reels from the tilt often.   120

Rod., Gris. Ha, ha, ha!

Ferd. Why do you laugh? Methinks you that are courtiers
should be my touch-wood, take fire, when I give fire;
that is, laugh when I laugh, were the subject never so
witty—   125

---

116. *Ferd.* How . . .] *conj. Samp, this ed.;* How . . . (*separate line and inset*) *Q*.
124. laugh when] *Q;* Not laugh but when *Q4;* laugh but when *Dyce i*.

---

116. *Ferd.*] The separate line 'How . . . jennet' is inset in Q as if Compositor B had placed a space in his composing-stick intending to set a
speech-prefix and had then forgotten to add it. Compositor A inset a line
in this way at v. iii. 35 where a prefix is clearly omitted.

A *jennet* is a light, sporting horse (cf. Painter; App. I, p. 181) and quite
inappropriate to the old Castruchio (cf. ii. iv. 44–5 and 53–6). Moreover,
Ferdinand alone introduces new topics of conversation in this small-talk
with sycophantic courtiers. Lucas, who followed most editors in giving the
question to Castruchio, argued that the jest at l. 120 would be too audacious
to apply to Ferdinand's horse. But this is probably the reason why Webster included the passage: he thus demonstrated Ferdinand's power in his
quenching of laughter suddenly—always an effective theatrical device for
centring attention on someone's ability to control others. Moreover, the
incident illustrates the precarious life of attendance at court: Silvio had
relaxed sufficiently to forget propriety and the rising enjoyment is rebuked
at once.

118. *Pliny's opinion*] Cf. *Natural History* (tr. 1601), xlii: 'In Portugall,
along the river Tagus, and about Lisbon, certaine it is, that when the West
wind bloweth, the mares set up their tailes, and turne them full against it,
and so conceive that genitall aire in steed of naturall seed: in such sort, as
they become great withall, and quicken in their time, and bring foorth
foles as swift as the wind . . .'

119. *ballasted with quicksilver*] The point is, probably, that the ballast
that should slow the horse down is itself *quick* and valuable.

120. *reels . . . tilt*] quibblingly: (1) the ballast rights the *tilt* (as of a boat),
and (2) the horse jibs (as in jousting). Possibly, Roderigo and Grisolan
laugh so noticeably because they sense the common bawdy meaning of *tilt*
(cf. *W.D.*, iii. i. 16 and note, and 66–73); Bosola's laughter is indicated in
the same way on talk of a codpiece (ii. ii. 39).

If Ferdinand silences bawdy laughter and yet speaks bawdily himself,
his sexual awareness will seem the more private and dangerous to an
audience.

124. *when I laugh*] i.e., and only then.

Cast. True, my lord, I myself have heard a very good jest,
        and have scorned to seem to have so silly a wit as to
        understand it.

Ferd. But I can laugh at your fool, my lord.

Cast. He cannot speak, you know, but he makes faces—my   130
        lady cannot abide him.

Ferd. No?

Cast. Nor endure to be in merry company: for she says too
        much laughing, and too much company, fills her too full
        of the wrinkle.   135

Ferd. I would then have a mathematical instrument made for
        her face, that she might not laugh out of compass:—I
        shall shortly visit you at Milan, Lord Silvio.

Sil. Your grace shall arrive most welcome.

Ferd. You are a good horseman, Antonio—you have excel-   140
        lent riders in France; what do you think of good horse-
        manship?

Ant. Nobly, my lord—as out of the Grecian horse issued
        many famous princes, so, out of brave horsemanship,
        arise the first sparks of growing resolution, that raise the   145
        mind to noble action.

Ferd. You have bespoke it worthily.

        Enter Cardinal, Duchess, CARIOLA, [*with* Attendants].

Sil. Your brother, the Lord Cardinal, and sister Duchess.

Card. Are the galleys come about?

Gris. They are, my lord.   150

147.1. *with Attendants*] *This ed.; and* Bosola *Q4; and* Julia *Dyce i.*

127–30. *so silly . . . faces*] Congenital imbeciles were kept as 'fools' in
great households: Castruchio's was a dumb idiot.

137. *out of compass*] immoderately, beyond due limits; with a pun on
compass as a 'mathematical instrument' (l. 136).

140. *You . . . Antonio*] Cf. Painter; App. I, p. 177.

140–1. *excellent . . . France*] The French were commonly held to be good
riders; cf. *W.D.*, IV. iii. 96.

149–50.] This exchange is never developed in narrative or in the relation-
ship between the two men: it is a brief, but theatrically effective, device for
suggesting the alert and independent intrigues behind the façade of formal
court-life.

Ferd. Here's the Lord Silvio, is come to take his leave.

Delio. Now sir, your promise: what's that cardinal?

I mean his temper? they say he's a brave fellow,
Will play his five thousand crowns at tennis, dance,
Court ladies, and one that hath fought single combats.   155

Ant. Some such flashes superficially hang on him, for form;
but observe his inward character:—he is a melancholy
churchman; the spring in his face is nothing but the
engendering of toads; where he is jealous of any man, he
lays worse plots for them than ever was imposed on   160
Hercules, for he strews in his way flatterers, panders,
intelligencers, atheists, and a thousand such political
monsters. He should have been Pope; but instead of
coming to it by the primitive decency of the church, he
did bestow bribes so largely, and so impudently, as if he   165
would have carried it away without heaven's knowledge.
Some good he hath done.

Delio. You have given too much of him: what's his brother?

Ant. The duke there? a most perverse, and turbulent nature:
What appears in him mirth, is merely outside;   170
If he laugh heartily, it is to laugh

---

160. them] *Q;* him *Haz.*   161. flatterers] *Q3;* Flatters *Q.*

---

154. *Will . . . tennis*] Cf. *W.D.*, II. i. 182, and note.

156. *form*] merely outward appearances; cf. *W.D.*, IV. iii. 144–9 where
the *form* is modesty, rather than *flashes* of youthful bravery. *O.E.D.* first
records *flash* = 'ostentation, *éclat*' in 1674, but = 'showy talk' in Jonson's
character 'Sir Petronell Flash' in *Eastward Ho* (1605).

158–9. *spring . . . toads*] Cf. Chapman, *Bussy* (1604), III. ii. 363–5:
'. . . thy gall / Turns all thy blood to poison, which is cause / Of that toad-
pool that stands in thy complexion'; see also *Mer.V.*, I. i. 88–9 and *Oth.*,
IV. ii. 59–64 (so Lucas).

159. *jealous*] suspicious (a common meaning).

162. *intelligencers*] informers, spies.

atheists] commonly used, in a general sense, for impious or wicked
persons.

163–6. *He . . .*] perhaps from Hall, *Characters* (1608), 'Ambitious': 'His
wit so contriues the likely plots of his promotion, as if hee would steale it
away without Gods knowledge'.

171–2. *If . . . fashion*] another possible debt to Hall, *Characters*, 'Profane': 'Euery vertue hath his slander and his iest to laugh it out of fashion'.

All honesty out of fashion.

Delio.					Twins ?

Ant.					In quality:—
He speaks with others' tongues, and hears men's suits
With others' ears; will seem to sleep o'th' bench
Only to entrap offenders in their answers;					175
Dooms men to death by information,
Rewards by hearsay.

Delio.					Then the law to him
Is like a foul black cobweb to a spider—
He makes it his dwelling, and a prison
To entangle those shall feed him.

Ant.					Most true:					180
He ne'er pays debts, unless they be shrewd turns,
And those he will confess that he doth owe.
Last, for his brother, there, the cardinal—
They that do flatter him most say oracles
Hang at his lips: and verily I believe them;					185
For the devil speaks in them.

---

181. shrewd] *Q2;* shewed *Q.*

---

172. *Twins ?*] Webster probably intended the two brothers and sister to look alike in appearance and age; Ferdinand later says that he and the duchess are twins (IV. ii. 267). See also I. i. 188–9.

173–7. *He . . . hearsay*] from *A.T.,* II. i. 570–8: 'Whilst he that rulde still needing to be rulde, / Spake but with others tongues, heard with their eares. / . . . / That of himselfe cannot discerne a crime: / But doomes by information men to death'.

information = 'reported intelligence' or 'accusation'.

177–80. *law . . . him*] Webster has adapted the common proverb, 'the law, like a cobweb, traps the little and allows the great to escape' (Tilley L116): Dyce, however, compared Field, *Woman is a Weathercock* (1612), II. i. 316–19; law 'is a Spiders web / Made to entangle the poore helplesse flies, / Whilst the great Spiders that did make it first, / And rule it, sit i' th midst secure and laugh . . .'

181–2.] Muriel Bradbrook (*M.L.R.,* 1947) compared Chapman, *Penitential Psalms* (1612), 'A Great Man': 'Paies neuer debt, but what he should not ow.'

shrewd turns = 'acts of ill will, injuries' (the opposite to a 'good turn').

184–5. *They . . . lips*] Cf. Hall, *Characters* (1608), 'Flatterer': 'He hangs vpon the lips which he admireth, as if they could let fall nothing but oracles . . .'

But for their sister, the right noble duchess—
You never fix'd your eye on three fair medals,
Cast in one figure, of so different temper:
For her discourse, it is so full of rapture   190
You only will begin then to be sorry
When she doth end her speech; and wish, in wonder,
She held it less vain-glory to talk much,
Than you penance to hear her: whilst she speaks,
She throws upon a man so sweet a look,   195
That it were able raise one to a galliard
That lay in a dead palsy, and to dote
On that sweet countenance: but in that look,
There speaketh so divine a continence
As cuts off all lascivious, and vain hope.   200
Her days are practis'd in such noble virtue
That sure her nights—nay more, her very sleeps—

---

188. your] *Q2;* you *Q.*   194. Than] *Q2;* Then *Q.*   you] *Anderson;*
your *Q.*   196. able] *Q;* able to *Q3.*

190–205. *For . . . her*] from Pettie, II. 241–2: 'her talke and discourses
are so delightfull, that you wyll only then beginne to bee sory, when shee
endeth to speake: and wishe that shee woulde bee no more weary to speake,
then you are to heare. . . She wyll also in talke cast oft times upon a man
such a sweete smyle, that it were enough to bryng him into a fooles Paradise,
but that her countenance conteineth such continencie in it, as is sufficient
to cut off all fond hope. . . I cannot sufficientlye set foorth unto you the
graces and perfections of this perfect peece, but for conclusion I will say,
that shee may well bee set for an example, whereto other women ought to
conforme them selves . . .'

In noting this source, Marcia Anderson untangled the confusion due to
Q's 'your' at l. 194.

196. *galliard*] a lively dance; Davies (*Orchestra*) called it 'gallant . . . /
With lofty turns and capriols in the air'.

198–9. *countenance . . . continence*] a quibble: both words are derived
from L. *continentia,* and in the 16th century were confused in spelling.

201–3.] Perhaps suggested by Donne, *Progress of the Soul* (1612), ll.
463–4: 'Whose twilights were more cleare, then our mid-day; / Who
dreamt devoutlier, then most use to pray' (so Lucas).

nay . . . sleeps alludes to the notion that dreams 'are certaine signes of ye
affections of ye minde . . .: the fearfull dreame that they flye daunger: the
couetous yt they imbrace riches', etc. (Bartholomeus, *De Proprietatibus
Rerum* (tr. 1582), VI. xxvii).

Are more in heaven than other ladies' shrifts.
Let all sweet ladies break their flatt'ring glasses,
And dress themselves in her.

Delio.   Fie Antonio,   205
You play the wire-drawer with her commendations.

Ant. I'll case the picture up:—only thus much—
All her particular worth grows to this sum:
She stains the time past, lights the time to come.

Cari. You must attend my lady, in the gallery,   210
Some half an hour hence.

Ant. I shall.

Ferd. Sister, I have a suit to you:—

Duch.   To me, sir?

Ferd. A gentleman here, Daniel de Bosola;
One that was in the galleys.

Duch.   Yes, I know him:—   215

Ferd. A worthy fellow h' is: pray let me entreat for
The provisorship of your horse.

Duch.   Your knowledge of him
Commends him, and prefers him.

Ferd.   Call him hither—
                              [*Exit* Attendant.]

We now are upon parting: good Lord Silvio,
Do us commend to all our noble friends   220
At the leaguer.

Sil.   Sir, I shall.

Duch.   You are for Milan?

212. shall] *Q;* shall. *Ex. Ant. Delio Q4.*   216. for] *Q;* for him *conj. Luc i.*
218.1.] *Dyce i.*   219. now are] *McIl;* now *Q;* are now *Q4.*   221.
leaguer] *Q2;* Leagues *Q.   Duch.*] *Samp; Ferd. Q.*

---

206. *play the wire-drawer*] spin out your words, make much of little.
207. *case*] close, cover; cf. III. ii. 139.
209.] from *A.T.,* III. ii. 1319: 'Staine of times past, and light of times to come'.
   stains = 'eclipses, puts in the shade' (a common sense in Webster's day).
221. *leaguer*] military camp.
   Duch.] The speech can hardly be Ferdinand's (as in Q) because he obviously knows Silvio's destination (cf. his previous speech and l. 151,

Sil. I am:—

Duch. Bring the caroches: we'll bring you down to the haven.

           [*Exeunt all except* Cardinal *and* FERDINAND.]

Card. Be sure you entertain that Bosola

    For your intelligence: I would not be seen in't;   225

    And therefore many times I have slighted him

    When he did court our furtherance, as this morning.

Ferd. Antonio, the great master of her household

    Had been far fitter:—

Card.   You are deceiv'd in him,

Enter BOSOLA.

    His nature is too honest for such business—   230

    He comes: I'll leave you.   [*Exit.*]

Bos.   I was lur'd to you.

Ferd. My brother here, the cardinal, could never

    Abide you.

Bos.   Never since he was in my debt.

Ferd. May be some oblique character in your face

    Made him suspect you!

Bos.   Doth he study physiognomy?   235

    There's no more credit to be given to th' face

    Than to a sick man's urine, which some call

    The physician's whore, because she cozens him:—

    He did suspect me wrongfully.

223.1.] *Dyce i subs.*   229.1.] *so this ed.; at l. 82.1* Q; *at l. 148* Q4; *after* leave you, *l. 231 Dyce i.*   231. *Exit*] *Dyce i.*

---

above) and would have no motive for uttering it as a statement rather than a question (question marks are found in Q for exclamations or full-stops); moreover, the duchess' next speech would be too curiously abrupt without this preparation. Compositor A confused speech-prefixes on at least one other occasion (cf. III. v. 105).

    223. *caroches*] coaches (of a stately kind).

    bring] accompany.

    229.1.] By marking Bosola's entrance thus early, the irony of the brothers' talk is enhanced. And Bosola and Antonio are clearly linked elsewhere as two men with similar opportunities for advancement (e.g. II. i. 84–107).

    In the first three Acts other early entries are effective in similar ways; cf. II. i. 107.1, note, and III. ii. 62.1.

Ferd.   For that
    You must give great men leave to take their times: 240
    Distrust doth cause us seldom be deceiv'd;—
    You see, the oft shaking of the cedar-tree
    Fastens it more at root.

Bos.   Yet take heed:
    For to suspect a friend unworthily
    Instructs him the next way to suspect you,   245
    And prompts him to deceive you.

Ferd.   There's gold.

Bos.   So:
    What follows? Never rain'd such show'rs as these
    Without thunderbolts in the tail of them;
    Whose throat must I cut?

Ferd. Your inclination to shed blood rides post   250
    Before my occasion to use you:—I give you that
    To live i'th' court, here; and observe the duchess,
    To note all the particulars of her 'haviour;
    What suitors do solicit her for marriage
    And whom she best affects: she's a young widow—   255
    I would not have her marry again.

Bos.   No, sir?

248–9.] *so this ed.; one line Q.*   248. in the] *This ed.;* i'th *Q.*

241.] Cf. the proverb, 'He who trusts not is not deceived' (Tilley T559).

242–3. *oft . . . root*] Dent compared Hall, *Epistles* (1608), IV. vi: 'the oft-shaking of the tree, fastens it more at the roote;' he noted that the more common 'sentence' expressed the opposite, that shrubs are safe when great trees perish in a storm (see Tilley C208).

The *cedar* was a symbol of greatness; cf. *Cymb.*, v. v. 453.

244–6. *to . . . you*] The idea is in Florio, III. ix; but, as Dent shows, Webster seems closer to the original Seneca (*Epist.*, III. 3).

next = 'nearest'.

247–9.] an allusion to the shower of gold, in which form Jupiter visited the imprisoned Danäe.

248–9.] These words are only just accommodated in the third line of type from the foot of the last page of Sheet B: Compositor A probably altered the lining of his copy and elided *in the* so that he could complete the text cast-off for this page. See Intro., pp. lxii–lxiii.

250. *post*] in haste.

Ferd. Do not you ask the reason: but be satisfied,
    I say I would not.

Bos.   It seems you would create me
    One of your familiars.

Ferd.   Familiar! what's that?

Bos. Why, a very quaint invisible devil, in flesh: 260
    An intelligencer.

Ferd.   Such a kind of thriving thing
    I would wish thee: and ere long, thou mayst arrive
    At a higher place by't.

Bos.   Take your devils
    Which hell calls angels: these curs'd gifts would make
    You a corrupter, me an impudent traitor,   265
    And should I take these they'd take me to hell.

Ferd. Sir, I'll take nothing from you that I have given:—
    There is a place that I procur'd for you
    This morning: the provisorship o'th' horse—
    Have you heard on't?

Bos.   No.

Ferd.   'Tis yours—is't not worth thanks?

Bos. I would have you curse yourself now, that your bounty, 271
    Which makes men truly noble, e'er should make
    Me a villain: O, that to avoid ingratitude
    For the good deed you have done me, I must do
    All the ill man can invent! Thus the devil   275
    Candies all sins o'er; and what heaven terms vile,

266. to] *Q4; not in Q.*   270. on't] *Q2* (ont); *out Q.*   276. o'er] *Q2*
(ore); *are Q.*

---

   259. *familiars*] (1) 'members of household', (2) 'intimate friends', and
(3) 'familiar spirits' (supposed to attend at a call). Lucas suggested that a
Jacobean audience might recall *familiar* = 'Officer of the Inquisition,
chiefly employed in arresting and imprisoning' (*O.E.D.*).

   260. *quaint*] skilful, cunning.

   263–4. *devils . . . angels*] In Webster's time there was a gold coin with St
Michael stamped on it (the noble) which was commonly called an *angel*.

   264–6. *these . . .*] probably from *A.T.*, v. i. 2791–8: 'I tolde, that such a
summe but seru'd, to make / Him a corrupter, me corrupted thought: /
And foule for him to giue, for me to take, . . .'

   275–6. *devil . . . o'er*] Cf. *W.D.*, v. vi. 58–60. *Candies* = 'sugars'.

That names he complimental.

Ferd.   Be yourself:
Keep your old garb of melancholy; 'twill express
You envy those that stand above your reach,
Yet strive not to come near 'em: this will gain   280
Access to private lodgings, where yourself
May, like a politic dormouse—

Bos.   As I have seen some
Feed in a lord's dish, half asleep, not seeming
To listen to any talk; and yet these rogues
Have cut his throat in a dream:—what's my place?   285
The provisorship o'th' horse? say then, my corruption
Grew out of horse-dung: I am your creature.

Ferd. Away.

Bos. Let good men, for good deeds, covet good fame,
Since place and riches oft are bribes of shame—   290
Sometimes the devil doth preach.   *Exit.*

[*Enter* Duchess *and* Cardinal.]

288. Away] *Q; Away. Exit Samp.*   291.1.] *This ed.; . . . and Cariola
Dyce i; Scene ii. | . . . | Enter Cardinal, Ferdinand, Duchess, and Cariola
Samp; . . . and Ferdinand conj. this ed.*

277. *complimental*] i.e., a polite accomplishment, or refinement; cf.
Troil., III. i. 42.

282. *dormouse*] Cf. III. i. 22. Pliny's *Natural History* (tr. 1601) tells how
dormice 'renue their age every yeare, by sleeping all Winter: for they lie by
it close, snug all the while, and are not to be seene. But come the Summer
once, they bee young and fresh againe' (VIII. lvii).

283. *Feed . . . dish*] dine at a lord's table; the usage is not recorded in
O.E.D., but cf. Marston, *Malcontent* (1604), II. iii: 'Lay one into his breast
shall sleepe with him, / Feede in the same dish, . . . / Who may discover any
shape of danger. . .'

291. *Sometimes . . . preach*] Cf. the proverbs: 'The devil can cite scripture
for his purpose' and 'The devil sometimes speaks truth' (Tilley D230 and
D266).

291.1] Possibly Ferdinand should leave the stage on 'Away' (l. 288) to
re-enter here with the cardinal and duchess; thus the change of location to
'the gallery' (l. 210) would be clearly indicated. Such an arrangement
would also (1) suggest that the family conference is in a less public place
than the presence chamber of the first part of Act I; (2) avoid the possible
awkwardness of Ferdinand suddenly breaking into an intimate duologue
(at l. 293) without the fact being remarked upon (the three could enter

Card. We are to part from you: and your own discretion
    Must now be your director.

Ferd.   You are a widow:
    You know already what man is; and therefore
    Let not youth, high promotion, eloquence—   295

Card. No, nor anything without the addition, honour,
    Sway your high blood.

Ferd.   Marry! they are most luxurious
    Will wed twice.

Card.   O fie!

Ferd.   Their livers are more spotted
    Than Laban's sheep.

Duch.   Diamonds are of most value   299
    They say, that have pass'd through most jewellers' hands.

Ferd. Whores, by that rule, are precious:—

Duch.   Will you hear me?
    I'll never marry:—

296.] *so Q;* No, / Nor . . . *Dyce i.*

---

already talking together); and (3) give Bosola a clear stage (and concentrated attention) for his couplet-soliloquy and comment upon it. However, if Crane transcribed the printer's copy from a MS. which had directions for Ferdinand's exit and re-entry, he would normally have marked a new scene after l. 291.

In a Jacobean theatre the curtains of some kind of inner-stage could be closed before Antonio's entry at l. 361 (perhaps concealing the thrones appropriate to the 'presence') and thus Webster's audience could easily accept the fiction of a change of place by the time it is undoubtedly required by the text; these curtains could be the 'arras' of l. 357. The action of *W.D.*, IV. ii moves from outside to inside the House of Convertites without exit and re-entry.

297. *high blood*] noble lineage; Ferdinand seems to take *blood* = 'passion, sensual appetite' (cf. *W.D.*, I. ii. 292 and note).

luxurious] lecherous, unchaste.

298. *livers*] The liver was thought to be the seat of love and violent passions: cf. *A.Y.L.*, III. ii. 441–4, where Rosalind promises 'to wash your liver as clean as a sound sheep's heart, that there shall not be one spot of love in 't'.

298–9. *more . . . sheep*] Cf. *Genesis*, xxx. 31–43; Webster probably found the phrase in Whetstone, *Heptameron* (1582), C3ᵛ: 'a company as spotted as Labans Sheepe', applied to members of the Church of Rome who have taken but broken a vow of chastity (so Dent).

Card.   So most widows say:
But commonly that <u>motion</u> lasts no longer   *resolve.*
Than the turning of an hour-glass—the funeral sermon
And it, end both together.
Ferd.   Now hear me: 305
You live in a rank pasture here, i'th' court—
There is a kind of honey-dew that's deadly:
'Twill poison your fame; look to't: be not cunning:
For they whose faces do belie their hearts
Are witches, ere they arrive at twenty years—   310
Ay: and give the devil suck.
Duch. This is terrible good counsel:—
Ferd. Hypocrisy is woven of a fine small thread,   *The net of very*
Subtler than <u>Vulcan's engine</u>: yet, believe 't, *fine thread.*
Your darkest actions—nay, your privat'st thoughts—   315
Will come to light.
Card.   You may flatter yourself,
And take your own choice: privately be married
Under the eaves of night.
Ferd.   Think 't the best voyage
That e'er you made; like the irregular crab,
Which though 't goes backward, thinks that it goes right,   320
Because it goes its own way: but observe,
Such weddings may more properly be said

---

303. *motion*] resolve.

307. *honey-dew*] a sweet, sticky substance found on leaves, etc., being excreted by aphides; formerly it was supposed to be a kind of dew (so *O.E.D.*).

313.] probably from Ariosto, *Satires*, tr. R. Tofte (1608), III: 'Hypocrisie is wouen of fine thrid'; it may be proverbial.

314. *Vulcan's engine*] the net of very fine thread (cf. l. 313) in which he caught Mars and Venus in adultery.

318. *Under . . . night*] The phrase was probably associated with bats and owls: Dent compared Dekker, *Whore of Babylon* (1607), III. i. 158, on being secretive: 'Flie with the Batt vnder the eeues of night', and T. Adams, *Gallant's Burden* (1612), D4ᵛ.

319–21. *like . . . way*] The crab's sideways motion is often alluded to, as in Sidney's *Arcadia*, II. iii (*Wks*, I. 164): it 'looks one way and goes another'; but its illusion of normality may well be Webster's addition.

 To be executed, than celebrated.

Card. The marriage night
 Is the entrance into some prison.

Ferd.   And those joys,   325
 Those lustful pleasures, are like heavy sleeps
 Which do fore-run man's mischief—

Card.   Fare you well.
 Wisdom begins at the end: remember it.   [*Exit.*]

Duch. I think this speech between you both was studied,
 It came so roundly off.

Ferd.   You are my sister—   330
 This was my father's poniard: do you see?
 I'd be loth to see 't look rusty, 'cause 'twas his:—
 I would have you to give o'er these chargeable revels;   *Costly*
 A visor and a mask are whispering-rooms
 That were ne'er built for goodness: fare ye well:—   335
 And women like that part which, like the lamprey,
 Hath ne'er a bone in't.

Duch.   Fie sir!

Ferd.   Nay,
 I mean the tongue: variety of courtship;—
 What cannot a neat knave with a smooth tale
 Make a woman believe? Farewell, lusty widow.   [*Exit.*] 340

---

328. *Exit*] *Q4*.   333. to] *Q; not in Q2*.   340. *Exit*] *Q4*.

---

 323. *executed*] Meanings ranged from 'carried out' (practically or legally) to 'put to death'; the word-play turns on the accepted meaning 'celebrated' (of ceremonies and rites).

 328. *Wisdom . . . end*] a counsel of prudence and a *memento mori*: cf. the proverbs 'Think on the end before you begin' and 'Remember the end' (Tilley E125 and E128).

 330. *roundly*] probably 'fluently'.

 333. *chargeable*] burdensome, costly.

 334. *whispering-rooms*] intimate, private closets, as at III. ii. 257; these are the only occurrences of the word recorded in *O.E.D.*

 336. *lamprey*] This eel-like fish with sucker mouth 'swimmeth all whole in flexible sort, and all alike bending hir bodie' (J. Maplet, *Green Forest* (1567), N3ᵛ).

 339–40. *What . . . believe*] Cf. Overbury, *Characters* (1614), 'A Good Woman': 'Shee leaues the neat youth telling his lushious tales' (so Lucas). *neat* = 'fine, elegant', or, in mod. slang, 'smooth'; cf. the description of

Duch. Shall this move me ? If all my royal kindred
    Lay in my way unto this marriage,
    I'd make them my low footsteps : and even now,
    Even in this hate, as men in some great battles,
    By apprehending danger, have achiev'd   345
    Almost impossible actions—I have heard soldiers say so—
    So I, through frights, and threat'nings, will assay
    This dangerous venture : let old wives report
    I wink'd and chose a husband. Cariola,

              [*Enter* CARIOLA.]

    To thy known secrecy I have given up   350
    More than my life, my fame :—
Cari.   Both shall be safe :
    For I'll conceal this secret from the world
    As warily as those that trade in poison
    Keep poison from their children.
Duch.   Thy protestation
    Is ingenious and hearty : I believe it.   355
    Is Antonio come ?
Cari.   He attends you :—
Duch.   Good dear soul,
    Leave me : but place thyself behind the arras,

349.1.] *This ed.*   355. ingenious] *Q;* ingenuous *Q3.*

Jack Donne as '*neat*', but not 'dissolute'. Following ll. 336–7, there is an
equivocation centring on *tale* for 'tail' (or penis); this was a common
quibble (see, e.g., *Rom.*, II. iv. 99–106).

343. *footsteps*] steps (as before an altar).

349. *I . . . chose*] 'I chose with my eyes shut'; a proverbial phrase first
noted by Tilley in 1621 (W501). However, here there may be a quibble
suggesting a premonition of moral condemnation, for to *wink* = 'to close
one's eyes', and also 'to shut one's eyes to wrong, to be complaisant'.

349.1.] Some editors direct Cariola to enter with her mistress at l. 291.1;
but a later entrance has the advantage of Ferdinand and the duchess being
alone when he says (ll. 330 ff.) what he seems to have restrained until the
cardinal's departure. It also makes it credible that Cariola, and not her
mistress, should know that Antonio is waiting (cf. l. 356).

355. *ingenious*] intelligent, sagacious (in opposition to 'hearty'); but the
word was often used for 'ingenuous', and this sense may also be required
here. Cf. the ambiguous use in *W.D.*, III. iii. 70.

Where thou mayst overhear us:—wish me good speed
For I am going into a wilderness,
Where I shall find nor path, nor friendly clew   360
To be my guide.   [*Cariola withdraws behind the arras.*]

[*Enter* ANTONIO.]

I sent for you—sit down:
Take pen and ink, and write: are you ready?

Ant.   Yes:—

Duch. What did I say?

Ant.   That I should write somewhat.

Duch. O, I remember:—

~~festivities~~ After these <u>triumphs</u>, and this large expense,   365
It's fit, like thrifty husbands, we inquire
What's laid up for tomorrow.

Ant. So please your beauteous excellence.

Duch.   Beauteous?
Indeed I thank you: I look young for your sake.
You have ta'en my cares upon you.

Ant.   I'll fetch your grace   370
The particulars of your revenue, and expense.

Duch. O, you are an upright treasurer: but you mistook,
For when I said I meant to make inquiry

361. *Cariola . . .*] *Dyce i subs.; Exit Car. Q4 (after l. 357), Samp (after l. 358).
Enter Antonio*] *Q4 (at l. 358), Dyce i (as here).*   365. *these*] *Dyce i; this Q.*
368-9. *Beauteous . . .*] *so Dyce i; one line Q.*   370-1. I'll . . .*] *so Dyce i;
. . . the / Particulars . . . Q.*   372.] *so Q; . . . are / An . . . Dyce i.*

---

361. Cariola . . . arras] If Cariola has to open a door for Antonio as well
as withdraw, the stage movement may be clumsy and involve a pause not
indicated by the metre or words. Probably the duchess lets the steward in
herself; this would explain his initial silence, and add to his surprise when
Cariola discloses her presence at l. 475. Possibly, Cariola should leave at the
end of l. 358; this would entail the addition of heavy punctuation after
'speed' and the duchess speaking the next two and a half lines as soliloquy (gaining closer attention from the audience and perhaps making her
courage and dignity appear studied).

365. *triumphs*] festivities.

366. *husbands*] husbanders, heads of households.

369. *for . . . sake*] (1) 'thanks to you', and (2) 'for love of you' (cf. *O.E.D.*,
sake, 6 and 6b).

What's laid up for tomorrow, I did mean
What's laid up yonder for me.

Ant.   Where?

Duch.   In heaven—   375
I am making my will (as 'tis fit princes should,
In perfect memory), and I pray sir, tell me
Were not one better make it smiling, thus,
Than in deep groans, and terrible ghastly looks,
As if the gifts we parted with procur'd   380
That violent distraction?

Ant.   O, much better.

Duch. If I had a husband now, this care were quit:
But I intend to make you overseer;—
What good deed shall we first remember? say.

Ant. Begin with that first good deed began i'th' world   385
After man's creation, the sacrament of marriage—
I'd have you first provide for a good husband,
Give him all.

Duch.   All?

Ant.   Yes, your excellent self.

Duch. In a winding sheet?

Ant.   In a couple.

Duch. Saint Winifred, that were a strange will!   390

Ant. 'Twere strange if there were no will in you
To marry again.

378. thus,] *Q3;* thus? *Q.*   381. distraction] *Q3;* distruction *Q.*   390.
Winifred] *Dyce i;* Winfrid *Q.*   391–2. 'Twere . . . again] *so Q; . . .* strange/
If . . . *Luc i.*   391. strange] *Q;* stranger *Dyce ii.*

383. *overseer*] person appointed by a testator to supervise or assist the
executors of the will.

389. *In . . . sheet*] i.e., fit to accompany her dead husband.

couple] i.e., of sheets; but with a quibble, for *couple* also meant both
'wedlock' and 'copulation'.

390. *Saint Winifred*] a 7th-century Welsh saint; her head was struck off
by Caradoc ap Alauc whose love she had refused, but she was restored to
life by St Bruno.

391. *strange*] Emendation is unnecessary and the metre satisfactory if
no and *will* are both stressed.

will] Besides the obvious quibble on 'testament' and 'desire, inclina-

Duch.   What do you think of marriage?

Ant. I take 't, as those that deny purgatory—
     It locally contains, or heaven, or hell;
     There's no third place in't.   *Feel towards.*

Duch.   How do you affect it?   395

Ant. My banishment, feeding my melancholy,
     Would often reason thus . . .

Duch.   Pray let's hear it.

Ant. Say a man never marry, nor have children,
     What takes that from him? only the bare name
     Of being a father, or the weak delight   400
     To see the little wanton ride a-cock-horse
     Upon a painted stick, or hear him chatter
     Like a taught starling.

Duch.   Fie, fie, what's all this?
     One of your eyes is blood-shot—use my ring to't,
     They say 'tis very sovereign—'twas my wedding ring,   405
     And I did vow never to part with it,
     But to my second husband.

Ant. You have parted with it now.

Duch. Yes, to help your eyesight.

Ant. You have made me stark blind.   410

Duch. How?

Ant. There is a saucy, and ambitious devil
     Is dancing in this circle.

Duch.   Remove him.

---

tion', there may be an allusion to *will* = 'carnal desire, passion' (as at III. i.
73).

   392–5. *What . . . in't*] Dent has shown that the usual maxim called
marriage purgatory or hell, *or* heaven or hell; Webster seems to have
responded to both forms in finding his own idiosyncratic 'sentence'.

   395. *affect*] fancy, feel towards.

   398–403. *Say . . . starling*] from Elyot, *Image of Governance* (1541),
PɪV: '. . . sterilitie can no more hurte me, but onely take from me the name
of a father, or the dotynge pleasure to se my lytell sonne ryde on a cokhorse,
or to here hymn chatter and speake lyke a wanton'.

   412–13. *devil . . . circle*] Magicians when raising spirits either protected
themselves with a magic circle or confined the spirit within one; the latter
practice is alluded to in *W. Ho*, IV. ii.

Ant.   How?

Duch. There needs small conjuration, when your finger
  May do it: thus—is it fit?

      [*She puts her ring upon his finger:*] *he kneels.*

Ant.   What said you?

Duch.   Sir,   415
  This goodly roof of yours is too low built,
  I cannot stand upright in't, nor discourse,
  Without I raise it higher: raise yourself,
  Or if you please, my hand to help you: so.   [*Raises him.*]

Ant. Ambition, madam, is a great man's madness,   420
  That is not kept in chains, and close-pent rooms,
  But in fair lightsome lodgings, and is girt
  With the wild noise of prattling visitants,
  Which makes it lunatic, beyond all cure—
  Conceive not I am so stupid but I aim   425
  Whereto your favours tend: but he's a fool
  That, being a-cold, would thrust his hands i'th' fire
  To warm them.

Duch.   So, now the ground's broke,
  You may discover what a wealthy mine
  I make you lord of.

Ant.   O, my unworthiness!   430

Duch. You were ill to sell yourself—
  This dark'ning of your worth is not like that
  Which tradesmen use i'th' city; their false lights
  Are to rid bad wares off: and I must tell you
  If you will know where breathes a complete man—   435

---

415. *She . . . finger*] Dyce i (*subs.*). *he kneels*] *so* Q2; *after* you Q. 419.
S.D.] *Dyce ii.* 435. will] *Q;* would *Q2.*

416.] Lucas compared Hall, *Characters*, 'Humble Man': 'He is . . . a
rich stone set in lead; and lastly, a true Temple of God built with a low
roofe'.

423. *prattling*] could be used in Webster's time of prating, or small-talk,
without suggesting childishness; Antonio pictures a great man surrounded
by courtiers who appear to speak about nothing, but are hoping to forward
their individual suits.

  I speak it without flattery—turn your eyes
  And progress through yourself.
Ant. Were there nor heaven nor hell,
  I should be honest: I have long serv'd virtue,
  And ne'er ta'en wages of her.
Duch.   Now she pays it!   440
  The misery of us that are born great—
  We are forc'd to woo, because none dare woo us:
  And as a tyrant doubles with his words,
  And fearfully equivocates, so we
  Are forc'd to express our violent passions   445
  In riddles, and in dreams, and leave the path
  Of simple virtue, which was never made
  To seem the thing it is not. Go, go brag
  You have left me heartless—mine is in your bosom,
  I hope 'twill multiply love there. You do tremble: 450
  Make not your heart so dead a piece of flesh
  To fear, more than to love me: sir, be confident—
  What is't distracts you? This is flesh, and blood, sir;
  'Tis not the figure cut in alabaster
  Kneels at my husband's tomb. Awake, awake, man! 455
  I do here put off all vain ceremony,
  And only do appear to you a young widow
  That claims you for her husband, and like a widow,
  I use but half a blush in't.

---

 437. *progress*] make a royal progress, or journey in state; i.e. 'you are ruler of such a man'.

 438–40.] from Hall, 'Honest Man': '. . . if there were no heauen, yet he would be vertuous', and, possibly, Hall, *Epistles* (1611), VI. x: 'Serue honestie euer, though without apparant wages: shee will pay sure, if slow'. *pays* = 'repays, rewards'.

 442. *woo . . . woo*] a pun, introduced by *misery* of the previous line; cf. *Rom.*, III. v. 120: 'Ere he that should be Husband comes to woe' (Q2) and Kökeritz, p. 85. For the sentiment, see Painter; App. I, p. 183.

 451–2. *Make . . . me*] possibly from Hall, *Characters*, 'Profane': 'To matter of Religion his heart is a peece of dead flesh, without feeling of loue, of feare. . .'

 453. *flesh, and blood*] Cf. the proverb, 'To be flesh and blood as others are' (Tilley F367).

Ant.   Truth speak for me:
   I will remain the constant sanctuary   460
   Of your good name.
Duch.   I thank you, gentle love,
   And 'cause you shall not come to me in debt,
   Being now my steward, here upon your lips
   I sign your *Quietus est*:—   [*Kisses him.*]
   This you should have begg'd now—   465
   I have seen children oft eat sweetmeats thus,
   As fearful to devour them too soon.
Ant. But for your brothers?
Duch.   Do not think of them—
   All discord, without this circumference,
   Is only to be pitied, and not fear'd: 470
   Yet, should they know it, time will easily
   Scatter the tempest.
Ant.   These words should be mine,
   And all the parts you have spoke, if some part of it
   Would not have savour'd flattery.
Duch. Kneel.   [CARIOLA *comes from behind the arras.*] 475
Ant. Hah?
Duch. Be not amaz'd, this woman's of my counsel—
   I have heard lawyers say, a contract in a chamber
   Per verba de presenti is absolute marriage:—

464–5.] *so this ed.; one line* Q.   464. S.D.] *This ed.*   475. S.D.] *Dyce* i;
Enter Cariola (after l. 474) Q4.   479. de] *Samp; not in* Q.   marriage]
Q; marriage. (*She and Antonio kneel Dyce* ii.

---

464. Quietus est] 'He is discharged, or acquitted of payment due'; the
phrase was also used of the 'release' of death, as in *Ham.*, III. i. 75 (and cf.
Tilley Q16). There is a sequence of allusions to death in this duologue; cf.
ll. 375–81, 389, 451, 454–5.

469. *without . . . circumference*] outside these bounds; they have embraced.

473. *parts*] 'part' in the same line suggests that this is used quibblingly:
(1) 'parts of speech' (cf. 'words', l. 472), and (2) 'matter, particulars' (see
O.E.D., sb. 2, a and c).

479. Per . . . presenti] When a couple declared that they were man and
wife (with or without a witness, and without a deposition in writing), they
were legally married. The church's official attitude was that these mar-

> Bless, heaven, this sacred Gordian, which let violence   480
> Never untwine.

Ant. And may our sweet affections, like the spheres,
> Be still in motion.

Duch.   Quickening, and make
> The like soft music.

Ant. That we may imitate the loving palms,   485
> Best emblem of a peaceful marriage,
> That ne'er bore fruit, divided.

---

riages were valid and binding, but also sinful and forbidden; offenders had to solemnize their marriage *in facie ecclesiae*. The consummation of such unions before public solemnizing was regarded as fornication and a deadly sin. In practice, however, sexual intercourse before the final religious ceremony was accepted behaviour for such contracted couples, despite the disapproval of puritans and some clergy. (See E. Schanzer, 'Marriage-Contracts', *Sh. S.*, xiii (1960), 81–9, which quotes contemporary English authorities.)

480. *Gordian*] Gordius, king of Gordium in Phrygia, tied a knot in the yoke of the oxen that pulled his chariot when he was chosen king: the oracle declared that whoever loosened it would rule Asia. Alexander the Great cut through the knot with his sword.

482–4.] The relevant properties of the planetary *spheres* are described in Florio's Montaigne, I. xxii; perpetual movement (*still* = 'continuously, always'), touching (*Quickening* = 'stimulating, exciting'), and unheard music (*soft*, or appropriate to the pleasures of a secret marriage) are all mentioned: 'Philosophers deeme of the celestiall musicke . . . that the bodies of it's circles, being solid smooth, and in their rowling motion, touching and rubbing one against another, must of necessitie produce a wonderfull harmonie. . . But that universally the hearing senses of these low world's creatures . . . cannot sensibly perceive or distinguish the same.'

485–7.] The idea was common, being found in Pliny's *Natural History* and often quoted as an *emblem* of marriage (see Dent). James Maxwell's *Monument of Remembrance* (1613) used it of the marriage of Princess Elizabeth (Sig. C4):

> . . . wise Nature doth vs show
> In the *Palme-trees*, which being set asunder
> From mutuall sight, no fruit is seene to grow
> Of either kinde; but faint, as if some thunder
> > Had blasted both; they pine and droope as dead,
> > And haue no heart once to hold up their head. . .

485, 489. *That* . . .] Antonio (but not the duchess), in praying to 'heaven', introduces new petitions with *That*, as in the Litany of the Church of England.

Duch. What can the church force more ?

Ant.   That Fortune may not know an accident,
         Either of joy or sorrow, to divide   490
         Our fixed wishes.

Duch.   How can the church bind faster ?
         We now are man and wife, and 'tis the church
         That must but echo this :—maid, stand apart—
         I now am blind.

Ant.   What's your conceit in this ?

Duch. I would have you lead your fortune by the hand,   495
         Unto your marriage bed :—
         (You speak in me this, for we now are one)
         We'll only lie, and talk together, and plot
         T'appease my humorous kindred ; and if you please,
         Like the old tale, in 'Alexander and Lodowick',   500
         Lay a naked sword between us, keep us chaste :—
         O, let me shroud my blushes in your bosom,

491. bind] *This ed.; build Q.*

---

488. *force*] enforce (of a law or regulation) ; or, possibly, 'care for' (cf.
O.E.D., s.v., 14), or 'urge'.

491. *bind*] Q's 'build' is not meaningful, whereas *bind* is in keeping
with associations of 'contract . . . Gordian . . . like . . . divided . . . divide
. . . faster . . . man and wife'. Crane occasionally used too many minim
strokes, so 'build' may be the compositor's attempt to make sense of
four minims between a 'b' and 'd' in his copy. Professor Leech compared
Spanish Gipsy (1623), v. iii : '—He is not married to thee.—In his faith /
He is ; and faith and troth I hope bind faster / Than any other ceremonies
can.'

494. *blind*] as Fortune ; see l. 489, and l. 495 (where the primary sense is
probably 'good fortune').

conceit] idea, fancy.

499. *humorous*] ill-humoured ; or, possibly, with irony, 'capricious'.

500-1.] The Admiral's Men performed a (now lost) play with this title
in 1597. The story was told in *The Seven Sages of Rome* and in a ballad to
the tune of *Flying Fame : The Two Faithful Friends* : 'the pleasant history
of Alexander and Lodwicke, who were so like one another, that none
could know them asunder : wherin is declared how Lodwike married
the Princesse of Hungaria in Alexander's name and how each night he
layd a naked sword betweene him and the Princesse, because he would
not wrong his friend' (reprinted, *Pepys Ballads*, ed. H. E. Rollins (1929),
I. 136 ff.).

Since 'tis the treasury of all my secrets.

[*Exeunt* Duchess *and* ANTONIO.]

Cari. Whether the spirit of greatness or of woman
Reign most in her, I know not, but it shows   505
A fearful madness; I owe her much of pity.   *Exit.*

503.1.] *Dyce i.*   506. *Exit*] *Dyce i; Exeunt Q.*

504–6.] Lucas compared the 'gloomy anticipations' in Webster's source
at this point; see App. I, pp. 184–5, 189.

Act II

ACTUS II, SCENA I.

Enter BOSOLA *and* CASTRUCHIO.

Bos. You say you would fain be taken for an eminent courtier?

Cast. 'Tis the very main of my ambition. aim.

Bos. Let me see, you have a reasonable good face for't already,
and your night-cap expresses your ears sufficient largely
—I would have you learn to twirl the strings of your band 5
with a good grace; and in a set speech, at th' end of every

II. i. 0.1.] *Q4; Bosola, Castruchio, an Old Lady, Antonio, Delio, Duchesse, Rodorico, Grisolan Q.* 4. sufficient] *Q;* sufficiently *McIl.*

II. i.] The preparatory entries without specific motivation, the casual talk as if waiting for something else, Bosola's bringing of a gift in expectation of presenting it, the duchess' address to Antonio and Bosola as if she expected them to be in attendance, and her reference to etiquette and 'the presence' (l. 120) all show that this is a formal presence-chamber scene, like I. i. Webster has repeated an effect with differences to clarify his drama: *now* the duchess is not attended by her brothers, and the formality ends in disorder.

2. *main*] aim, purpose (perhaps originating as a term of archery).

4. *your . . . largely*] Cf. *W. Ho*, I. i. 213–14: 'put case this night-cap be to little for my eares or forehead, can any man tell mee where my Night-cap wringes me, except I be such an asse to proclaime it', and *W.D.*, I. ii. 87–9. Bosola says that Castruchio evidently has the long ears of an ass.

In *W. Ho* and *W.D.* the wearers are cuckolds, and so is Castruchio. But he is also a would-be lawyer (cf. l. 9) and Webster used *night-cap* elsewhere of a lawyer's white coif or skull-cap (so Sykes, but not recorded in *O.E.D.*): cf. *A.V.*, IV. i. 121 and *D.L.C.*, IV. i. 69–73: 'such vild suits . . . make honest Lawyers / Stop their own eares, whilst they plead, & thats the reason / Your yonger men that haue good conscience, / Weare such large Night-caps'. Bosola certainly mocks Castruchio as a lawyer, and perhaps as a husband.

5. *band*] neck-band; here, probably, a lawyer's white tabs (so Lucas). But, possibly, there is a reference to a growing fashion among courtiers, in the early 17th century in England, for elaborate bands; in Jonson's *Cynthia's Revels*, V. iv. 158, the frenchified Amorphus makes an 'accost' which includes some 'solemne' play with his 'band string'.

    sentence, to hum, three or four times, or blow your nose
    till it smart again, to recover your memory; when you
    come to be a president in criminal causes, if you smile
    upon a prisoner, hang him, but if you frown upon him and   10
    threaten him, let him be sure to 'scape the gallows.

Cast. I would be a very merry president—

Bos. Do not sup o'nights, 'twill beget you an admirable wit.

Cast. Rather it would make me have a good stomach to
    quarrel, for they say your roaring boys eat meat seldom,   15
    and that makes them so valiant. But how shall I know
    whether the people take me for an eminent fellow?

Bos. I will teach a trick to know it: give out you lie a-dying,
    and if you hear the common people curse you, be sure you
    are taken for one of the prime night-caps—   20

Enter an Old Lady.

    You come from painting now?

Old Lady. From what?

Bos. Why, from your scurvy face-physic—to behold thee not
    painted inclines somewhat near a miracle: these, in thy
    face here, were deep ruts and foul sloughs the last pro-   25
    gress. There was a lady in France, that having had the
    smallpox, flayed the skin off her face to make it more
    level; and whereas before she looked like a nutmeg-
    grater, after she resembled an abortive hedgehog.

Old Lady. Do you call this painting?   30

Bos. No, no, but careening of an old morphewed lady, to make

20.1.] *so Dyce i; at l. o.1* Q.   24. these,] *McIl;* These *Q;* These . . . *Luc i;*
these dimples *conj. Luc i.*   31. but] *McIl;* but you call *Q;* but you ca‖ it
Q3; but I call it *Luc i.*

---

    15. *roaring boys*] slang for 'rowdies'.

    20. *night-caps*] lawyers; cf. *D.L.C.*, II. i. 43. *O.E.D.* glosses 'nocturnal
bullies', but quotes Webster only.

    20.1.] She is to act as midwife; see II. ii. 3.1, note.

    26–8. *lady . . . level*] probably from Florio, I. xl: 'Who hath not heard of
hir at Paris, which onely to get a fresher hew of a new skinne, endured to
have hir face flead all over'.

    31. *but*] Q is obviously corrupt, and McIlwraith's emendation is prob-

her disembogue again—there's rough-cast phrase to your
plastic.

Old Lady. It seems you are well acquainted with my closet.

Bos. One would suspect it for a shop of witchcraft, to find in   35
it the fat of serpents, spawn of snakes, Jews' spittle, and
their young children's ordure—and all these for the face:
I would sooner eat a dead pigeon, taken from the soles of
the feet of one sick of the plague, than kiss one of you
fasting. Here are two of you, whose sin of your youth is   40
the very patrimony of the physician, makes him renew
his footcloth with the spring and change his high-prized
courtezan with the fall of the leaf: I do wonder you do not
loathe yourselves—observe my meditation now:

What thing is in this outward form of man   45
To be belov'd ? we account it ominous
If nature do produce a colt, or lamb,

---

37. children's ordure] *Q2;* children ordures *Q;* children's ordures *Luc i.*
42. high-prized] *Q* (-priz'd)*; high-priced *Dyce i.*

---

ably the most satisfactory; some memory, or sight, of 'you call' immediately above caused the error.

31–2. *careening . . . again*] i.e., 'scraping clean an old scurfy lady, as if she
were the hull of a ship, so that she can look for new adventures, like a ship
leaving harbour for sea again'.

32–3. *rough-cast . . . plastic*] coarse (harsh, brutal) plaster . . . (fine,
artistic) modelling.

34–7.] probably from Ariosto, *Satires*, tr. Tofte (1608), IV: 'He knowes
not, did he know it he would spewe, / That paintings made with spettle of
a Iewe, / (For they the best sell) nor that loathsome smell, / (Though mixt
with muske and amber nere so well), / Can they with all their cunning take
away / The fleame and snot so ranke in it doth stay. / Little thinks he that
with the filthy doung, / Of their small circumcised infants young, / The fat
of hideous serpents, spaune of snakes, / Which slaues from out their
poisonous bodies takes.'

38–9. *dead . . . plague*] A broadsheet of *Remedies Against the Plague* told
how the rump of a cock, pullet, or chicken should be bared and held to the
plague-sore until the creature died; this should be repeated 'so long as any
doe die', for when all the poison is 'drawn foorth' the bird will live; 'This
Medicine is necessarie to driue the venome from the heart' (reproduced in
F. P. Wilson, *The Plague* (1927), opp. p. 8).

42. *footcloth*] a rich cloth laid over the back of a horse to protect the
rider from mud and dust; it was a sign of dignity and rank.

A fawn, or goat, in any limb resembling
A man; and fly from't as a prodigy.
Man stands amaz'd to see his deformity   50
In any other creature but himself.
But in our own flesh, though we bear diseases
Which have their true names only ta'en from beasts,
As the most ulcerous wolf, and swinish measle;
Though we are eaten up of lice and worms,   55
And though continually we bear about us
A rotten and dead body, we delight
To hide it in rich tissue: all our fear—
Nay, all our terror—is lest our physician
Should put us in the ground, to be made sweet.   60
Your wife's gone to Rome: you two couple, and get you
to the wells at Lucca, to recover your aches.

                    [*Exeunt* CASTRUCHIO *and* Old Lady.]

I have other work on foot:—I observe our duchess
Is sick o' days, she pukes, her stomach seethes,
The fins of her eyelids look most teeming blue,   65
She wanes i'th' cheek, and waxes fat i'th' flank;
And (contrary to our Italian fashion)
Wears a loose-body'd gown—there's somewhat in't!
I have a trick may chance discover it,

61–2.] *so Dyce i;* . . . you / To . . . *Q.*   62.1.] *Dyce i.*

53–4.] Cf. Topsell, *History of Four-Footed Beasts* (1607), Sig. Xxx 1ᵛ:
'There is a disease called a wolfe, because it consumeth and eateth vp the
flesh in the bodie next the sore, and must euery day be fed with fresh meat,
as Lambes, Pigeons, and such other things wherein is bloode, or else it consumeth al the flesh of the body, leauing not so much as the skin to couer **the**
bones.'

Webster says that the common human disease of measles (earlier used in
the singular) was given the name of a skin disease in swine caused by tape-
worm; according to *O.E.D.*, both human and *swinish* measle were confused
with 'mesel' (leper, leprous).

62. *Lucca*] The town was famous as a spa in the 16th and 17th centuries.

65. *fins*] probably 'eyelids' (so *O.E.D.*, 2b, quoting Marston), and so
tautologous here.

68. *loose-body'd gown*] In Webster's England loose, unwaisted gowns
were worn 'by older women' (Cunningham, *English Costume in 16th
Century* (1954), p. 167).

A pretty one: I have bought some apricocks,   70
The first our spring yields.

Enter ANTONIO *and* DELIO[, *talking apart*].

Delio.   And so long since married?
  You amaze me.
Ant.   Let me seal your lips for ever,
  For did I think that anything but th' air
  Could carry these words from you, I should wish
  You had no breath at all:—   75
  [*To Bosola*] Now sir, in your contemplation? You are
  studying to become a great wise fellow?
Bos. O sir, the opinion of wisdom is a foul tetter that runs all
  over a man's body: if simplicity direct us to have no evil,
  it directs us to a happy being; for the subtlest folly pro-   80
  ceeds from the subtlest wisdom: let me be simply honest.
Ant. I do understand your inside.
Bos. Do you so?
Ant. Because you would not seem to appear to the world
  puffed up with your preferment, you continue this out-   85
  of-fashion melancholy—leave it, leave it.

71. S.D. *Enter . . . Delio*] *so Q4; at l. 0.1 Q.   talking apart*] *Samp
subs.   75–7.*] *so this ed.; . . .* contemplation / You . . . (*two lines*) *Q.*
76. S.D.] *Luc i.   84–6.*] *as prose this ed.; . . .* world / Puff'd . . . continue /
This . . . *Q.*

76–107.] This small-talk—opinionated, ironic, and complimental—
presents two ambitious men sparring for advantage. Bosola out-plays
Antonio by pretending at one point to reveal all (l. 88) and then turning
defence into attack.
  78–81. *opinion . . . wisdom*] from three or four pages of Florio, II. xii:
'The opinion of Wisedome is the plague of man. . . Whence proceedes the
subtilest follie, but from the subtilest wisdome? . . . I say therefore, that if
simplicitie directeth vs to have no evil, it also addresseth vs, according to
our condition to a most happy estate'.   *tetter* = 'sore'.
  85–6. *out-of-fashion melancholy*] Cf. I. i. 76, note. Bosola's *melancholy* is
out-of-fashion now because he has got preferment.
  L. Babb has suggested that this is a topical allusion, the affectation of
melancholy becoming less popular after the first decade of the 17th century
(*Eliz. Malady* (1951), pp. 83–4); but Webster can hardly have intended
this, for the malcontent was still a recognizable type-character delineated

Bos. Give me leave to be honest in any phrase, in any compli-
        ment whatsoever—shall I confess myself to you ? I look
        no higher than I can reach: they are the gods that must
        ride on winged horses; a lawyer's mule of a slow pace   90
        will both suit my disposition and business: for mark me,
        when a man's mind rides faster than his horse can gallop,
        they quickly both tire.

Ant. You would look up to heaven, but I think
        The devil, that rules i'th' air, stands in your light.   95

Bos. O sir, you are lord of the ascendant, chief man with the
        duchess, a duke was your cousin-german removed:—
        say you were lineally descended from King Pepin, or he
        himself, what of this ? search the heads of the greatest

---

in Overbury's *Characters* (1614) and A. Nixon, *Strange Foot-Post* (1613),
and other writings.

88–9. *I . . . reach*] Cf. the proverbs 'Things that are above us are nothing
to us' and 'One may look at a star, but not reach at it' (Tilley T206 and
S825).

89–90. *they . . . horses*] from Florio, I. xlii: 'Al the true commodities that
Princes have, are common vnto them with men of meane fortune. It is for
Gods to mount winged horses, and to feed on Ambrosia.'

91. *mark me*] talk of horsemanship also points the generalizations at
Antonio (cf. I. i. 140–7).

95.] Cf. *Ephesians*, ii. 2: the devil 'ruleth in the ayre' (Bishops' Bible);
Webster links this with the proverbial criticism of men who 'stand in their
own light' (Tilley L276).

96. *lord . . . ascendant*] Astrologers divided the heavens into 12 'houses'
(shaped like sections of an orange by imaginary lines drawn through the
north and south points of the horizon). The 'first house', or 'house of *the
ascendant*', is that section of the sky which is at the moment rising in the
east, extending from 5° above to 25° below the horizon. The *lord of the
ascendant* was any planet within the first house.

Bosola speaks with (unintentional) irony in so calling Antonio, for the
lord of the ascendant was supposed to have a special influence upon the life
of a child then born and Antonio's son is born in the same scene; cf. the
dramatic irony at I. i. 88.

97. *cousin-german removed*] first cousin once removed.

98. *King Pepin*] King of the Franks, who died in 768; in *W.D.* (v. vi.
107–12) Webster ranked him with great rulers like Alexander and Caesar.

99–101. *search . . . water*] probably from Florio, II. xii: laws 'swell, and
grow greater and greater, as do our rivers: follow them vpward, vnto their
sourse, & you shall find them but a bubble of water, scarse to be discerned,
which in gliding-on swelleth so proud, & gathers so much strength.'

rivers in the world, you shall find them but bubbles of   100
water. Some would think the souls of princes were
brought forth by some more weighty cause than those of
meaner persons—they are deceived, there's the same
hand to them: the like passions sway them, the same
reason that makes a vicar go to law for a tithe-pig and   105
undo his neighbours, makes them spoil a whole province, and batter down goodly cities with the cannon.

Enter Duchess [*with* Attendants *and* Ladies.]

Duch. Your arm Antonio—do I not grow fat?
    I am exceeding short-winded:—Bosola,
    I would have you, sir, provide for me a litter,   110
    Such a one as the Duchess of Florence rode in.
Bos. The duchess us'd one when she was great with child.
Duch. I think she did:—Come hither, mend my ruff—
    Here, when? thou art such a tedious lady; and
    Thy breath smells of lemon pills—would thou hadst done—

107.1. *Enter Duchess*] so *Q4; at l. 0.1 Q; after* water, *l. 101 conj. this ed.*
with . . . Ladies] *This ed.*; Ladies *Q4.*   115. pills] *Q3;* pils *Q;* peel *Q4;*
peels *Thorn.*

101-7. *Some . . . cannon*] from Florio, II. xii: 'The soules of Emperours
and Coblers are all cast in one same mold. Considering the importance of
Princes actions, and their weight, wee perswade our selves, they are
brought forth by some as weighty and important causes; we are deceived:
They are mooved, stirred and remooved in their motions, by the same
springs and wardes, that we are in ours. The same reason that makes vs
chide and braule, and fall out with anie of our neighbours, causeth a warre
to follow between Princes; The same reason that makes vs whippe or beate
a lackey, maketh a Prince (if he apprehend it) to spoyle and waste a whole
Province.'

107.1. *Attendants*] suitable for a presence chamber; see note on the
scene-heading above. The entry of the duchess *enceinte* for the first time
should, perhaps, be marked earlier, as Bosola comments, 'some would
think . . . the like passions sway them'; this would give an effect comparable
to Vittoria's entry during Flamineo's speech in *W.D.*, I. ii. 113. See, also,
I. i. 229.1, note.

111. *Duchess of Florence*] Editors have been unable to suggest any particular reference; cf. IV. i. 112–14, note on 'Lauriola'.

114. *tedious*] troublesome, dilatory (cf. *O.E.D.*, 2 and 4).

115. *pills*] rinds, peel.

Shall I swoon under thy fingers ? I am   116
  So troubled with the mother. *hysteria.*
Bos. [*Aside*]   I fear too much.
Duch. I have heard you say that the French courtiers
  Wear their hats on 'fore the king.
Ant.   I have seen it.
Duch. In the presence ?   120
Ant. Yes:—
Duch.   Why should not we bring up that fashion ?
  'Tis ceremony more than duty, that consists
  In the removing of a piece of felt:
  Be you the example to the rest o' th' court,
  Put on your hat first.
Ant.   You must pardon me: 125
  I have seen, in colder countries than in France,
  Nobles stand bare to th' prince; and the distinction
  Methought show'd reverently.
Bos. I have a present for your grace.
Duch.   For me sir ?
Bos. Apricocks, madam.

---

116. swoon] *Dyce i;* sound *Q;* swound *Q2.*   117. *Aside*] *Dyce ii.*   121.
Duch.] *Q4; not in Q.*

---

116. *swoon*] Q's 'sound' was a common form, and (with 'under your fingers') implies a secondary meaning of 'sounding' (as a musical instrument).

117. *the mother*] hysteria; the pun is common.

118–19. *I . . . king*] a much debated question at the time (see Boklund, pp. 35–6): cf. Florio, I. xliii: 'Our Kings have the power to addresse all these externall reformations. . . "Whatsoever Princes doe, that they seeme to command." The rest of France takes the modell of the court as a rule unto it selfe to follow. Let Courtiers first begin to leave off . . . that against our forefathers manner, and the particular libertie of our French nobilitie, we should stand bare-headed, aloofe-off from them, wheresoever they be.'

In its context, this is not casual talk. The duchess wants the private excitement of seeing Antonio with his hat on before the rest of the court as if he were publicly acknowledged to be her equal. Antonio turns the secret jest, saying that he has seen 'Nobles *stand bare* to the prince' (meaning himself before the duchess, his 'prince'). See ll. 142–3, note, below, and III. ii. 5 where the duchess clearly talks of Antonio as a 'nobleman'.

126. *colder countries*] Lucas suggested an allusion to English loyalty.

Duch.   O sir, where are they?   130
    I have heard of none to-year. this year.

Bos. [*Aside*]   Good, her colour rises.

Duch. Indeed I thank you; they are wondrous fair ones:
    What an unskilful fellow is our gardener!
    We shall have none this month.

Bos. Will not your grace pare them?   135

Duch. No, they taste of musk, methinks; indeed they do:—

Bos. I know not: yet I wish your grace had par'd 'em:—

Duch. Why?

Bos.   I forgot to tell you the knave gard'ner
    (Only to raise his profit by them the sooner)
    Did ripen them in horse-dung.

Duch.   O you jest:—   140
    You shall judge; pray taste one.

Ant.   Indeed madam,
    I do not love the fruit.

Duch.   Sir, you are loth
    To rob us of our dainties:—'tis a delicate fruit,
    They say they are restorative.

Bos.   'Tis a pretty art,
    This grafting.

Duch.   'Tis so: a bettering of nature.   145

Bos. To make a pippin grow upon a crab,
    A damson on a blackthorn:—[*Aside*] how greedily she
    eats them!

---

131. *Aside*] Dyce ii.   144–5. 'Tis . . . grafting] *so* Dyce i; . . . pretty /
Art. . . *Q.*   147. *Aside*] *Q4* (*at end of line*).

---

131. *to-year*] this year (like 'today').

142–3. *you . . . dainties*] another *double entendre: dainties* = 'choice
foods', and (2) 'things delighted in, luxuries'. In *A.Q.L.*, III. i. 147–8,
'Tastes . . . of the daintiest Dish' is used with an unmistakeable sexual
innuendo; see also Marston, *Sophonisba* (1606), I (*Wks*, II. 17): 'These
dainties, this first fruits of nuptials'.

144–5. *'Tis . . . grafting*] Lucas compared the *double entendre* in Florio,
II. xii, the page from which Webster borrowed for ll. 99–101 above: 'graft
the forked tree'.

146–7. *pippin . . . blackthorn*] Dent illustrated Webster's choice of trees

A whirlwind strike off these bawd farthingales,
For, but for that, and the loose-body'd gown,
I should have discover'd apparently   150
The young <u>springal</u> cutting a caper in her belly.

stridling ·

Duch. I thank you, Bosola, they were right good ones—
    If they do not make me sick.
Ant.   How now madam?
Duch. This green fruit and my stomach are not friends—
    How they swell me!
Bos. [*Aside*]   Nay, you are too much swell'd already.
Duch. O, I am in an extreme cold sweat!   156
Bos. I am very sorry:—
Duch. Lights to my chamber: O good Antonio,
    I fear I am undone.   *Exit.*
Delio.   Lights there, lights!
                    [*Exeunt all except* ANTONIO *and* DELIO.]
Ant. O my most trusty Delio, we are lost!   160
    I fear she's fall'n in labour; and there's left
    No time for her remove.
Delio.   Have you prepar'd
    Those ladies to attend her? and procur'd
    That politic safe conveyance for the midwife
    Your duchess plotted?   165
Ant. I have:—
Delio.   Make use then of this forc'd occasion:
    Give out that Bosola hath poison'd her
    With these apricocks; that will give some <u>colour</u> *pretext.*
    For her keeping close.

---

155. *Aside*] *Q4*.   157. sorry:] *Q;* sorry. *Exit. Q4*.   159.1.] *Q4 subs.*

from Breton, *Will of Wit* (1606), I1: 'is not the Damson tree to be accounted
off, aboue the Blackthorne tree? is not the Pippin tree to be esteemed aboue
the crabtree? the Abricock aboue the common plum?'
    Webster probably gave prominence to *pippin* to echo 'Pepin' (an alter-
native spelling) of l. 98; he so punned on the king's name in *W.D.*
    150. *apparently*] manifestly, visibly.
    151. *springal*] stripling.
    168. *colour*] pretext.

Ant.   Fie, fie, the physicians
     Will then flock to her.
Delio.   For that you may pretend   170
     She'll use some prepar'd antidote of her own,
     Lest the physicians should re-poison her.
Ant. I am lost in amazement: I know not what to think on't.

                                                        Exeunt.

SCENA II.

Enter BOSOLA.

Bos. So, so: there's no question but her tetchiness and most
     vulturous eating of the apricocks are apparent signs of
     breeding—

                    Enter Old Lady.

     Now?
Old Lady. I am in haste, sir.   5
Bos. There was a young waiting-woman had a monstrous
     desire to see the glass-house.
Old Lady. Nay, pray let me go:—
Bos. And it was only to know what strange instrument it was
     should swell up a glass to the fashion of a woman's belly.   10
Old Lady. I will hear no more of the glass-house—you are
     still abusing women!
Bos. Who I? no, only (by the way now and then) mention
     your frailties. The orange tree bears ripe and green fruit,

II. ii. 0.1.] *Dyce i; Bosola, old Lady, Antonio, Rodorigo, Grisolan: seruants,*
Delio, Cariola Q; Enter Bosola, Lady Q4.   3.1.] *so Dyce i; at l. 0.1*
Q, Q4.   12. women!] *Kel;* woemen? *Q;* women. *Haz.*   14. bears]
Q3; beare *Q.*

     II. ii. 1. *tetchiness*] irritability, testiness; *O.E.D.* first records the word in
1623, but 'tetchy' is known earlier (e.g. *Rom.*, I. iii. 32).
     3.1.] She is 'in haste' (l. 5) to act as midwife (cf. II. i. 164 and l. 24, below);
she may carry some parcel or bag to make this clear to Bosola and the
audience.
     7. *glass-house*] glass-factory; there was one near the Blackfriars
theatre.
     14–21. *orange . . . them*] i.e., some women make love in youth and for

and blossoms all together: and some of you give enter-   15
tainment for pure love; but more, for more precious
reward. The lusty spring smells well; but drooping
autumn tastes well: if we have the same golden showers
that rained in the time of Jupiter the Thunderer, you have
the same Danäes still, to hold up their laps to receive   20
them:—didst thou never study the mathematics?

Old Lady. What's that, sir?

Bos. Why, to know the trick how to make a many lines meet in
one centre:—go, go; give your foster-daughters good
counsel: tell them that the devil takes delight to hang at a   25
woman's girdle, like a false rusty watch, that she cannot
discern how the time passes.   [*Exit* Old Lady.]

Enter ANTONIO, DELIO, RODERIGO, GRISOLAN.

Ant. Shut up the court gates:—

Rod.   Why sir? what's the danger?

Ant. Shut up the posterns presently: and call
All the officers o' th' court.

Gris.   I shall instantly.   [*Exit.*]   30

Ant. Who keeps the key o' th' park gate?

Rod.   Forobosco.

15. all together] *Dyce ii;* altogether *Q.*   20. Danäes] *Q4;* Danes *Q.*
27. S.D.] *Dyce i.*   27.1.] *so Dyce i; at l. 0.1 Q; after* gates, *l. 28 Q4.*
30. Exit] *Dyce i.*

'pure love's' sake, others (like the '*Old* Lady') when they are *drooping*, for
the sake of the *reward*.

For the *orange tree*, cf. J. Maplet, *Green Forest* (1567), H7ᵛ: 'This tree
is at all seasons of ye yeare fruit bearing or fruitfull: insomuch that it is
neuer found without fruit, . . . for when the first of their fruit is mellow, and
readie ripe: then the second you shall espie greene and sower: and the
thirde newe blosoming and in flower.'

For *Danäes*, see I. i. 247–9, note.

23–4. *many . . . centre*] proverbial, usually in the form, 'many ways meet
in one town' (Tilley W176); for the *double entendre* Lucas compared
Florio, III. v: 'All the worlds motions bend and yeelde to this [sexual] con-
iunction: it is a matter euery-where infused; and a Centre whereto all lines
come, all things looke.'

29. *presently*] at once.

31. *Forobosco*] See Intro., p. lxvii.

Ant. Let him bring 't presently.

Enter [GRISOLAN *with*] Officers.

1st. Off. O, gentlemen o'th' court, the foulest treason!

Bos. [*Aside*] If that these apricocks should be poison'd now,
    Without my knowledge!   35

1st. Off. There was taken even now a Switzer in the duchess'
    bedchamber.

2nd. Off. A Switzer?

1st. Off. With a pistol in his great cod-piece.

Bos. Ha, ha, ha!   40

1st. Off. The cod-piece was the case for 't.

2nd. Off. There was a cunning traitor. Who would have
    searched his cod-piece?

1st. Off. True, if he had kept out of the ladies' chambers:—
    and all the moulds of his buttons were leaden bullets.   45

2nd. Off. O, wicked cannibal! a fire-lock in 's cod-piece!

1st. Off. 'Twas a French plot, upon my life.

32.1.] *so Dyce i; at l.* 0.1 *Q.*   *Grisolan with*] *Dyce i subs.*   33, *et seq.*
1st. Off.] *This ed.; Seru. Q subs.*   34. *Aside*] *Q4.*   36–7.] *so Dyce i;*
. . . *Switzer* / *In* . . . *Q;* . . . *now* / *A* . . . *Luc i.*   38, *et seq.* 2*nd. Off.*]
This ed.; 2. Seru. Q subs.   42–5.] *so Dyce i;* . . . *traitor,* / *Who* . . . *cod-*
piece? / *Seru.* . . . *chambers:* / *And* . . . *Q, Luc i.*

36–48.] from Nashe, *Unfortunate Traveller* (1594), *Wks*, II. 223, of a
Switzer captain whom Wilton duped: 'after hee was throughly searched;
. . . the molds of his buttons they turnd out, to see if they were not bullets
couered ouer with thred; the cod-peece in his diuels breeches (for they wer
then in fashion) they said plainly was a case for a pistol. . .'

Switzer = Swiss mercenary; these were frequently used in feuds between Italian noblemen. A *cod-piece* was a necessary accessary of close-
fitting hose or breeches; it was often enlarged and ornamented (cf. *W.D.*,
v. iii. 99–101), and sometimes used as a pocket for handkerchief, purse or
even oranges. But cod-pieces were discarded by the fashionable in England
in the 1590s (see Nashe's parenthesis), and by all soon after 1600. (See
C. W. & P. Cunnington, *English Costume in 16th Century* (1954), p. 118.)

40.] This is bawdy laughter; Bosola probably hears a pun on pizzle
(= penis), for the 'current colloquial pronunciation of *pistol* [was] without
the medial *t* as in castle' (H. Kökeritz, *Shakespeare's Pronunciation* (1953),
p. 135). There is a pun on Pistol's name in *2H4*.

47. *French*] Among other judgements, it was said that the *French* were
courteous, hasty, and lustful.

2nd. Off. To see what the devil can do!

Ant. All the officers here?

Off. We are:—   50

Ant. Gentlemen,
    We have lost much plate you know; and but this evening
    Jewels, to the value of four thousand ducats
    Are missing in the duchess' cabinet—
    Are the gates shut?

Off.   Yes.

Ant.   'Tis the duchess' pleasure   55
    Each officer be lock'd into his chamber
    Till the sun-rising; and to send the keys
    Of all their chests, and of their outward doors,
    Into her bedchamber:—she is very sick.

Rod. At her pleasure.   60

Ant. She entreats you take 't not ill: the innocent
    Shall be the more approv'd by it.

Bos. Gentleman o'th' wood-yard, where's your Switzer now?

1st. Off. By this hand, 'twas credibly reported by one o' the
    black guard.   [*Exeunt all except* ANTONIO *and* DELIO.]

Delio. How fares it with the duchess?

Ant.   She's expos'd   66
    Unto the worst of torture, pain, and fear:—

Delio. Speak to her all happy comfort.

Ant. How I do play the fool with mine own danger!
    You are this night, dear friend, to post to Rome;   70
    My life lies in your service.

Delio.   Do not doubt me—

Ant. O, 'tis far from me: and yet fear presents me
    Somewhat that looks like danger.

---

49. All] *Q;* Are all *Q4.*   officers] *Q2;* Offices *Q.*   50, 55. *Off.*] *This ed.;*
Seru. Q subs.   65. S.D. *Dyce i subs.*

---

54. *cabinet*] private apartment, boudoir.

63. *Gentleman o'th' wood-yard*] Bosola mocks the 'Gentleman o'th'
court' (cf. l. 33, above). There was a 'wood-yard' in London, being an out-
lying and disreputable part of Whitehall between the Tilt-yard and the
Thames.

Delio.   Believe it,
    'Tis but the shadow of your fear, no more:
    How superstitiously we mind our evils!   75
    The throwing down salt, or crossing of a hare,
    Bleeding at nose, the stumbling of a horse,
    Or singing of a cricket, are of pów'r
    To daunt whole man in us. Sir, fare you well:
    I wish you all the joys of a bless'd father;   80
    And, for my faith, lay this unto your breast—
    Old friends, like old swords, still are trusted best.   [*Exit.*]

Enter CARIOLA.

Cari. Sir, you are the happy father of a son—
    Your wife commends him to you.
Ant.   Blessed comfort:
    For heaven-sake tend her well; I'll presently   85
    Go set a figure for's nativity.   *Exeunt.*

---

82. *Exit*] Dyce i.   82.1.] *so* Dyce i; *at* l. 0.1 Q; *Enter Cariola with a Child Q4.*

75–9. *How . . . us*] Cf. Florio, II. xii, on a page used for II. i. 99–101:
'A gust of contrarie winds, the croking of a flight of Ravens, the false pase
of a Horse, the casuall flight of an Eagle, a dreame . . . are enough to overthrow, sufficient to overwhelme, and able to pul him [man] to the ground'.

Crossing of a hare boded disordered senses (so Lucas, quoting Fletcher's
Wit at Several Weapons, II. iii), or the presence of a witch (cf. G. Giffard,
Dialogue concerning Witches (1593), B1: 'I am afraide, for I see nowe and
then a Hare; which my conscience giueth me is a witch, or some witches
spirite'). A *stumbling horse* and *singing cricket* boded death (cf. *R3*, III. iv.
86–8 and *W.D.*, v. iv. 85–7).

79. *whole man*] Cf. *W.D.*, I. i. 45: 'Have a full man within you' (be fully
fortified and resolved).

82.] a rephrasing of the proverbial 'Old friends and old wine are best'
(Tilley F755); see also Tilley F321 and W740.

86. *set . . . nativity*] cast a horoscope, calculate the aspects of the astro-
logical houses (see II. i. 96, note), for the time of the child's birth. Such
practice was common despite satirical attacks upon it: e.g. Henry IV of
France summoned an astrologer at the moment of Louis XIII's birth.

See D. C. Allen, *Star-Crossed Renaissance* (1941), *passim.*

SCENA III.

Enter BOSOLA[, *with a dark lantern*].

Bos. Sure I did hear a woman shriek: list, hah?
      And the sound came, if I receiv'd it right,
      From the duchess' lodgings: there's some stratagem
      In the confining all our courtiers
      To their several wards: I must have part of it,   5
      My intelligence will freeze else:—list again!
      It may be 'twas the melancholy bird,
      Best friend of silence and of solitariness,
      The owl, that scream'd so:—

Enter ANTONIO.

                              hah? Antonio!
Ant. I heard some noise: who's there? what art thou? speak.   10
Bos. Antonio? Put not your face nor body
      To such a forc'd expression of fear—
      I am Bosola; your friend.
Ant.   Bosola!—
      [*Aside*] This mole does undermine me—[*To him*] heard
          you not
      A noise even now?
Bos.   From whence?
Ant.   From the duchess' lodging.
Bos. Not I: did you?
Ant.   I did: or else I dream'd.   16
Bos. Let's walk towards it.
Ant.   No: it may be 'twas
      But the rising of the wind:—

II. iii. 0.1.] *Q4; Bosola, Antonio Q.*   9. S.D.] *so this ed.; at l. 0.1 Q; at
end of line Q4; Enter Antonio, with a Candle his Sword drawn Q4.*   14.
S.Ds.] *Dyce ii subs.;* This . . . me *within brackets Q.*

II. iii. 0.1. dark lantern] a lantern with an arrangement for concealing its
light (cf. l. 54, below); *O.E.D.* first records the phrase in 1650 but one is
mentioned in *D.M.* at v. iv. 43.
  6. *freeze*] *O.E.D.* does not record a similar figurative usage.

Bos.   Very likely.
    Methinks 'tis very cold, and yet you sweat:
    You look wildly.

Ant.   I have been setting a figure   20
    For the duchess' jewels:—

Bos.   Ah: and how falls your question?
    Do you find it radical?

Ant.   What's that to you?
    'Tis rather to be question'd what design,
    When all men were commanded to their lodgings,
    Makes you a night-walker.

Bos.   In sooth I'll tell you: 25
    Now all the court's asleep, I thought the devil
    Had least to do here; I came to say my prayers—
    And if it do offend you I do so,
    You are a fine courtier.

Ant. [*Aside*]   This fellow will undo me:—
    [*To him*] You gave the duchess apricocks today,   30
    Pray heaven they were not poison'd!

Bos.   Poison'd! a Spanish fig
    For the imputation.

Ant.   Traitors are ever confident,
    Till they are discover'd:—there were jewels stol'n too—

29–30. S.Ds.] *Q4 subs.*

20–1. *setting . . . jewels*] i.e., casting a horoscope to inquire about the
recovery of the stolen goods; so, it was said, thieves could be identified,
hiding places revealed, and the course of recovery or final loss foretold.

22. *radical*] *O.E.D.* quoted (*adj.* 6) Lilly, *Christian Astrology* (1647),
p. 121: 'The question then shall be taken for radicall, or fit to be judged,
when as the Lord of the hour at the time of proposing the question . . . and
the Lord of the Ascendant . . . , are of one Triplicity [i.e., in one group of
three houses] or be one'; its earliest quotation is from Burton (1621).

25. *night-walker*] commonly used of thieves, rogues, etc.

31. *Spanish fig*] According to Nashe, those who 'swallow Spanish figs'
are men who 'deuoure anie hooke baited for them' (*Wks*, II. 299). The
phrase was doubly appropriate, for a *Spanish fig* was also a synonym for the
poison supposed to be administered with it (cf. *W.D.*, IV. ii. 61).

Lucas suggested that Bosola 'gave the fig' on saying this (i.e., thrust his
thumb between the first and middle finger with a phallic implication; this
was a common offensive gesture).

In my conceit, none are to be suspected
More than yourself.

Bos.   You are a false steward.   35

Ant. Saucy slave! I'll pull thee up by the roots;—

Bos. May be the ruin will crush you to pieces.

Ant. You are an impudent snake indeed, sir,
Are you scarce warm, and do you show your sting?

＊   ＊   ＊

Ant. You libel well, sir.

Bos.   No sir, copy it out,   40
And I will set my hand to't.

Ant. [*Aside*]   My nose bleeds:
One that were superstitious would count
This ominous;—when it merely comes by chance.
Two letters, that are wrought here for my name,
Are drown'd in blood!   45
Mere accident:—[*To him*] for you, sir, I'll take order:
I'th' morn you shall be safe:—[*Aside*] 'tis that must colour

38. *Ant.*] *Q; omit conj. this ed.*   39. * * *] *Luc i (prefixing [Bos.]).*   40.
Ant.] *Q; not in Q2.*   40–1. No . . . to't] *Dyce i; . . . sir,) / Copy . . . Q.*
41–51. S.Ds.] *Dyce ii subs.*   41–2. My . . . count] *so Dyce i; one line Q.*
44. wrought] *Q;* wrote *Q3.*   45–6.] *so Dyce i; one line Q.*   46. order:]
Q; order *Dyce i.*

---

34. *conceit*] opinion.

37. *ruin*] falling down (cf. *O.E.D.*, 1 and 1b).

38, 40. *Ant.*] Two consecutive prefixes for Antonio in Q probably imply that a speech for Bosola is missing. But ll. 38–9 might belong to Bosola,
continuing his speech of l. 37 and referring, like l. 35, to Antonio, the up-
start ('fine courtier', l. 29), threatening ('I'll pull thee up . . .', l. 36) and
strangely prosperous ('snake') steward. Compositor A might have anticipated the next speech-prefix for Antonio and, not realizing his error, set
it again at the correct place; he certainly confused and omitted prefixes
elsewhere in Q.

39. *scarce warm*] just out of hibernation; i.e., only recently having
obtained preferment.

40. *copy it out*] i.e., the supposed 'libel'.

41. *set . . . to't*] sign it.

41–3. *My . . .*] Cf. II. ii. 75–9, and note.

44. *wrought*] i.e., on a handkerchief; busied with this, he drops the copy
of the horoscope.

Her lying-in:—[*To him*] sir, this door you pass not:
I do not hold it fit that you come near
The duchess' lodgings, till you have quit yourself.   50
[*Aside*] *The great are like the base—nay, they are the same—*
When they seek shameful ways, to avoid shame.   *Exit.*

Bos. Antonio hereabout did drop a paper—
Some of your help, false friend—O, here it is:
What's here ? a child's nativity calculated!   55
[*Reads*] *The duchess was delivered of a son,'tween the hours*
twelve and one, in the night: Anno Dom. 1504,—that's
this year—decimo nono Decembris,—that's this night—
taken according to the meridian of Malfi—that's our
duchess: happy discovery!—The lord of the first house,   60
being combust in the ascendant, signifies short life: and Mars
being in a human sign, joined to the tail of the Dragon, in the
eighth house, doth threaten a violent death; caetera non
scrutantur.
Why now 'tis most apparent: this precise fellow   65

---

50. quit] *Q3;* quite *Q.*   51–2.] *italicized Q.*   56. *Reads*] *Dyce ii.*
56–64.] *so italicized Q4 subs.; all italicized except Latin words Q.*

---

54. *false friend*] i.e., his dark lantern.

56–64.] J. Parr (*Tamburlaine's Malady* (1953), pp. 94–100) has shown
that the configurations described never occurred in the early years of the
16th century. The horoscope was probably invented by Webster (or a professional astrologer) to prognosticate a violent death as clearly as possible.
'combust' = 'burnt up', signifying that a planet is positioned within 8½° of
the sun; this implies that its benign influence is almost destroyed.

Parr has shown that for 19 Dec. in any year, Capricorn must be the sign
in the first house (cf. II. i. 96, note), and that Saturn is the ruler of Capricorn.

The 'human signs' of the zodiac are Gemini, Virgo, Sagittarius, and
Aquarius. The 'tail of the Dragon' is the point in the heavens where the
moon crosses the sun's ecliptic in her descent into southern latitude; it was
thought to exert a sinister influence.

The son whose nativity is calculated here is the one child surviving at the
end of the play from the marriage of the duchess and Antonio. An astrologer would suspect that some benevolent influence, as of Jupiter or Venus,
was exerted before the 'combustion' and so delayed the disaster; by adding
caetera non scrutantur Webster made it clear that the horoscope was not
fully investigated.

65. *precise*] scrupulous, correct.

Is the duchess' bawd:—I have it to my wish;
This is a parcel of intelligency
Our courtiers were cas'd up for! It needs must follow
That I must be committed on pretence
Of poisoning her; which I'll endure, and laugh at:—   70
If one could find the father now! but that
Time will discover. Old Castruchio
I'th' morning posts to Rome; by him I'll send
A letter, that shall make her brothers' galls
O'erflow their livers—this was a thrifty way.   75
Though lust do mask in ne'er so strange disguise,
She's oft found witty, but is never wise.   [*Exit.*]

SCENA IV.

Enter Cardinal *and* JULIA.

Card. Sit: thou art my best of wishes—prithee tell me
    What trick didst thou invent to come to Rome
    Without thy husband.
Julia.   Why, my lord, I told him
    I came to visit an old anchorite
    Here, for devotion.
Card.   Thou art a witty false one:—   5
    I mean to him.
Julia.   You have prevail'd with me
    Beyond my strongest thoughts: I would not now
    Find you inconstant.

68. cas'd] *Q2;* caside *Q.*   76–7.] *italicized Q (and indented).*   76. *mask*]
Q4; masque *Q.*   ne'er] *Q3 (ne're);* nea'r *Q.*   77. *Exit*] *Q4.*

II. iv. 0.1.] *Q4;* Cardinall, and Iulia, Seruant, and Delio *Q.*

---

67. *parcel*] item, piece.
68. *cas'd*] III. ii. 139 suggests that it is unnecessary to look further for an
explanation of Q's 'caside'.
76–7.] Only the second line is likely to have been proverbial (so Dent).
76. *mask*] 'Masque' and *mask* were not differentiated in spelling.

II. iv. 5. *devotion*] The same quibble is found in *W.D.,* II. i. 150.
witty] This echoes the 'sentence' at the end of the previous scene.

Card.   Do not put thyself
    To such a voluntary torture, which proceeds
    Out of your own guilt.
Julia.   How, my lord?
Card.   You fear   10
    My constancy, because you have approv'd
    Those giddy and wild turnings in yourself.
Julia. Did you e'er find them?
Card.   Sooth, generally for women:
    A man might strive to make glass malleable,
    Ere he should make them fixed.
Julia.   So, my lord—   15
Card. We had need go borrow that fantastic glass
    Invented by Galileo the Florentine,
    To view another spacious world i'th' moon
    And look to find a constant woman there.
Julia. This is very well, my lord.
Card.   Why do you weep?   20
    Are tears your justification? the self-same tears
    Will fall into your husband's bosom, lady,
    With a loud protestation, that you love him
    Above the world:—come, I'll love you wisely,
    That's jealously, since I am very certain   25
    You cannot me make cuckold.
Julia.   I'll go home
    To my husband.

10–11. You . . .] *so Dyce i; one line* Q.   12. turnings] *Q3;* turning *Q.*
13. generally] *Q;* generally; *Haz.*   women:] *Q;* women, *Dyce i, Haz.*
26. me make] *Q;* make me *Q2.*

16–19.] Cf. Donne, *Ignatius his Conclave* (1611), pp. 116–17: 'I will
write to the Bishop of Rome: he shall call Galilaeo the Florentine to him;
who by this time hath throughly instructed himselfe of all the hills, woods,
and Cities in the new world, the Moone. And since he effected so much
with his first Glasses, . . . he may draw the Moone . . . as neere the earth as
he will' (so Marcia Anderson, *ap.* Dent).

25. *jealously*] probably, 'ardently' or 'solicitously' (cf. *O.E.D.*, 1 and 3,
and *Jealous, a,* 1–3); he is assuring her that love is better without marriage.
There may be a quibble on the more usual meaning of *jealously.*

Card.   You may thank me, lady,
 I have taken you off your melancholy perch,
 Bore you upon my fist, and show'd you game,
 And let you fly at it:—I pray thee kiss me—   30
 When thou wast with thy husband, thou wast watch'd
 Like a tame elephant:—still you are to thank me—
 Thou hadst only kisses from him, and high feeding,
 But what delight was that? 'twas just like one
 That hath a little fing'ring on the lute,   35
 Yet cannot tune it:—still you are to thank me.
Julia. You told me of a piteous wound i'th' heart,
 And a sick liver, when you woo'd me first,
 And spake like one in physic.
Card.   Who's that?—
 Rest firm: for my affection to thee,   40
 Lightning moves slow to't.

Enter Servant.

Serv.   Madam, a gentleman,
 That's come post from Malfi, desires to see you.
Card. Let him enter, I'll withdraw.   *Exit.*
Serv.   He says,
 Your husband, old Castruchio, is come to Rome,
 Most pitifully tir'd with riding post.   [*Exit.*] 45

Enter DELIO.

41. S.D.] *so this ed.; at l. 0.1 Q; after l. 39 Dyce i.*   45. Exit] *Dyce i.*
45.1.] *so Q4; at l. 0.1 Q.*

 28–30. *perch . . . fist . . . fly*] terms of falconry.
 31–2. *watch'd . . . elephant*] Cf. *A.Q.L.*, I. i. 158–60: 'she rail'd vpon me
when I should sleep, / And that's, you know, intollerable; for indeed /
'Twill tame an Elephant.' *watch'd* = (1) 'kept awake' (cf. *O.E.D.*, 2 and
13), and, perhaps, (2) 'kept in sight'.
 38. *liver*] Cf. I. i. 298, note.
 40–1. *Rest . . . to't*] The comparison was not unusual, but normally it
illustrated love's impermanence or destruction: cf., e.g., *Bussy*, v. i. 177–8:
'O what a lightning / Is man's delight in women! what a bubble, . . .'
to't = 'in comparison with it'.

Julia. [*Aside*] Signior Delio! 'tis one of my old suitors.

Delio. I was bold to come and see you.

Julia.   Sir, you are welcome.

Delio. Do you lie here?

Julia.   Sure, your own experience
    Will satisfy you, no—our Roman prelates
    Do not keep lodging for ladies.

Delio.   Very well: 50
    I have brought you no commendations from your husband,
    For I know none by him.

Julia.   I hear he's come to Rome?

Delio. I never knew man and beast, of a horse and a knight,
    So weary of each other—if he had had a good back,
    He would have undertook to have borne his horse,   55
    His breech was so pitifully sore.

Julia.   Your laughter
    Is my pity.

Delio.   Lady, I know not whether
    You want money, but I have brought you some.

Julia. From my husband?

Delio.   No, from mine own allowance.

Julia. I must hear the condition, ere I be bound to take it.   60

Delio. Look on't, 'tis gold—hath it not a fine colour?

Julia. I have a bird more beautiful.

Delio. Try the sound on't.

Julia.   A lute-string far exceeds it;
    It hath no smell, like cassia or civet,
    Nor is it physical, though some fond doctors   65

---

46. *Aside*] *Dyce ii.*   47. you are] *Q2;* your are *Q;* you're *conj. this ed.*
52. Rome?] *Q;* Rome. *Q2.*   53. of] *Q;* or *conj. Leech.*

---

   53. *of*] The General Editor suggests 'or', but the stiff sentence structure
may be appropriate to Delio's careful approach.

   54. *had ... back*] implying that he is impotent as well as weak; cf. II. v. 73
and *W.D.*, I. ii. 33–4.

   64. *cassia*] properly, an inferior kind of cinnamon; but, influenced by the
Bible (e.g., *Psalms*, xlv. 8) and perhaps Vergil and Ovid, poets often used it
for a plant of great fragrance (so *O.E.D.*, I and 3).

   65. *physical*] medicinal.

Persuade us seethe 't in cullises—I'll tell you,
This is a creature bred by . . .

[*Enter* Servant.]

Serv.   Your husband's come,
    Hath deliver'd a letter to the Duke of Calabria,
    That, to my thinking, hath put him out of his wits.   [*Exit.*]
Julia. Sir, you hear—   70
    Pray let me know your business and your suit,
    As briefly as can be.
Delio.   With good speed—I would wish you
    (At such time as you are non-resident
    With your husband) my mistress.
Julia. Sir, I'll go ask my husband if I shall,   75
    And straight return your answer.   *Exit.*
Delio.   Very fine!
    Is this her wit or honesty that speaks thus ?
    I heard one say the duke was highly mov'd
    With a letter sent from Malfi:—I do fear
    Antonio is betray'd. How fearfully   80
    Shows his ambition now! unfortunate fortune!
    They pass through whirlpools and deep woes do shun,
    Who the event weigh, ere the action's done.   *Exit.*

---

67. S.D.] *Q4* (*at end of line*).   68–9.] *so Dyce i;* . . . that, / To . . . *Q.*
69. *Exit*] *Q4 subs.*   82–3.] *italicized Q4;* "They . . . *Q.*

---

66. *cullises*] broths.
67. *This . . . by*] Cf. *Characters* (1615), 'A Devillish Usurer': 'He puts his
money to the vnnaturall Act of Generation'; Julia is about to say that gold
is 'a breed for barren metal' (*Mer.V.*, I. iii. 135).
74. *my mistress*] Lucas suggested that Delio intended to use Julia as a
means of gaining information about Antonio's enemies (as Bosola does
later, and Francisco uses Zanche in *W.D.*); but this notion is nowhere
stated or developed.
Perhaps Webster purposely avoided an 'explanation' or 'development'
of this incident, and so used it to aggravate the audience's sense of a growing
web of intrigue and an increasing complexity of character.

SCENA V.

Enter Cardinal, *and* FERDINAND *with a letter*.

Ferd. I have this night digg'd up a mandrake.

Card.   Say you?

Ferd. And I am grown mad with't.

Card.   What's the prodigy?

Ferd. Read there—a sister damn'd; she's loose i'th' hilts: *unchaste*

Grown a notorious strumpet.

Card.   Speak lower.

Ferd.   Lower?

Rogues do not whisper 't now, but seek to publish 't   5

(As servants do the bounty of their lords)

Aloud; and with a covetous searching eye

To mark who note them:—O confusion seize her!

II. v. 0.1.] *Q4 subs.; Cardinall, . . . Q.*   1. digg'd] *Q^b (dig'd); dig Q^a.*

II. v. 1–2. *I . . . with't*] A *mandrake* (i.e., mandragora) is a poisonous plant formerly used medicinally for its narcotic and emetic properties. When forked its root can look like a caricature of the human form. Gerarde's *Herbal* (1597), S4^v–5, recounts some 'ridiculous tales' about it, and in his two main tragedies Webster alludes to several of these: it was said to utter a shriek when pulled from the ground (cf. *W.D.*, v. vi. 67), to feed on blood (cf. *W.D.*, III. iii. 114–15), and to have the power to madden by its shriek any who pulled it up (see this passage). Webster also mentions its poisonous qualities (cf. *W.D.*, III. i. 50–2). He once calls it 'mandragora' when he alludes to its narcotic properties (cf. *D.M.*, IV. ii. 235).

But Ferdinand's cry is still puzzling. That he feels himself *grown mad* could have been said simply: the *mandrake* adds fantasy, sensationalism, and an association with shrieks and the human body (of either his sister or her son). Yet why should he think of *digging* rather than pulling, if the shriek were the supposed cause of madness?

Ferdinand's reaction to the news of the birth of his sister's son is not due wholly to thwarted political intrigue as he says later (cf. IV. ii. 281–5), or to outraged honour and pride of family as he implied in Act I; the cry shows, at the beginning of this crucial scene, which is the climax of Act II, that his reaction involves, in some fantastic way, horror, violence, and sex.

3. *loose . . . hilts*] unchaste. A *hilt* is the handle of a sword or dagger. The phrase was used proverbially in several ways (cf. Tilley H472), but the first record in *O.E.D.* of this sexual connotation is Howell, *Cotgrave's Dict.* (1650), Ded.: 'In French *Cocu* is taken for one whose wife is loose in the hilts.'

7. *covetous*] because they hope to be paid for future silence, or further information.

She hath had most cunning bawds to serve her turn,
And more secure conveyances for lust   10
Than towns of garrison for service.

Card.   Is't possible?
Can this be certain?

Ferd.   Rhubarb, O for rhubarb
To purge this choler! here's the cursed day
To prompt my memory, and here 't shall stick
Till of her bleeding heart I make a sponge   15
To wipe it out.

Card.   Why do you make yourself
So wild a tempest?

Ferd.   Would I could be one,
That I might toss her palace 'bout her ears,
Root up her goodly forests, blast her meads,
And lay her general territory as waste   20
As she hath done her honours.

Card.   Shall our blood,
The royal blood of Arragon and Castile,
Be thus attainted?

---

9. *serve her turn*] be useful to her, answer her purpose. The phrase could be used with sexual innuendo; cf. *Tit.*, II. i. 95–6.

11. *service*] 'supplies' (cf. *O.E.D.*, *sb*¹., 23); and, quibblingly, 'sexual indulgence' (cf. *O.E.D.*; *serve, v.*, 52).

12–13. *rhubarb . . . choler*] *choler*, or 'bile', was considered to be one of the 'four humours' contributing to the 'complexion' or temperament of a man; *rhubarb* was a common prescription for dealing with an excess of it.

P. Charron, *Of Wisdom* (tr. 1608), G4, says *choler* 'stirreth vp furious vapors in our spirits, which blinde vs and cast vs headlong to whatsoeuer may satisfie the desire which we haue of reuenge'.

13. *here's*] Lucas suggested that Ferdinand refers to the horoscope which Bosola has sent to Rome, and at 'here 't shall stick' thrusts it back into his bosom. But this gesture might be too difficult for an actor to effect quickly enough for this 'wild' scene. Ferdinand's following words are highly figurative—'Till of her bleeding heart I make a sponge'—and he may be speaking so already: like Hamlet, he may allude to the 'table of his memory' and the 'book and volume of his brain' (*Ham.*, I. v. 97–104). This would fittingly indicate the ineradicable nature of his sensations, and the mingling of fact and fiction.

23. *attainted*] The cardinal seems to use the word legally, as 'held to be stained or corrupted' (*O.E.D.*, 6); Ferdinand to understand it more physic-

Ferd.   Apply desperate physic:
          We must not now use balsamum, but fire,
          The smarting cupping-glass, for that's the mean   25
          To purge infected blood, such blood as hers:—
          There is a kind of pity in mine eye,
          I'll give it to my handkercher; and now 'tis here,
          I'll bequeath this to her bastard.
Card.   What to do?
Ferd. Why, to make soft lint for his mother's wounds,   30
          When I have hew'd her to pieces.
Card.   Curs'd creature!
          Unequal nature, to place women's hearts
          So far upon the left side!
Ferd.   Foolish men,
          That e'er will trust their honour in a bark
          Made of so slight, weak bulrush as is woman,   35
          Apt every minute to sink it!
Card. Thus ignorance, when it hath purchas'd honour,
          It cannot wield it.
Ferd.   Methinks I see her laughing—

---

28. handkercher] *Q;* handkerchief *Q3*.   30. mother's] *Q2;* mother *Q.*
37.] *so Samp;* Thus / Ignorance . . . *Q.*

---

ally, as 'infected' (cf. l. 26), and he speaks of 'her' blood rather than 'our
blood'. For the cardinal, *blood* = 'noble lineage'; and for Ferdinand, 'life-
blood' or 'passion, sensual appetite' (cf. I. i. 297, note, and I. i. 453).

24. *balsamum*] balm, aromatic resin mixed with oils.

25. *cupping-glass*] surgical vessel in which a vacuum is created by the
application of heat, and then is used to draw off blood.

32-3. *place . . . side*] Cf. Matthieu, *History of Louis XI* (1614), V2ᵛf.:
'The hearts of men lie on the left side; they are full of deceit; Truth, freedome and loyalty are rare, vnknowne and exiled qualities'; and in the
margin, 'Aristotle . . . saith that man onely hath his hart on the left side, and
all beasts haue it in the middest of their brests' (so Dent). See also Painter,
where the duchess' brother says that women 'seem to be procreated and
borne against all order of nature, . . .' (App. I, p. 199). *Unequal* = 'unjust'.

37-8. *Thus . . . it*] Cf. Hall, *Characters*, 'The Truly Noble': 'He so
studies, as one that knowes ignorance can neither purchase honour, nor
wield it.'   *purchas'd* = 'obtained' (as often).

38-9. *Methinks . . . hyena*] The cry of a *hyena* sounds like a laugh.
Topsell's *Four-Footed Beasts* (1607), pp. 435-42, distinguishes four kinds

Excellent hyena!—talk to me somewhat, quickly,
Or my imagination will carry me   40
To see her, in the shameful act of sin.

Card. With whom?

Ferd.   Happily with some strong thigh'd bargeman;
Or one o'th' wood-yard, that can quoit the sledge,
Or toss the bar, or else some lovely squire
That carries coals up to her privy lodgings.   45

Card. You fly beyond your reason.

Ferd.   Go to, mistress!
'Tis not your whore's milk that shall quench my wild-fire,
But your whore's blood.

Card. How idly shows this rage! which carries you,
As men convey'd by witches through the air,   50
On violent whirlwinds—this intemperate noise
Fitly resembles deaf men's shrill discourse,
Who talk aloud, thinking all other men
To have their imperfection.

Ferd.   Have not you
My palsy?

Card.   Yes—I can be angry   55

43. o'th'] *Q3;* th' *Q.*   49–50.] *so Dyce i;* . . . rage? / Which . . . *Q.*
55. Yes—] *Luc i;* Yes, *Q;* Yes, but *Dyce ii;* Yes; *Haz;* Yet *conj. Samp;*
Yes, yet *McIl.*

---

of hyena. The 'first and vulgar kind' cannot 'see one quarter so perfectly in
the day as in the night; . . . the female is far more subtill then the male, and
therefore more seldome taken . . .' She can kill a sleeping man 'with . . .
some secret worke of nature by stretching her body vpon him'. So the
animal became a type of treachery, especially in woman.

But since Ferdinand seems to see and hear the duchess as if she were
present, Topsell's second kind of *hyena* may be alluded to: 'their voices are
so shrill and sounding, that although they be very remote and farre off, yet
do men heare them as if they were hard by . . . they barke onely in the night
time.'

42. *Happily*] commonly used as 'haply'.

43. *wood-yard*] Cf. II. ii. 63, note.
quoit the sledge] throw the hammer.

45. *carries coals*] a proverbial phrase, = 'do any dirty work' or 'submit
to indignity' (cf. *O.E.D.,* coal, 12).

55. *palsy*] paralysis.

Without this rupture: there is not in nature
A thing that makes man so deform'd, so beastly,
As doth intemperate anger:—chide yourself.
You have divers men who never yet express'd
Their strong desire of rest, but by unrest,   60
By vexing of themselves:—come, put yourself
In tune.

Ferd.   So; I will only study to seem
The thing I am not. I could kill her now,
In you, or in myself, for I do think
It is some sin in us, heaven doth revenge   65
By her.

Card.   Are you stark mad?

Ferd.   I would have their bodies
Burnt in a coal-pit, with the ventage stopp'd,
That their curs'd smoke might not ascend to heaven:
Or dip the sheets they lie in, in pitch or sulphur,
Wrap them in't, and then light them like a match;   70
Or else to boil their bastard to a cullis,
And give 't his lecherous father, to renew
The sin of his back.

Card.   I'll leave you.

Ferd.   Nay, I have done—
I am confident, had I been damn'd in hell
And should have heard of this, it would have put me   75
Into a cold sweat:—In, in; I'll go sleep—

---

56. rupture] *Q;* rapture *conj. Dyce ii.*

---

56. *rupture*] Dyce's 'rapture' is followed by several editors and supported
by Compositor B's setting of 'distruction' for 'distraction' (I. i. 381); but
'palsy' of the previous line and 'deform'd' of the following suggest a
sequence of word-play on physical disabilities.

62–6. *So . . . her*] See Intro., p. liii.

67. *coal-pit*] a pit for making charcoal.

69–70.] Cf. Painter's account of Otho's 'butcherly' cruelty (App. I,
p. 204).

76–7. *I'll . . . stir*] This is echoed and, perhaps, revalued at the beginning of the next Act (III. i. 21–2). Webster has been taken to task for allowing Ferdinand to be inactive for two or three years following the discovery

Till I know who leaps my sister, I'll not stir:
That known, I'll find scorpions to string my whips,
And fix her in a <u>general</u> eclipse. ~~total~~.   *Exeunt.*

---

of the duchess' child. But his response to this news is both wild and
paralysed (cf. 'palsy', l. 55): while he wants to act (and does act in fantasy),
he is unable to bring himself to do so. Such a state of being is consistently
portrayed in this scene and later: his talk of a husband (an absurd one) for
his sister may be both a probe and a self-indulgence; his silence on coming
into her chamber in III. ii and his subsequent questions, generalizations,
cruelty, and refusal to act are best understood as a mixture of passion and
paralysis. 'I will never see thee more' (ll. 136 and 141) is followed by rapid
action, in riding away (cf. ll. 161–2).

78. *scorpions . . . whips*] Cf. *W.D.*, II. i. 245. The idea derives from
I *Kings*, xii. 11: 'my father hath chastised you with whips, but I will
chastise you with scorpions'—where 'scorpions' is thought to mean
knotted or barbed scourges (so *O.E.D.*).

79. *general*] total.

Act III

Enter ANTONIO *and* DELIO.

Ant. Our noble friend, my most beloved Delio!
    O, you have been a stranger long at court—
    Came you along with the Lord Ferdinand?
Delio. I did sir; and how fares your noble duchess?
Ant. Right fortunately well: she's an excellent   5
    Feeder of pedigrees; since you last saw her,
    She hath had two children more, a son and daughter.
Delio. Methinks 'twas yesterday: let me but wink,
    And not behold your face, which to mine eye
    Is somewhat leaner, verily I should dream   10
    It were within this half-hour.
Ant. You have not been in law, friend Delio,
    Nor in prison, nor a suitor at the court,
    Nor begg'd the reversion of some great man's place,
    Nor troubled with an old wife, which doth make   15
    Your time so insensibly hasten.
Delio.   Pray sir, tell me,
    Hath not this news arriv'd yet to the ear
    Of the Lord Cardinal?
Ant.   I fear it hath—
    The Lord Ferdinand, that's newly come to court,
    Doth bear himself right dangerously.
Delio.   Pray why?   20
Ant. He is so quiet, that he seems to sleep
    The tempest out, as dormice do in winter:

III. i. 0.1.] *Q4; Antonio, and Delio, Duchesse, Ferdinand, Bosola Q.*

III. i. 22. *dormice*] Cf. I. i. 282, and note. 'To sleep like a dormouse' was a proverb (Tilley D568).

> Those houses that are haunted are most still,
> Till the devil be up.

Delio.   What say the common people?

Ant. The common rabble do directly say   25
> She is a strumpet.

Delio.   And your graver heads,
> Which would be politic, what censure they? *judge*

Ant. They do observe I grow to infinite purchase
> The left-hand way, and all suppose the duchess
> Would amend it, if she could: for, say they,   30
> Great princes, though they grudge their officers
> Should have such large and unconfined means
> To get wealth under them, will not complain
> Lest thereby they should make them odious
> Unto the people—for other obligation   35
> Of love, or marriage, between her and me,
> They never dream of.

Enter FERDINAND *and* Duchess.

Delio.   The Lord Ferdinand
> Is going to bed.

Ferd.   I'll instantly to bed,
> For I am weary:—I am to bespeak
> A husband for you.

Duch.   For me, sir! pray who is't?   40

Ferd. The great Count Malateste.

Duch.   Fie upon him,—

---

37. S.D.] *so Luc i; at l. o.1 Q; at end of line Q4; after going to bed, l. 38,
Dyce i.   Duchess*] *This ed.; Dutchess, and Bosola Q4; Duchess and
Attendants Dyce ii subs.*   39. to] *Q2;* to be *Q.*

---

25. *directly*] plainly, simply.
27. *censure*] judge.
28. *purchase*] acquisitions, wealth.
31–5. *Great . . . people*] from Donne, *Ignatius his Conclave* (1611), p. 92:
'. . . Princes, who though they enuy and grudge, that their great Officers
should haue such immoderate meanes to get wealth; yet they dare not
complaine of it, least thereby they should make them odious and contemptible to the people' (so Marcia Anderson, *ap.* Dent).

> A count! he's a mere stick of sugar-candy,
> You may look quite thorough him: when I choose
> A husband, I will marry for your honour.

Ferd. You shall do well in't:—how is't, worthy Antonio?   45

Duch. But sir, I am to have private conference with you
> About a scandalous report, is spread
> Touching mine honour.

Ferd.   Let me be ever deaf to't:
> One of Pasquil's paper bullets, court-calumny,
> A pestilent air which princes' palaces   50
> Are seldom purg'd of: yet, say that it were true,—
> I pour it in your bosom—my fix'd love
> Would strongly excuse, extenuate, nay, deny
> Faults, were they apparent in you: go be safe
> In your own innocency.

Duch.   O bless'd comfort!   55
> This deadly air is purg'd.   *Exeunt [all except* FERDINAND].

---

54. were] *Q3;* where *Q.*   55. Duch.] *Q; Duch. (aside) Dyce ii.*   56. *all
except Ferdinand] Dyce ii subs.; manent Ferd. Bosola Q4.*

---

42. *sugar-candy] Cf. D.L.C.,* II. i. 153–5: 'You are a foole, a precious one
—you are a meere sticke of Sugar Candy, a man may looke quite thorow
you'.

45. *how . . . Antonio]* Ferdinand supposes him to be the duchess' bawd,
and here tries to make him betray his complicity; the duchess immediately
tries to divert attention.

49. *Pasquil's . . . bullets]* Pasquil was, reputedly, a schoolmaster (some
authorities say a cobbler) who lived in Rome in the 15th century and had
a bitter tongue; his name was transferred to an old statue placed in Piazza
Navona to which it was a custom to attach topical lampoons. The original
Latin pasquinades were collected and published in 1544; the form had its
greatest vogue in Italy in 1585–90.

For *bullets,* cf. *Ado,* II. iii. 249–50: 'quips and sentences and these paper
bullets of the brain'.

52. *pour . . . bosom]* assure you, confide in you: as Dent has shown, this
is a common phrase, but it may have retained a special implication of ardour
and intimacy for Webster; he used it for Bracciano's first appeal to
Vittoria (*W.D.,* I. ii. 205).

52–4. *my . . . you]* from *A.T.,* IV. i. 1994–6: 'Loue cannot finde an imperfection forth: / But doth excuse, extenuate, or denie / Faults where it likes,
with shaddowes of no woorth.'

Ferd.   Her guilt treads on
    Hot-burning coulters:—

                Enter BOSOLA.

                Now Bosola,
    How thrives our intelligence?
Bos.   Sir, uncertainly:
    'Tis rumour'd she hath had three bastards, but
    By whom, we may go read i'th' stars.
Ferd.   Why some   60
    Hold opinion, all things are written there.
Bos. Yes, if we could find spectacles to read them—
    I do suspect there hath been some sorcery
    Us'd on the duchess.
Ferd.   Sorcery! to what purpose?
Bos. To make her dote on some desertless fellow   65
    She shames to acknowledge.
Ferd.   Can your faith give way
    To think there's pow'r in potions, or in charms,
    To make us love, whether we will or no?
Bos. Most certainly.
Ferd. Away, these are mere gulleries, horrid things   70
    Invented by some cheating mountebanks
    To abuse us:—do you think that herbs or charms
    Can force the will? Some trials have been made

---

57. S.D.] *so Dyce ii; at l. 0.1 Q; at l. 37 Q4.*

    56–7. *Her . . . coulters*] Ordeal by red-hot *coulters*, or ploughshares, was known in Old English law. Emma, the mother of Edward the Confessor, walked 'barefoot upon nine culters red hote in Winchester Church without harme (an usuall kind of triall in those daies and then called *Ordalium*) and so cleered her selfe of that imputation, that she made her chastitie by so great a miracle more famous to posterity' (Camden's *Britain* (tr. 1610), p. 211). In the course of discussing 'Symptoms of Jealousy', Burton (*Anatomy*, III. iii. 2) lists numerous women who vindicated their chastity in this way.
    66–79. *Can . . . her*] This digression is detailed to show how readily Ferdinand is drawn to question the sources of love.
    73. *will*] In view of 'force To make . . . mad' (ll. 75–6) and 'rank blood' (l. 78 below), *will* here means 'carnal desire, appetite' (*O.E.D.*, 2), rather than 'wish, intention, power of choice', etc. Cf. Muriel Bradbrook's dis-

In this foolish practice; but the ingredients
Were lenitive poisons, such as are of force   75
To make the patient mad; and straight the witch
Swears, by equivocation, they are in love.
The witchcraft lies in her rank blood: this night
I will force confession from her. You told me
You had got, within these two days, a false key   80
Into her bed-chamber.

Bos.   I have.

Ferd.   As I would wish.

Bos. What do you intend to do?

Ferd.   Can you guess?

Bos.   No:—

Ferd. Do not ask then:
He that can compass me, and know my drifts,
May say he hath put a girdle 'bout the world   85
And sounded all her quicksands.

Bos.   I do not
Think so.

Ferd.   What do you think then? pray?

Bos.   That you
Are your own chronicle too much; and grossly
Flatter yourself.

Ferd.   Give me thy hand, I thank thee:

87–8. That . . .] *so Samp;* . . . are / Your . . . *Q.*

---

cussion of *will* in Middleton's *Changeling* (1622), in her *Themes and Conventions* (1935), pp. 214–16. And see, also, III. ii. 116–18, note.

75. *lenitive*] soothing. Lucas considered the epithet 'forced' and suggested that Q's 'lenative' was derived from L. *lenare*, to prostitute. But Webster used 'lenative' in its ordinary sense in *A.Q.L.*, I. i. 91 and often showed particular interest in poisons that work secretly (cf. *W.D.*, II. i. 285–7 and note, and V. i. 69–75). Ferdinand means that these potions were sweet to take, but poisonous in that they rendered the takers crazy.

82.] Probably the metre stresses 'Can *you* guess'.

85. *put . . . world*] a proverbial phrase often used of Drake's circumnavigation: see, e.g., G. Whitney, *Emblems* (1586), p. 203, or the ambitious Bussy's opening speech (*Bussy*, I. i. 23).

87–8. *you . . . much*] Cf. *W.D.*, V. i. 100–1: ''Tis a ridiculous thing for a man to be his own chronicle', and *Troil.*, II. iii. 165–6: 'pride is his own glass, his own trumpet, his own chronicle.'

I never gave pension but to flatterers,   90
Till I entertained thee. Farewell:
That friend a great man's ruin strongly checks
Who rails into his belief all his defects.   *Exeunt.*

SCENA II.

Enter Duchess, ANTONIO *and* CARIOLA.

Duch. Bring me the casket hither, and the glass:—
　　You get no lodging here tonight, my lord.
Ant. Indeed, I must persuade one:—
Duch.   Very good:
　　I hope in time 'twill grow into a custom
　　That noblemen shall come with cap and knee,   5
　　To purchase a night's lodging of their wives.
Ant. I must lie here.
Duch.   Must? you are a lord of mis-rule.
Ant. Indeed, my rule is only in the night.
Duch. To what use will you put me?
Ant.   We'll sleep together:—
Duch. Alas, what pleasure can two lovers find in sleep?   10
Cari. My lord, I lie with her often; and I know
　　She'll much disquiet you:—
Ant.   See, you are complain'd of.
Cari. For she's the sprawling'st bedfellow.
Ant. I shall like her the better for that.

92–3.] *italicized Q.*

III. ii. 0.1] *Q4 subs.; Dutchesse, Antonio, Cariola, Ferdinand, Bosola,*
Officers Q.   10.] *so Q;* Alas, / What . . . *Dyce i.*   14.] *so Q;* . . . her /
The . . . *McIl.*

III. ii. 5. *with . . . knee*] an informal way of saying 'with cap in hand and
bended knee'.

7. *lord of mis-rule*] one chosen to preside over feasts and revels at Court,
universities, great houses, etc.; he was very young or of low degree, and so
reversed the usual hierarchies. See E. K. Chambers, *Medieval Stage* (1903),
I.403–19, and E. Welsford, *The Fool* (1935), ch. ix.
　　Q's hyphen may be retained to point the quibble.

8. *my . . . night*] probably suggested by Painter; App. I, p. 189.

Cari.　Sir, shall I ask you a question?　　　　　　　　　15

Ant.　I pray thee, Cariola.

Cari.　Wherefore still when you lie with my lady *always*.
　　　Do you rise so early?

Ant.　　　　　　　　　Labouring men
　　　Count the clock oft'nest Cariola,
　　　Are glad when their task's ended.

Duch.　　　　　　　　　I'll stop your mouth.　　20
　　　　　　　　　　　　　　[*Kisses him.*]

Ant.　Nay, that's but one—Venus had two soft doves
　　　To draw her chariot: I must have another.　　[*Kisses her.*]
　　　When wilt thou marry, Cariola?

Cari.　　　　　　　　　Never, my lord.

Ant.　O fie upon this single life! forgo it!

---

16. I] *Q; Ay, Dyce* i.　　20.1.] *Dyce* ii.　　22. S.D.] *Luc* i; *She kisses him again Dyce* ii.

---

17. *still*] always.

20. *I'll . . . mouth*] The phrase was proverbial (Tilley M1264), and its application to a kiss common; cf. *W.D.*, IV. ii. 192–3 and *Ado*, II. i. 321–3.

24–32.] from Whetstone, *Heptameron* (1582), C4: 'And where Isma-rito, attributes such Glorie unto a Single lyfe, because that Daphne was metamorphosed into a Bay tree, whose Branches are alwayes greene: In my opinion, his reason is fayre like the Bay Tree; for the Bay Tree is barren of pleasant fruict, & his plesing words of weighty matter. Furthermore, what remembrance is theare of faire Sirinx coynesse, refusing to be God Pans wife? other then that she was metamorphosed into a fewe unprofitable Reedes: Or of Anaxaretes chaste crueltie towardes Iphis, [other] then that she remaineth an Image of Stone in Samarin. . . But in the behalf of Mariage, thousands haue ben changed into Olyue, Pomegranate, Mulberie, and other fruictfull trees, sweete flowers, Starres, and precious stones, by whom the worlde is beautified, directed and noorished' (so Dent, who noted that in the 1593 edn, titled *Aurelia*, 'Pans' was misprinted 'Paris' and so may have led Webster on to consider 'Paris' case', ll. 33–42).

Daphne was wooed by Apollo (Ovid, *Met.*, i. 452, etc.). Pan made his pipe from the reed into which *Syrinx* was changed (*Met.*, i. 691, etc.). Iphis hanged himself at *Anaxarete*'s door and then Venus changed her to stone for being unaffected as his body was taken to its grave (*Met.*, xiv. 74, etc.).

The *olive* and *pomegranate* are not associated with any well-known or appropriate metamorphosis: the *mulberry*'s fruit was turned to red from the blood of Pyramus, who slew himself because he thought Thisbe was dead (*Met.*, iv. 55–165).

We read how Daphne, for her peevish flight,   25
Became a fruitless bay-tree; Syrinx turn'd
To the pale empty reed; Anaxarete
Was frozen into marble: whereas those
Which marry'd, or prov'd kind unto their friends,
Were, by a gracious influence, transshap'd   30
Into the olive, pomegranate, mulberry;
Became flow'rs, precious stones, or eminent stars.

Cari. This is a vain poetry: but I pray you tell me,
If there were propos'd me, wisdom, riches, and beauty,
In three several young men, which should I choose?   35

Ant. 'Tis a hard question: this was Paris' case
And he was blind in't, and there was great cause;
For how was't possible he could judge right,
Having three amorous goddesses in view,
And they stark naked? 'twas a motion   40
Were able to benight the apprehension
Of the severest counsellor of Europe.
Now I look on both your faces so well form'd,
It puts me in mind of a question I would ask.

Cari. What is't?

Ant.   I do wonder why hard-favour'd ladies,   45
For the most part, keep worse-favour'd waiting-women

---

25. flight] *Dyce i;* slight *Q.*   33. is a] *Q;* is *conj. Samp.*   41. apprehension] Q^b (apprehention); approbation Q^a.

---

25. *flight*] Dent suggested that Q's 'slight' might be correct because 'Webster's source refers only to Daphne's refusal'. But, according to *O.E.D.*, 'slight' was not used for 'display of contemptuous indifference or disregard' etc. until 1701; in Webster's day it meant a 'small matter, trifle'. Moreover, '*peevish* slight' would be unusefully tautologous. There are other misprints in the following lines.

29. *friends*] often used of lovers, or 'paramours', of either sex; see, for example, *Meas.*, I. iv. 29 and *Wint.*, I. ii. 108–9.

34–42.] Cf. Alexander, *J.C.*, I. i. 59–60, where Juno complains of the judgement of Paris: 'No wonder too though one all iudgement lost, / That had three naked goddesses in sight.'

40. *motion*] Lucas glossed 'puppet-show', quoting (after *O.E.D.*) Jonson; but 'incitement' (cf. *O.E.D.*, 9 and 10) is possibly more apposite.

 To attend them, and cannot endure fair ones.
Duch. O, that's soon answer'd.
 Did you ever in your life know an ill painter
 Desire to have his dwelling next door to the shop   50
 Of an excellent picture-maker ? 'twould disgrace
 His face-making, and undo him:—I prithee,
 When were we so merry ?—my hair tangles.
Ant. Pray thee, Cariola, let's steal forth the room
 And let her talk to herself; I have divers times   55
 Serv'd her the like, when she hath chaf'd extremely:
 I love to see her angry:—softly, Cariola. *Exit with* CARIOLA.
Duch. Doth not the colour of my hair 'gin to change ?
 When I wax gray, I shall have all the court
 Powder their hair with arras, to be like me:—   60
 You have cause to love me; I enter'd you into my heart
 Before you would vouchsafe to call for the keys.

    Enter FERDINAND [*behind*].

 We shall one day have my brothers take you napping:
 Methinks his presence, being now in court,
 Should make you keep your own bed: but you'll say   65
 Love mix'd with fear is sweetest. I'll assure you
 You shall get no more children till my brothers

50. his] *Q^b*; the *Q^a*.   57. S.D.] *Dyce i subs.; Exeunt Q.*   62.1.] *so Dyce i; at l. o.1 Q; after l. 61 (. . . unseen) Q4.*

---

 50. *his*] press-corrections in this forme may be authorial; see Intro., pp. lxiii f.
 53. *When . . . merry*] 'A lightening' of the spirits was said to precede death (Tilley L277): cf. *W.D.*, I. ii. 269: 'Woe to light hearts—they still forerun our fall', and *Rom.*, v. iii. 88–90.
 60. *Powder . . . arras*] Powdered orris, or iris, root was used for whitening and perfuming hair. In England in the 17th century, orris was often called *arras* (properly, a rich tapestry fabric) as in *W.D.*, v. iii. 117, and that form is kept in this text for its luxurious associations.
 61–2.] Cf. Sidney, *Arcadia*, I. xi (*Wks*, I. 69): '. . . his fame had so framed the way to my mind, that his presence, so full of beauty, sweetnes, and noble conversation, had entred there before he vouchsafed to call for the keyes'.

Consent to be your gossips:—have you lost your tongue?

[*Turns and sees Ferdinand.*]

'Tis welcome:

For know, whether I am doom'd to live or die,   70

I can do both like a prince.   *Ferdinand gives her a poniard.*

Ferd.   Die then, quickly!

Virtue, where art thou hid? what hideous thing

Is it that doth eclipse thee?

Duch.   Pray sir, hear me:—

Ferd. Or is it true, thou art but a bare name,

And no essential thing?

Duch.   Sir:—

Ferd.   Do not speak.

Duch.   No sir: 75

I will plant my soul in mine ears to hear you.

Ferd. O most imperfect light of human reason,

That mak'st us so unhappy, to foresee

What we can least prevent! Pursue thy wishes,

And glory in them: there's in shame no comfort   80

But to be past all bounds, and sense of shame.

Duch. I pray sir, hear me: I am married.

Ferd.   So:—

Duch. Happily, not to your liking: but for that,

68–9.] *so Q4; one line Q.*   68.1.] *Luc i subs.*   71. S.D.] *Q^b (to right of two lines of type for l. 71); not in Q^a.*   75–6. No . . .] *so Q; one line McIl.* 78. us] *Q4; not in Q.*

---

68. *gossips*] godfathers (to your child).

70–1. *know . . . prince*] from *Arcadia*, I. iv (*Wks*, I. 25): 'Lastly, whether your time call you to live or die, doo both like a prince.'

71. *poniard*] presumably his father's (cf. I. i. 331–2); it has been strangely presented before, and is so now (cf. ll.149–54).

72–5. *Virtue . . . thing*] from *Arcadia*, II. i. (*Wks*, I. 146): 'O Vertue, where doost thou hide thy selfe? or what hideous thing is this which doth eclips thee? or is it true that thou weart never but a vaine name, and no essentiall thing . . . ?'

77–81.] from the same soliloquy in *Arcadia* as Ferdinand's previous speech: 'O imperfect proportion of reason, which can too much forsee, & too little prevent. . . In shame there is no comfort, but to be beyond all bounds of shame.' See, also, *W.D.*, v. vi. 180, and note.

83. *Happily*] haply, perhaps.

    Alas, your shears do come untimely now

    To clip the bird's wings that's already flown!   85

    Will you see my husband?

Ferd.   Yes, if I could change

    Eyes with a basilisk:—

Duch.   Sure, you came hither

    By his confederacy.

Ferd.   The howling of a wolf

    Is music to thee, screech-owl, prithee peace!

    Whate'er thou art, that hast enjoy'd my sister,—   90

    For I am sure thou hear'st me—for thine own sake

    Let me not know thee: I came hither prepar'd

    To work thy discovery, yet am now persuaded

    It would beget such violent effects

    As would damn us both:—I would not for ten millions   95

    I had beheld thee; therefore use all means

    I never may have knowledge of thy name;

    Enjoy thy lust still, and a wretched life,

    On that condition.—And for thee, vile woman,

    If thou do wish thy lecher may grow old   100

    In thy embracements, I would have thee build

    Such a room for him as our anchorites

    To holier use inhabit: let not the sun

86–7. Yes . . . basilisk] *so Dyce i;* . . . I / Could . . . *Q.*   88. confederacy]
Q3; consideracy *Q.*   89. thee] *Q4;* the *Q.*   95. damn] *Q2* (damne);
dampe *Q.*

    84–5.] from *Arcadia*, II. v (*Wks*, I. 177), where Philoclea is warned not
to fall in love: 'Alas thought Philoclea to her selfe, your sheeres come to late
to clip the birds wings that already is flowne away.' To *clip . . . wings* was
a proverbial saying (Tilley W498).

    86–7. *if . . . basilisk*] For the repartee, Lucas compared *R3*, I. ii. 150–1:
'—Thine eyes, sweet lady, have infected mine.—Would they were
basilisks, to strike thee dead!'

    A *basilisk*, or cockatrice, was a fabled reptile 'brought forth of a Cockes
egge' and hatched by a Snake or Toad (Topsell, *Serpents* (1608), p. 119).
According to Pliny (*Nat. History* (tr. 1601), XXIX. iv) 'all other serpents doe
flie from and are afraid of [it] . . . and (by report) if he do but set his eye on
a man, it is enough to take away his life'.

    89. *to thee*] i.e., 'compared to thee'.

Shine on him, till he's dead; let dogs and monkeys
Only converse with him, and such dumb things   105
To whom nature denies use to sound his name;
Do not keep a paraquito, lest she learn it.
If thou do love him, cut out thine own tongue
Lest it bewray him.

Duch.   Why might not I marry?
I have not gone about, in this, to create   110
Any new world, or custom.

Ferd.   Thou art undone:
And thou hast ta'en that massy sheet of lead
That hid thy husband's bones, and folded it
About my heart.

Duch.   Mine bleeds for't.

Ferd.   Thine? thy heart?
What should I name 't, unless a hollow bullet   115
Fill'd with unquenchable wild-fire?

Duch.   You are, in this,
Too strict: and were you not my princely brother
I would say too wilful: my reputation
Is safe.

Ferd.   Dost thou know what reputation is?
I'll tell thee—to small purpose, since th' instruction   120
Comes now too late:
Upon a time, Reputation, Love, and Death

---

115. *bullet*] cannon-ball: explosive shells were introduced in the place of solid ones during the 16th century.

116. *wild-fire*] used of explosives; but cf. II. v. 47.

116–18. *You . . . wilful*] Cf. Cesario to Clarissa in *Fair Maid of the Inn*, I. i, after counselling her not to marry without his approval: '*Clarissa.* You haue my hand for't;—*Cesario.* Which were it not my sisters, I should kisse / With too much heate.' The duchess' *wilful* probably means 'passionate'; cf. the '*wilful* shipwreck' of Bracciano's 'lascivious dream' (*W.D.*, II. i. 32–42). See also III. i. 73, and note.

122–33. *Upon . . . again*] based on P. Matthieu, *Henry IV* (tr. 1612), Ss1ᵛ: 'Reputation . . . the goddesse of great courages is so delicate, as the least excesse doth blemish it, an vniust enterprise dishonoreth it. . . It is a spirit that goes and returnes no more. They report that water, fire, and

Would travel o'er the world; and it was concluded
That they should part, and take three several ways:
Death told them, they should find him in great battles,   125
Or cities plagu'd with plagues; Love gives them counsel
To inquire for him 'mongst unambitious shepherds,
Where dowries were not talk'd of, and sometimes
'Mongst quiet kindred that had nothing left
By their dead parents: 'Stay', quoth Reputation,   130
'Do not forsake me; for it is my nature
If once I part from any man I meet
I am never found again.' And so, for you:
You have shook hands with Reputation,
And made him invisible:—so fare you well.   135
I will never see you more.

Duch.   Why should only I,
Of all the other princes of the world,
Be cas'd up, like a holy relic? I have youth,
And a little beauty.

Ferd.   So you have some virgins   140
That are witches:—I will never see thee more.   *Exit.*

Enter ANTONIO *with a pistol*[*, and* CARIOLA].

141.1] *so Q4 (subs.); after* apparition, *l. 142 Q; . . . and Cariola Dyce i.*

---

reputation, vndertooke to goe throughout the world, and fearing they
should goe astray, they gaue signes one vnto another: Water said that they
should find her where as they sawe reeds, and fire whereas the smoke
appeared, loose me not said reputation, for if I get from you, you will neuer
finde mee againe.'

137–9. *Why . . . relic*] possibly from Pettie, II. 75: '. . . not to suffer a
mayde to go abrode but once or twise in the yeare, and to keepe her in-
closed like a holy relique, is the way to make her . . . more easie to bee
caughte in a net.'

140–1. *virgins . . . witches*] Cf. III. i. 78, and Intro., pp. xliii f.

141. *I . . . more*] preparing for IV. i (see esp. ll. 23–8). The repetition (from
l. 136) gives force to the words; IV. i. 23 suggests that they were meant to be
both 'solemn' and 'rash'. Perhaps this is a response to his sister's 'beauty'
(l. 140), or to a 'wilful' attraction to her (l. 118). In Fletcher's *King and No
King* (1611), when Arbaces believes he lusts after his sister, he tells her:
'thy dwelling must be dark and close / Where I may never see thee.' (IV. iv.
77–8). For the effect of this line in performance, see Intro., p. lviii.

Duch. You saw this apparition ?

Ant.   Yes : we are
    Betray'd ; how came he hither ? I should turn
    This to thee, for that.

Cari.   Pray sir, do : and when
    That you have cleft my heart, you shall read there   145
    Mine innocence.

Duch.   That gallery gave him entrance.

Ant. I would this terrible thing would come again,
    That, standing on my guard, I might relate
    My warrantable love :—   *She shews the poniard.*
                ha, what means this ?

Duch. He left this with me :—

Ant.   And it seems did wish   150
    You would use it on yourself ?

Duch.   His action seem'd
    To intend so much.

Ant.   This hath a handle to't
    As well as a point—turn it towards him,
    And so fasten the keen edge in his rank gall :—
                              [*Knocking within.*]
    How now ! who knocks ? more earthquakes ?

Duch.   I stand   155
    As if a mine, beneath my feet, were ready
    To be blown up.

Cari.   'Tis Bosola :—

Duch.   Away !
    O misery ! methinks unjust actions
    Should wear these masks and curtains, and not we :—   159

149. S.D.] *so Dyce ii; to right of two lines of type for l. 150 Q.*   151–2. His
. . . much] *so Samp;* . . . Action / Seem'd . . . *Q.*   153–4.] *so Q;* . . . and /
So . . . *Samp.*   154.1.] *Dyce ii.*

---

142. *apparition*] Meanings ranged from 'spectre' and 'illusion', to
'phenomenon' and 'appearance'.

   144. *This . . . that*] i.e., the pistol to Cariola for betrayal.

   158. *unjust*] faithless, dishonest (cf. *O.E.D.*, 2).

You must instantly part hence; I have fashion'd it already.

Exit ANTONIO.

Enter BOSOLA.

Bos. The duke your brother is ta'en up in a whirlwind,
  Hath took horse, and's rid post to Rome.
Duch.   So late?
Bos. He told me, as he mounted into th' saddle,
  You were undone.
Duch.   Indeed, I am very near it.
Bos. What's the matter?   165
Duch. Antonio, the master of our household,
  Hath dealt so falsely with me, in's accounts:
  My brother stood engag'd with me for money
  Ta'en up of certain Neapolitan Jews,
  And Antonio lets the bonds be forfeit.   170
Bos. Strange!—[*Aside*] This is cunning:—
Duch.   And hereupon
  My brother's bills at Naples are protested
  Against:—call up our officers.
Bos.   I shall.   *Exit.*

[*Enter* ANTONIO.]

Duch. The place that you must fly to is Ancona,
  Hire a house there. I'll send after you   175
  My treasure and my jewels: our weak safety

160.2.] *so Q4; at l. 0.1 Q.* 171. *Aside*] *Dyce ii.* 173.1.] *Q4.*

168–70.] i.e., Ferdinand was security (*stood engaged*) for money that the
duchess (*with me*) had borrowed (*ta'en up*), and Antonio, by some breach
of contract (as a failure to pay due interest) causes, or allows (*lets*), Ferdinand to become liable for the sum borrowed (*bonds be forfeit*).

172–3. *My . . . Against*] i.e., it has been formally declared (*protested*) that
his bills of exchange, or promissory notes (*bills*), are not acceptable.

176–7. *our . . . wheels*] 'The world runs on wheels' was a proverb (Tilley
W893), implying haste and impermanence. Perhaps *enginous* is, simply,
'like an engine'; for which Dyce quoted Dekker, *Whore of Babylon* (1607),
I. ii. 165–6: 'For that one Acte giues like an enginous wheele, / Motion to
all.' But it was also used for 'clever, crafty, cunning' (cf. *O.E.D.*, 1).

Runs upon enginous wheels; short syllables
Must stand for periods. I must now accuse you
Of such a feigned crime as Tasso calls
Magnanima menzogna: a noble lie   180
'Cause it must shield our honours:—hark! they are coming.

Enter [BOSOLA *and*] Officers.

Ant. Will your grace hear me?
Duch. I have got well by you: you have yielded me
    A million of loss; I am like to inherit
    The people's curses for your stewardship.   185
    You had the trick in audit-time to be sick,
    Till I had sign'd your *quietus*; and that cur'd you
    Without help of a doctor.—Gentlemen,
    I would have this man be an example to you all:
    So shall you hold my favour; I pray let him,   190
    For h'as done that, alas, you would not think of,
    And, because I intend to be rid of him,
    I mean not to publish:—use your fortune elsewhere.
Ant. I am strongly arm'd to brook my overthrow,
    As commonly men bear with a hard year: 195
    I will not blame the cause on't; but do think
    The necessity of my malevolent star
    Procures this, not her humour. O the inconstant

---

177. enginous] *Dyce i*; engenous *Q*; ingenious *Q2*.   181.1.] *Q4 subs.*;
Officers (*at l. o.1*) *Q*.

179–80. feigned ... menzogna] from *Gerus. Lib.*, II. 22; Soprina takes the
blame for rescuing a statue of the Virgin from a mosque, in order to prevent
wholesale persecution of Christians.
    183. I ... by you] The first of a series of *doubles entendres*, comparable to
those in II. i. 118 ff. At l. 187, 'quietus' echoes the 'Quietus est' of I. i. 464.
Other quibbling phrases are: 'I pray let him' (i.e., 'be an example for ill' *or*
'for good'; or, possibly, *let him* = 'let him go' *or* 'let him remain'—see
O.E.D. 9, 10, and 1, and *1H4*, I. i. 91 and *Wint.*, I. ii. 41); 'h'as done that
... I mean not to publish'; 'use your fortune elsewhere' (cf. I. i. 495 and,
possibly, *use* = 'have intercourse with'—see *O.E.D.*, 10b); 'brook' ('profit
from' *or* 'bear with'—see *O.E.D.*, 1 and 3); 'I am all yours, ... All mine
should be so'; 'your pass' ('permission to go' *or* 'approval'—see *O.E.D.*,
8 and 3); and 'what 'tis to serve ... with body, and soul'.

And rotten ground of service!—you may see:
'Tis ev'n like him, that in a winter night   200
Takes a long slumber o'er a dying fire,
As loth to part from't; yet parts thence as cold
As when he first sat down.

Duch.   We do confiscate,
Towards the satisfying of your accounts,
All that you have.   205

Ant. I am all yours: and 'tis very fit
All mine should be so.

Duch.   So, sir; you have your pass.

Ant. You may see, gentlemen, what 'tis to serve
A prince with body, and soul.   *Exit.*

Bos. Here's an example, for extortion: what moisture is   210
drawn out of the sea, when foul weather comes, pours
down and runs into the sea again.

Duch. I would know what are your opinions of this Antonio.

2nd. Off. He could not abide to see a pig's head gaping: I
thought your grace would find him a Jew.   215

3rd. Off. I would you had been his officer, for your own sake.

4th. Off. You would have had more money.

1st. Off. He stopp'd his ears with black wool; and to those
came to him for money, said he was thick of hearing.

2nd. Off. Some said he was an hermaphrodite, for he could   220
not abide a woman.

4th. Off. How scurvy proud he would look, when the treasury was full! Well, let him go:—

---

202. As loth] *Q*^{c}; A-loth *Q*^{a}.   213.] *so this ed.;* . . . opinions / Of . . . *Q.*

210–12.] a commonplace: cf. Cotgrave, *Dictionary* (1611), *s.v.* Mer:
'*Les Rivieres retournent en la mer*: Prov. (Said when Princes doe squeeze out
of their spungie Officers the moisture which they haue purloyned from
them.)' (so Dent).

214–15.] a conflation of two proverbs: 'Some cannot abide to see a pig's
head gaping' (of irrational fads, as at *Mer.V.*, IV. i. 47), and 'Invite not a
Jew either to pig or pork' (Tilley P310 and J50).

218. *black wool*] An old cure for deafness was said to be 'take the gall of
an Hare, mixe it with the greace of a Foxe, and with blacke wooll, instill
this into the eare' (Bartholomeus, *De Prop. Rerum* (tr. 1582), VII. xxi).

1st. Off. Yes, and the chippings of the buttery fly after him,
    to scour his gold chain.   225

Duch. Leave us.   *Exeunt* Officers.
    What do you think of these?

Bos. That these are rogues, that in's prosperity,
    But to have waited on his fortune, could have wish'd
    His dirty stirrup riveted through their noses,   230
    And follow'd after's mule, like a bear in a ring;
    Would have prostituted their daughters to his lust;
    Made their first-born intelligencers; thought none happy
    But such as were born under his bless'd planet,
    And wore his livery: and do these lice drop off now?   235
    Well, never look to have the like again:
    He hath left a sort of flatt'ring rogues behind him—
    Their doom must follow: princes pay flatterers
    In their own money; flatterers dissemble their vices
    And they dissemble their lies: that's justice—   240
    Alas, poor gentleman!

Duch. Poor? he hath amply fill'd his coffers.

Bos.   Sure
    He was too honest: Pluto, the god of riches,

226–7.] *so Dyce i; one line Q.*   226. S.D.] *so Dyce i; after l. 225 Q subs.;*
after l. 227 Q4.   233. first-born] *Q^c;* first-borne and *Q^a.*   242–3.
Sure . . .] *so this ed.; one line Q.*

---

224. *chippings*] 'parings of the crust of a loaf' (*O.E.D.*, 2).

225. *gold chain*] a steward's badge of office; cf. *Tw.N.*, II. iii. 128–9: 'Go,
Sir, rub your chain with crumbs'.

231. *in a ring*] i.e., led on a ring (cf. Abbott §160).

235. *lice . . . now*] a common image for flatterers: lice were supposed to
leave a body as soon as the blood failed.

237. *sort*] set, gang.

238–40. *princes . . .*] from Matthieu, *Henry IV* (1612), Cc3: 'Princes pay
flatterers, in their owne money: Flatterers dissemble their vices, and they
dissemble their lies, that's Justice.'

243–7. *Pluto . . .*] derived, probably through some intermediary, from
Lucian, *Timon*, 20 (so Dent).

The *god of riches* was properly called Plutus, but he was sometimes given
the name of the god of the underworld. In their original forms the names
are related, and *Pluto* may have been transferred to the other god as a pro-

When he's sent by Jupiter to any man
He goes limping, to signify that wealth   245
That comes on god's name comes slowly: but when he's sent
On the devil's errand, he rides post and comes in by scuttles.
Let me show you what a most unvalu'd jewel
You have, in a wanton humour, thrown away,
To bless the man shall find him: he was an excellent   250
Courtier, and most faithful, a soldier that thought it
As beastly to know his own value too little
As devilish to acknowledge it too much:
Both his virtue and form deserv'd a far better fortune.
His discourse rather delighted to judge itself, than show
   itself.   255
His breast was fill'd with all perfection,
And yet it seem'd a private whisp'ring-room,
It made so little noise of 't.
Duch.   But he was basely descended.
Bos. Will you make yourself a mercenary herald,
Rather to examine men's pedigrees than virtues ?   260
You shall want him,

---

247. On] *Q2;* One *Q.*   258. It] *Q;* He *conj. Samp.*

---

pitiatory euphemism or as a mark of the 'devil' (so Bacon, 'Of Riches'), or
because wealth comes from underground (so Lucas).

247. *scuttles*] *O.E.D.* glosses 'short hurried runs', but this passage is the
only illustration before Addison (1712): moreover 'scuttling' hardly agrees
with riding *post* (i.e., express, in haste). Perhaps Webster drops the per-
sonification and *scuttles* = 'large baskets' (as used for vegetables, etc.).

248. *unvalu'd*] (1) 'invaluable', and (2) 'not regarded as of value'.

254.] from Jonson's dedication to Prince Henry of *The Masque of
Queens* (1609): '. . . both yor vertue, & yor forme did deserue yor fortune'.
Webster drew on this dedication in *Monumental Column* (1613), and on the
masque in *W.D.,* III. ii. 135.

255.] from *Arcadia,* I. v (*Wks,* I. 32), describing Parthenia: 'a wit which
delighted more to judge it selfe, then to showe it selfe'. *discourse* = 'wit,
faculty of reasoning'.

256–8. *His . . . of 't*] Cf. *Monumental Column,* ll. 78–9: 'Who had his
breast instated with the choice / Of vertues, though they made no ambitious
noise'.

259–60.] from *Arcadia,* I. ii (*Wks,* I. 15): '. . . I am no herald to enquire
of mens pedigrees, it sufficeth me if I know their vertues.'

For know an honest statesman to a prince
Is like a cedar, planted by a spring:
The spring bathes the tree's root, the grateful tree
Rewards it with his shadow: you have not done so—   265
I would sooner swim to the Bermudas on
Two politicians' rotten bladders, tied
Together with an intelligencer's heart-string,
Than depend on so changeable a prince's favour.
Fare thee well, Antonio; since the malice of the world   270
Would needs down with thee, it cannot be said yet
That any ill happened unto thee,
Considering thy fall was accompanied with virtue.

Duch. O, you render me excellent music.

Bos.   Say you?

Duch. This good one that you speak of, is my husband.   275

Bos. Do I not dream? can this ambitious age
Have so much goodness in't, as to prefer
A man merely for worth, without these shadows
Of wealth, and painted honours? possible?

Duch. I have had three children by him.

Bos.   Fortunate lady!   280
For you have made your private nuptial bed
The humble and fair seminary of peace:

266–9.] *so Dyce i;* . . . Politicians / Rotten . . . -string / Then . . . *Q.*   272–
3.] *so Samp;* . . . fall, / Was . . . *Q.*   282–3. peace: . . . but] *Q3;* peace,
. . . but: *Q;* peace, . . . but *Q2.*

262–5. *For . . . shadow*] probably indebted to *Arcadia,* I. xv (*Wks,* I. 96):
'. . . a little River neere hand, which for the moisture it bestowed upon
rootes of some flourishing Trees, was rewarded with their shadowe'.

266. *Bermudas*] Especially after a wreck in 1609, these 'still-vexed'
islands were famous for wild noises and strange creatures, as for storms
(cf. *A.Q.L.,* v. i. 350–67 and *Tempest,* ed. F. Kermode (1954), Intro.).

270–3. *since . . .*] a Senecan theme and commonplace, which Webster
found in *Arcadia,* I. iv (*Wks,* I. 24): '. . . if the wickedness of the world
should oppresse it [prosperity], it can never be said, that evil hapneth to
him, who falles accompanied with vertue.'

279. *painted*] false, specious; cf. *W.D.,* I. i. 51: 'Leave your painted
comforts'.

282. *seminary*] seed-bed, breeding-place, nursery.

No question but many an unbenefic'd scholar
Shall pray for you for this deed, and rejoice
That some preferment in the world can yet   285
Arise from merit. The virgins of your land
That have no dowries, shall hope your example
Will raise them to rich husbands: should you want
Soldiers, 'twould make the very Turks and Moors
Turn Christians, and serve you for this act.   290
Last, the neglected poets of your time,
In honour of this trophy of a man,
Rais'd by that curious engine, your white hand,
Shall thank you, in your grave, for't; and make that
More reverend than all the cabinets   295
Of living princes. For Antonio,
His fame shall likewise flow from many a pen,
When heralds shall want coats to sell to men.

Duch. As I taste comfort in this friendly speech,
So would I find concealment.   300

Bos. O, the secret of my prince,
Which I will wear on th' inside of my heart.

Duch. You shall take charge of all my coin and jewels,
And follow him; for he retires himself
To Ancona.

Bos.   So.

Duch.   Whither, within few days,   305
I mean to follow thee.

Bos.   Let me think:
I would wish your grace to feign a pilgrimage

---

293. *curious*] skilfully or beautifully made, exquisite; cf. Venus of Adonis (*Ven.*, l. 734): 'the curious workmanship of nature'.
   engine] instrument, device (cf. *O.E.D.*, 10b).
   298. *heralds . . .*] The granting of arms by the Heralds' College was subject to abuse; in 1619, a Royal Commission was set up to inquire into the sale of pedigrees, etc. The wealthy clown Sogliardo in *Every Man Out of His Humour* buys his arms for £30.
   302. *wear . . . heart*] Cf. *Ham.*, III. ii. 77–8: 'I will wear him / In my heart's core, ay, in my heart of heart.'
   307–12. *I . . . you*] By seeming to aid her escape Bosola may aim at

To our Lady of Loretto, scarce seven leagues
From fair Ancona; so may you depart
Your country with more honour, and your flight   310
Will seem a princely progress, retaining
Your usual train about you.

Duch.   Sir, your direction
Shall lead me by the hand.

Cari.   In my opinion,
She were better progress to the baths
At Lucca, or go visit the Spa   315
In Germany, for, if you will believe me,
I do not like this jesting with religion,
This feigned pilgrimage.

Duch. Thou art a superstitious fool—
Prepare us instantly for our departure: 320
Past sorrows, let us moderately lament them,
For those to come, seek wisely to prevent them.

Exit [with CARIOLA].

Bos. A politician is the devil's quilted anvil—

313–15. In . . .] *so Q; . . .* opinion, / *She . . .* Lucca, / *Or . . . Dyce i; . . .*
progresse / *To . . . (2 lines) Samp.*   322.1. *with Cariola] Q4 subs.*

---

entering the duchess' confidence more deeply or, as Lucas suggested, aim
at dishonouring her still more by encouraging her to 'jest with religion' and
desert her Duchy (as Francisco 'instructs' Bracciano to 'marry a whore';
see *W.D.*, IV. iii. 52–6).

315–16. *Lucca . . . Germany*] The spas are mentioned in Florio, in a
passage (II. xv) also speaking of Loretto and Ancona (so Lucas). *Spa* is
in Belgium, some 16 m. south of Liège; the Belgians were often known by
the more general term of Germans.

317–18.] Cariola voices a serious objection: cf. III. iii. 60–2, and Marston,
Malcontent (1604), IV. iii: 'A fellow that makes Religion his stawking horse,/
He breedes a plague.'

321–2.] from Alexander, *Croesus*, III. i. 1019–22: 'we should such past
misfortunes pretermit, / At least no more immoderately lament them, /
And as for those which are but comming yet, / Vse ordinary meanes for to
preuent them.'

323–5. *A . . . heard*] Cf. Chapman, *Byron's Tragedy* (1608), I. ii. 53–4:
'. . . great affairs will not be forg'd / But upon anvils that are lin'd with
wool', and T. Adams, *Gallant's Burden* (1612), C1ᵛ–2: 'an insensible
Heart is the Deuils Anuile, he fashioneth all sinnes on it, and the blowes
are not felt.'

He fashions all sins on him, and the blows
Are never heard: he may work in a lady's chamber,   325
As here for proof. What rests, but I reveal
All to my lord? O, this base quality
Of intelligencer! why, every quality i'th' world
Prefers but gain or commendation:
Now, for this act I am certain to be rais'd,   330
And men that paint weeds to the life are prais'd.   *Exit.*

SCENA III.

Enter Cardinal *with* MALATESTE, FERDINAND *with* DELIO *and*
SILVIO, *and* PESCARA.

Card. Must we turn soldier then?
Mal.   The Emperor,
  Hearing your worth that way, ere you attain'd
  This reverend garment, joins you in commission
  With the right fortunate soldier, the Marquis of Pescara,
  And the famous Lannoy.
Card.   He that had the honour   5
  Of taking the French king prisoner?
Mal.   The same—
  Here's a plot drawn for a new fortification
  At Naples.
Ferd. This great Count Malateste, I perceive,
  Hath got employment?
Delio.   No employment, my lord;   10
  A marginal note in the muster-book, that he is
  A voluntary lord.

331.] *italicized Q4;* "And ... Q.

III. iii. 0.1–2.] *Q4 subs.; Cardinall, Ferdinand, Mallateste, Pescara, Siluio,
Delio, Bosola Q.*

329. *Prefers*] assists in bringing about, promotes (cf. *O.E.D.*, 2).

III. iii. 1–3.] For the source of these details, see Intro., p. xxxiii. The
Emperor was Charles V.
  7. *plot*] plan.
  12. *voluntary*] volunteer.

Ferd.   He's no soldier?

Delio. He has worn gunpowder in's hollow tooth,
    For the toothache.

Sil. He comes to the leaguer with a full intent   15
    To eat fresh beef and garlic, means to stay
    Till the scent be gone, and straight return to court.

Delio. He hath read all the late service
    As the City Chronicle relates it,
    And keeps two painters going, only to express   20
    Battles in model.

Sil.   Then he'll fight by the book.

Delio. By the almanac, I think—
    To choose good days, and shun the critical.
    That's his mistress' scarf.

Sil.   Yes, he protests
    He would do much for that taffeta—   25

Delio. I think he would run away from a battle
    To save it from taking prisoner.

Sil.   He is horribly afraid
    Gunpowder will spoil the perfume on't—

Delio. I saw a Dutchman break his pate once
    For calling him pot-gun; he made his head   30

13–14.] *so Luc i; one line Q.*   20. painters] *Q^c;* Pewterers *Q^a.*   21.
he'll] *Q2;* hel; *Q.*

---

    15. *leaguer*] military camp.
    18. *service*] military operations.
    20. *painters*] Press-corrections in this forme are probably authorial.
    21. *model*] scale drawing, ground-plan (cf. *O.E.D.*, 1).
    by the book] a common phrase for 'according to rule, in set phrase or
manner'; but here, also, 'theoretically, rather than practically' (cf. *W.D.*,
v. iii. 21).
    22–3.] Cf. C. Dariot, *Introduction to Astrological Judgement* (1598), R2:
'I will shew you how in the beginning of any matter the constitution and
due disposition of the Heauens and heauenly bodyes is to bee obserued and
marked, for euery houre of the day is not apt or fit for the beginning of
euery work. . .'
    25. *taffeta*] 'plain-wove, glossy silk' (*O.E.D.*).
    30. *pot-gun*] a child's toy, made of elder (sometimes called a 'pop-gun'),
and hence used contemptuously of a braggart or boaster; this passage is the
first occurrence recorded in *O.E.D.* Cf. *H5*, IV. i. 209–10 (Williams to the

          Have a bore in't, like a musket.
Sil.   I would he had made a touch-hole to't.
          He is indeed a guarded sumpter-cloth,
          Only for the remove of the court.

                    Enter BOSOLA.

Pes.   Bosola arriv'd! what should be the business?   35
          Some falling out amongst the cardinals.
          These factions amongst great men, they are like
          Foxes: when their heads are divided
          They carry fire in their tails, and all the country
          About them goes to wreck for't.
Sil.   What's that Bosola?   40
Delio. I knew him in Padua—a fantastical scholar, like such

---

32. to't.] to 't. / *Del.* (=*Catchword*) Q.   33. He] *Q; Delio.* He *conj. this
ed.*   34.1.] *so Q4; at ll. o.1-2 Q.*   41-7.] *so Dyce i;* . . . scholler, / Like
. . . in / Hercules . . . was, / Or . . . -ach, / He . . . the / True . . . this / He . . .
Q; . . . scholler, / Like . . . knots / Was . . . was, / Or . . . -ach— / He . . .
know / The . . . -horne, / And . . . did / To . . . *Luc i.*

---

disguised king): 'That's a perilous shot out of an elder-gun . . . 'tis a foolish
saying'.

    33. *He*] Q's catch-word (on G4ᵛ), its full-stop after l. 32, and the intro-
duction of a fresh notion with 'indeed', all suggest either that ll. 33-4 should
be Delio's or that some lines are missing. Compositor B probably omitted
a speech-prefix at I. i. 116.

    33-4. *guarded* . . .] ornamented (*guarded*) cloth covering a pack-horse
when the beast is employed in changing the place of residence of the court;
cf. *W.D.*, I. ii. 50-1, where Camillo's wit is said to be 'Merely an ass in's
foot-cloth'.

    37-40. *These . . . for't*] an allusion to Samson who tied pairs of foxes
together by their tails and attached firebrands to them, so that they
destroyed the Philistines' harvest (cf. *Judges*, xv. 4-5); this was a popular
story in moralizing writings of the time.

    41-7.] from Matthieu, *Henry IV* (1612), Qq3ᵛ: 'The study of vaine
things is a toilsome idlenesse, and a painful folly. The spirits beeing once
stroken with this disease . . . spend whole nights to finde how many knots
were in Hercules club, and of what colour Achilles beard was. . .' Florio
also provides a slight parallel (I. xxxviii): 'This man, whom about midnight, when others take their rest, thou seest come out of his studie meagre-
looking, with eyes-trilling, fleugmatike, squalide, and spauling, doost thou
thinke, that plodding on his bookes he doth seek how he shal become an
honester man; or more wise, or more content? There is no such matter.

who study to know how many knots was in Hercules'
club, of what colour Achilles' beard was, or whether
Hector were not troubled with the toothache; he hath
studied himself half blear-eyed to know the true sym-   45
metry of Caesar's nose by a shoeing-horn; and this he did
to gain the name of a speculative man.

Pes. Mark Prince Ferdinand:
A very salamander lives in's eye,
To mock the eager violence of fire.   50

Sil. That cardinal hath made more bad faces with his oppression than ever Michael Angelo made good ones; he lifts
up's nose, like a foul porpoise before a storm—

51–3.] so Dyce i; . . . oppression / Then . . . ones, / He . . . Q, Luc i (. . .
before / A . . .).

Hee will either die in his pursute, or teach posterity the measure of Plautus
verses, and the true Orthography of a Latine worde.'

Dent called this a 'lamentable intrusion', inconsistent with what we
know of both Delio and Bosola. But young, ambitious men, like Gabriel
Harvey, or Thomas Overbury, or Flamineo (see *W.D.*, I. ii. 319–27), came
from the universities to seek preferment with 'great men'; to gain a reputation for 'speculation' would be a recommendation for attention at court.
Chapman's Bussy called himself a 'scholar' in his encounter with Maffé
(*Bussy*, Q1, I. i. 183).

41. *Padua*] This 'nursery of Arts' (*Shr.*, I. i. 2) was one of the most famed
universities of the time, being founded in 1238.

47. *speculative*] 'theorizing', and also 'deeply searching'; *O.E.D.* cites
Bacon, *Advancement* (1605), I. iii. 7: 'To be speculative into another man,
to the end to know how to worke him, . . . proceedeth from a heart that is
double.'

49–50.] Salamanders were supposed to live in *fire*, and *fire* was emblematic of passion, destruction, or torment; cf. R.C., *Time's Whistle* (1616;
E.E.T.S. ed., 1871), 119: 'Yet he can live no moe without desire, / Then
can the salamandra without fire.'

51–2. *made . . . ones*] Dent compared Dallington, *View of France* (1604),
N2: 'when I was in Italy, ye should heare them say in derision, that the
King of Spayne [by failing to pay his debts] had made more ill faces vpon
the Exchange, in one day, then Michael Angelo, . . . had euer made good
faces in all his life.'

The *bad faces* are those of the victims of the cardinal's oppressive
acts.

52–3. *lifts . . . storm*] Cf. the proverb, 'The porpoise plays before a storm'
(Tilley P483). The primary sense of *lifts up's nose* is illustrated by *Tp.*, IV.
i. 177–8: 'lifted up their noses As they smelt music', but there may also be

Pes. The Lord Ferdinand laughs.

Delio.   Like a deadly cannon
    That lightens ere it smokes.   55

Pes. These are your true pangs of death,
    The pangs of life that struggle with great statesmen—

Delio. In such a deformed silence, witches whisper
    Their charms.

Card. Doth she make religion her riding-hood   60
    To keep her from the sun and tempest?

Ferd.   That!
    That damns her:—methinks her fault and beauty,
    Blended together, show like leprosy,
    The whiter, the fouler:—I make it a question
    Whether her beggarly brats were ever christen'd.   65

Card. I will instantly solicit the state of Ancona
    To have them banish'd.

Ferd.   You are for Loretto?
    I shall not be at your ceremony: fare you well—
    Write to the Duke of Malfi, my young nephew
    She had by her first husband, and acquaint him   70
    With's mother's honesty.

Bos.   I will.

Ferd.   Antonio!
    A slave, that only smell'd of ink and counters,
    And ne'er in's life look'd like a gentleman,

58–9.] *so Samp; one line* Q.   61–3. That . . .] *so Dyce i;* . . . *and /* Beauty
. . . *(two lines)* Q.   73. life] *Q2;* like Q.

---

an allusion to 'to hold up one's nose' = 'to be proud or haughty' (*O.E.D.*,
nose, 8d).

   62–4. *methinks . . . fouler*] Crawford compared Chapman, *Penitential
Psalms* (1612), 'A Great Man', ll. 17–19: 'Ill vpon ill he layes: th' embro-
derie / Wrought on his state, is like a leprosie, / The whiter, still the
fouler.'

   65. *beggarly brats*] 'beggar's brats' was a proverbial, contemptuous
phrase (so *O.E.D.*).

   69–70. *Duke . . . husband*] The only reference to this son; he is ignored
in Ferdinand's hope of treasure (IV. ii. 283–5) and Delio's assertion of the
rights of Antonio's son (V. vi. 107–8 and 111–13).

But in the audit-time—go, go presently,
Draw me out an hundred and fifty of our horse,   75
And meet me at the fort-bridge.   *Exeunt.*

SCENA IV.

Enter Two Pilgrims *to the Shrine of our Lady of Loretto.*

1st. Pil. I have not seen a goodlier shrine than this,
      Yet I have visited many.
2nd. Pil. The Cardinal of Arragon
      Is this day to resign his cardinal's hat;
      His sister duchess likewise is arriv'd   5
      To pay her vow of pilgrimage—I expect
      A noble ceremony.
1st. Pil.   No question:—they come.

Here the ceremony of the Cardinal's *instalment in the habit of a
soldier, performed in delivering up his cross, hat, robes and ring at the
shrine, and investing him with sword, helmet, shield and spurs; then*
ANTONIO, *the* Duchess *and their* Children, *having presented themselves at the shrine, are (by a form of banishment in dumb-show
expressed towards them by the cardinal and the state of Ancona)
banished: during all which ceremony, this ditty is sung, to very solemn
music, by divers* Churchmen; *and then exeunt* [*all, except the*
                                      Two Pilgrims].

Arms and honours deck thy story	The author
To thy fame's eternal glory !	disclaims
Adverse fortune ever fly thee,	this ditty 10
No disastrous fate come nigh thee !	to be his.

      I alone will sing thy praises,
      Whom to honour virtue raises,
      And thy study, that divine is,

III. iv. 0.1.] Dyce i; Two . . . Q.   7.1. habit] Q*b*; order Q*a*.   of a] Q2;
a Q.   7.5. in dumb-show] Q*b*; not in Q*a*.   7.7. ditty] Q*b*; Hymne Q*a*.
7.8–9. all . . . Pilgrims] Dyce ii.   8. Arms] Q*b*; The Hymne. | Armes Q*a*.
8–11. The . . . his] Q*b* (to right of ll. 10–13, approx.); not in Q*a*.

> *Bent to martial discipline is:*   15
> *Lay aside all those robes lie by thee;*
> *Crown thy arts with arms, they'll beautify thee.*
>
> *O worthy of worthiest name, adorn'd in this manner,*
> *Lead bravely thy forces on under war's warlike banner !*
> *O, mayst thou prove fortunate in all martial courses !*   20
> *Guide thou still, by skill, in arts and forces !*
> *Victory attend thee nigh whilst Fame sings loud thy pow'rs;*
> *Triumphant conquest crown thy head, and blessings pour down*
> *   show'rs !*

1st. Pil. Here's a strange turn of state! who would have thought
So great a lady would have match'd herself   25
Unto so mean a person ? yet the cardinal
Bears himself much too cruel.
2nd. Pil.   They are banish'd.
1st. Pil. But I would ask what power hath this state
Of Ancona to determine of a free prince ?
2nd. Pil. They are a free state sir, and her brother show'd   30
How that the Pope, fore-hearing of her looseness,
Hath seiz'd into th' protection of the church
The dukedom, which she held as dowager.
1st. Pil. But by what justice ?
2nd. Pil.   Sure, I think by none,
Only her brother's instigation.   35
1st. Pil. What was it with such violence he took
Off from her finger ?
2nd. Pil.   'Twas her wedding ring,
Which he vow'd shortly he would sacrifice
To his revenge.
1st. Pil.   Alas, Antonio !
If that a man be thrust into a well,   40

30. sir] Q^b; *not in* Q^a.   32. Hath] Q^b; Had Q^a.

---

20. courses] encounters.
29. *determine of*] judge, decide concerning (cf. *O.E.D.*, 5).
40–2. *If . . . bottom*] from Florio, II. xxxi: 'the mischiefe [of losing one's

No matter who sets hand to't, his own weight
Will bring him sooner to th' bottom:—come, let's hence.
Fortune makes this conclusion general:
All things do help th' unhappy man to fall.   *Exeunt.*

SCENA V.

Enter ANTONIO, Duchess, Children, CARIOLA, Servants.

Duch. Banish'd Ancona!
Ant.   Yes, you see what pow'r
Lightens in great men's breath.
Duch.   Is all our train
Shrunk to this poor remainder ?
Ant.   These poor men,
Which have got little in your service, vow
To take your fortune: but your wiser buntings,   5
Now they are fledg'd, are gone.
Duch.   They have done wisely—
This puts me in mind of death: physicians thus,
With their hands full of money, use to give o'er
Their patients.
Ant.   Right the fashion of the world:

44.] *italicized this ed.; "*All . . . *Q.*

III. v. 0.1.] *Q4; Antonio, . . . Seruants, Bosola, Souldiers, with Vizards Q.*
1. Ancona!] *Dyce i; Ancona ? Q.*

---

temper] is, that after you are once falne into the pit, it is no matter who
thrusts you in, you never cease till you come to the bottome. The fall
presseth, hasteneth, mooveth and furthereth it selfe.'
44.] from *A.T.*, IV. i. 1931: 'All things must help th' vnhappy man to
fall.'
III. v. 1. *Banish'd Ancona*] an echo of the opening word of *W.D.*
5. *buntings*] a kind of bird, allied to larks but without song; cf. Lafeu of
the braggart Parolles: 'I took this lark for a bunting' (*All's W.*, II. v. 6–7);
this was proverbial (cf. Tilley B722).
7–9. *physicians . . . patients*] Dent suggested this was proverbial; he
quoted Painter, *Palace*, ii (1567), 'Lord of Virle', p. 277ᵛ: 'And therfore
dispairing of his helth [he was love-sick], with handes full of money they
[his doctors] gaue him ouer.'
9. *Right*] just, exactly.

From decay'd fortunes every flatterer shrinks;   10
Men cease to build where the foundation sinks.
Duch. I had a very strange dream tonight.
Ant.   What was't?
Duch. Methought I wore my coronet of state,
And on a sudden all the diamonds
Were chang'd to pearls.
Ant.   My interpretation   15
Is, you'll weep shortly, for to me, the pearls
Do signify your tears:—
Duch. The birds that live i' th' field
On the wild benefit of nature, live
Happier than we; for they may choose their mates,   20
And carol their sweet pleasures to the spring:—

    Enter BOSOLA [*with a letter*].

Bos. You are happily o'erta'en.
Duch.   From my brother?
Bos. Yes, from the Lord Ferdinand, your brother,
All love and safety—
Duch.   Thou dost blanch mischief,
Wouldst make it white:—see, see, like to calm weather   25
At sea, before a tempest, false hearts speak fair
To those they intend most mischief.

21.1.] *Q4; Bosola Q (at l. o.1).*

12–17.] from Matthieu, *Henry IV* (1612), H3: 'Some few daies before this fatall accident shee [the queen] had two dreames, the which were true predictions, when as the Iewelers and Lapidaries prepared her crowne she drempt that the great diamonds and all the goodly stones which shee had giuen them to inrich it were turned into Pearles, the which the interpreters of dreames take for teares.'

18–19. *live . . . nature*] perhaps from *Arcadia*, IV (*Wks*, II. 119): 'to have for foode the wilde benefites of nature'; the phrase is repeated in *A.Q.L.*, IV. i. 81–2, a strong indication of its being taken from Webster's common-place book.

24. *blanch*] blanch over, 'whitewash' (cf. *O.E.D.*, v^1., 5).

25–6. *calm . . . tempest*] Cf. the proverb, 'After a calm comes a storm' (Tilley C24).

(Reads) Send Antonio to me; I want his head in a business:—
A politic equivocation!
He doth not want your counsel, but your head;   30
That is, he cannot sleep till you be dead.
And here's another pitfall, that's strew'd o'er
With roses; mark it, 'tis a cunning one:
[*Reads*] *I stand engaged for your husband, for several debts*
at Naples: let not that trouble him, I had rather have his   35
heart than his money.
And I believe so too.

Bos.   What do you believe?

Duch. That he so much distrusts my husband's love,
He will by no means believe his heart is with him
Until he see it: the devil is not cunning enough   40
To circumvent us in riddles.

Bos. Will you reject that noble and free league
Of amity and love which I present you?

Duch. Their league is like that of some politic kings,
Only to make themselves of strength and pow'r   45
To be our after-ruin: tell them so.

Bos. And what from you?

Ant.   Thus tell him: I will not come.

Bos. And what of this?

Ant.   My brothers have dispers'd

---

28. Reads] Q4; A Letter. (rom. and inset) Q.   28–9.] so Dyce i; one line Q.
28.] italicized Q.   34. Reads] Dyce ii.   34–6.] italicized Q.

28–31.] Louis XI played this trick on Louis of Luxembourg, Constable
of France, sending a letter saying he 'wanted his head', and so being able
to kill him (so Dent).

35–6. I . . . money] See Camden's *Remains* (1605), Ee4ᵛ (of Richard III):
'. . . when diverse shires of England offered him a benevolence, hee
refused it, saying, I know not in what sence: "I had rather have your hearts,
than your money"' (so Dent).

39–40. believe . . . it] from Donne, *Ignatius his Conclave* (1611), p. 89:
'wee consider not the entrails of Beasts, but the entrails of souls, in con-
fessions, and the entrails of Princes, in treasons; whose hearts wee do not
beleeue to be with vs, till we see them' (so Dent).

48. this] i.e., the letter.

Bloodhounds abroad; which till I hear are muzzled,
No truce, though hatch'd with ne'er such politic skill   50
Is safe, that hangs upon our enemies' will.
I'll not come at them.

Bos.   This proclaims your breeding.
Every small thing draws a base mind to fear,
As the adamant draws iron; fare you well sir,
You shall shortly hear from's.   *Exit.* 55

Duch. I suspect some ambush:
Therefore by all my love, I do conjure you
To take your eldest son, and fly towards Milan:
Let us not venture all this poor remainder
In one unlucky bottom.

Ant.   You counsel safely:—   60
Best of my life, farewell: since we must part
Heaven hath a hand in't; but no otherwise
Than as some curious artist takes in sunder
A clock or watch when it is out of frame,
To bring 't in better order.   65

Duch. I know not which is best,
To see you dead, or part with you:—farewell boy;
Thou art happy, that thou hast not understanding
To know thy misery, for all our wit
And reading brings us to a truer sense   70

50–1.] *so Q; after l. 47 conj. Craik; after l. 46 (spoken by Duch.) conj. this ed.*
61. farewell: . . part] *Q;* farewell, . . . part: *Dyce i.*

50–1.] from *A.T.*, v. iii. 3250–3: 'For all the fauour that she could procure, / Was leaue to liue a priuate person still; / And yet of that she could
not be made sure, / Which did depend vpon her enemies will.'

T. W. Craik suggested (quoted in Lucas, ii) that these lines should
follow l. 47; but 'at them' of l. 52 is then a little awkward referring to the
'brothers' rather than 'bloodhounds'. If the lines are misplaced, they might
be moved to follow l. 46, to become part of the duchess' speech which in
Q ends with a semi-colon.

54. adamant] loadstone.

59–60. venture . . . bottom] Cf. the proverb, 'Venture not all in one bottom' (Tilley A209); *bottom* = 'hold, ship'.

68–71. happy . . . sorrow] Cf. *Ecclesiastes*, i. 18: 'For in much wisdom is
much grief: and he that increaseth knowledge, increaseth sorrow.'

Of sorrow:—in the eternal church, sir,
I do hope we shall not part thus.

Ant.   O, be of comfort!
Make patience a noble fortitude,
And think not how unkindly we are us'd:
Man, like to cassia, is prov'd best, being bruis'd.   75

Duch. Must I, like to a slave-born Russian,
Account it praise to suffer tyranny?
And yet, O Heaven, thy heavy hand is in't.
I have seen my little boy oft scourge his top
And compar'd myself to't: naught made me e'er   80
Go right but heaven's scourge-stick.

Ant.   Do not weep:
Heaven fashion'd us of nothing; and we strive
To bring ourselves to nothing:—farewell Cariola,
And thy sweet armful: if I do never see thee more,
Be a good mother to your little ones,   85
And save them from the tiger: fare you well.

Duch. Let me look upon you once more; for that speech
Came from a dying father: your kiss is colder

75.] *italicized this ed.;* "Man . . . *Q*ᵇ.   80–1.] *so Dyce i;* . . . right, /
But, . . . *Q.*

71–2. *in . . . thus*] Cf. *Arcadia*, II. xiii (*Wks*, I. 233): 'when she thought
him dead, she sought all meanes (as well by poyson as by knife) to send her
soule, at least, to be maried in the eternall church with him.'

74. *unkindly*] with unnatural cruelty.

75.] a form of the proverb, 'If you beat spice it will smell the sweeter'
(Tilley S746); for the force of *prov'd*, see *W.D.*, I. i. 48–51: 'Perfumes the
more they are chaf'd the more they render / Their pleasing scents, and so
affliction / Expresseth virtue, fully, whether true, / Or else adulterate.'

76–7.] from Sidney, *Astrophel & Stella*, ii: 'and now like slave-borne
Muscovite: / I call it praise to suffer tyrannie.'

78–81. *Heaven . . . stick*] Lucas suggested this was from *Arcadia*, II. xii
(*Wks*, I. 227 f.): 'Griefe onely makes his wretched state to see / (Even like
a toppe which nought but whipping moves) / . . . / But still our dazeled eyes
their way do misse, / While that we do at his sweete scourge repine, / The
kindly way to beate us to our blisse.'

82–3. *Heaven . . . nothing*] from Donne, *First Ann.*, ll. 155–7: 'Wee seeme
ambitious, Gods whole worke t'undoe; / Of nothing hee made us, and we
strive too, / To bring our selves to nothing backe.'

Than that I have seen an holy anchorite
Give to a dead man's skull.   90
Ant. My heart is turn'd to a heavy lump of lead,
With which I sound my danger: fare you well.

                              Exit[, with his elder Son].
Duch. My laurel is all withered.
Cari. Look, madam, what a troop of armed men
Make toward us.

              Enter BOSOLA *with a* Guard, *with visards.*

Duch.   O, they are very welcome: 95
When Fortune's wheel is overcharg'd with princes,
The weight makes it move swift. I would have my ruin
Be sudden:—I am your adventure, am I not?

92.1. with . . . Son] Dyce i subs.   94. a] Q^b; not in Q^a.   95. Enter . . .
Guard] Q^b; not in Q^a; Souldiers (at l. 0.1) Q; after sudden, l. 98 Dyce ii.
with visards] Q (at l. 0.1); disguis'd Q4; vizarded (after 'Bosola') Dyce ii.
97. move] Q^b; more Q^a.

93.] Although *laurel* was, proverbially, 'ever green' (Tilley L95), it was
supposed to wither on the death of a king; Lucas suggested an echo of
Cleopatra's cry on the death of Antony: 'O, wither'd is the garland of the
war' (*Ant.*, IV. xv. 64).

95. S.D. with visards] Q's entry-direction at the head of this scene is
ambiguous. Probably the soldiers and Bosola wear visards, for 'What devil
art thou . . .' (l. 100) suggests that the duchess does not recognize Bosola at
first, and 'I'd beat that counterfeit face into thy other' (l. 118) might imply
that she has seen through a disguise. But possibly none wear visards, or
only the soldiers, for the simple '*Enter Bosola with a Guard*' was probably
Webster's own direction (cf. Intro., p. lxiv), and 'counterfeit' of l. 118
could refer simply to Bosola's apparent change of sides already evident
from his earlier, undisguised entry.

96–7. When . . . swift] from *A.T.*, v. i. 2836–8: 'The wheele of Fortune
still must slippery proue, / And chiefly when it burdend is with kings, /
Whose states as weightiest most must make it moue.'

97–8. I . . . sudden] Cf. Jonson, *Sejanus*, IV. 3–4: 'O, my fortune, / Let
it be sodaine thou prepar'st against me'; Webster probably borrowed the
retort immediately preceding for *W.D.*, III. ii. 270.

98. I . . . adventure] The usage is unusual: perhaps, ironically, 'You
wished to meet me by chance', or 'I am what matters to you, what is going
to be perilous for you' (cf. *O.E.D.*, 1 and 2 and 3–8). Sykes glossed 'quarry',
a sense not quoted in *O.E.D.*; he compared Marmion, *Holland's Leaguer*
(1632): 'I have a bird i' th' wind, I'll fly thee on him: He shall be thy
adventure, thy first quarry.'

Bos. You are, you must see your husband no more—

Duch. What devil art thou, that counterfeits heaven's thunder?

Bos. Is that terrible? I would have you tell me   101
    Whether is that note worse that frights the silly birds
    Out of the corn, or that which doth allure them
    To the nets? you have hearken'd to the last too much.

Duch. O misery! like to a rusty o'ercharg'd cannon,   105
    Shall I never fly in pieces? come: to what prison?

Bos. To none:—

Duch.   Whither then?

Bos.   To your palace.

Duch.   I have heard
    That Charon's boat serves to convey all o'er
    The dismal lake, but brings none back again.

Bos. Your brothers mean you safety, and pity.

Duch.   Pity!   110
    With such a pity men preserve alive
    Pheasants and quails, when they are not fat enough
    To be eaten.

Bos. These are your children?

Duch.   Yes:—

Bos.   Can they prattle?

---

101. *Bos.*] *Q^b*; not in *Q^a*.   101–2.] *so Q*; ... whether / Is ... *Dyce i.*
105. *Duch.*] *Q^b*; *Ant. Q^a*.   o'ercharg'd] *Q2 subs.*; ore-char'd *Q*.   107–
9. I ... again] *so Dyce i*; ... conuay / All ... (*two lines*) *Q*.   110–11.
Pity ...] *so Dyce i*; *one line Q*.   111. a] *Q^b*; *not in Q^a*.

---

102. *silly*] ignorant, lowly (see l. 132, below); but there may be an
instinctive or ironic sympathy in Bosola's speech, for *silly* also = 'frail,
defenceless, innocent, deserving of pity'.

105–6. *like ... pieces*] Cf. Donne, *Of the Progress of the Soul*, ll. 181–2,
of the soul leaving the body at death: 'Thinke that a rustie Peece, dis-
charg'd is flowne / In peeces ...'

108–9.] from Alexander, *J.C.*, v. i. 2577–8: 'Ah, th' vnrelenting Charons
restlesse barge / Stands to transport all ouer, but brings none backe.'

dismal (from L. *dies mali*) retained its original senses of 'fatal, disastrous,
terrible'; *O.E.D.* does not cite the modern senses of 'dark' or 'cheerless'
until 1617.

111–13.] from *Arcadia*, III. xxiii (*Wks*, I. 488 f.): 'with the same pittie as
folkes keepe foule, when they are not fatte inough for their eating'.

Duch.   No:
But I intend, since they were born accurs'd,   115
Curses shall be their first language.
Bos.   Fie, madam,
Forget this base, low fellow.
Duch.   Were I a man
I'd beat that counterfeit face into thy other.
Bos. One of no birth—
Duch.   Say that he was born mean:
Man is most happy when 's own actions   120
Be arguments and examples of his virtue.
Bos. A barren, beggarly virtue.
Duch. I prithee, who is greatest? can you tell?
Sad tales befit my woe: I'll tell you one.
A salmon, as she swam unto the sea,   125
Met with a dog-fish, who encounters her
With this rough language: 'Why art thou so bold
To mix thyself with our high state of floods,
Being no eminent courtier, but one
That for the calmest and fresh time o'th' year   130
Dost live in shallow rivers, rank'st thyself
With silly smelts and shrimps? and darest thou
Pass by our dog-ship, without reverence?'
'O', quoth the salmon, 'sister, be at peace:
Thank Jupiter we both have pass'd the net!   135
Our value never can be truly known

---

118. *counterfeit*] See l. 95 S.D., note, above.

120–1.] Cf. Dedication, ll. 14–15; Dent compared Hall, *Epistles*, VI. ix: 'It is an happy thing when our owne actions may be either examples, or arguments of good.'

126. *dog-fish*] 'a name given to various small sharks' (*O.E.D.*, 1); it was also applied opprobriously to persons.

128.] Cf. *2H4*, V. ii. 129–33: 'The tide of blood in me / Hath proudly flow'd in vanity till now: / Now doth it turn and ebb back to the sea, / Where it shall mingle with the state of floods / And flow henceforth in formal majesty.'

132. *smelts*] small fish, sparlings; used by Jonson, Dekker, etc. for 'simpletons'.

Till in the fisher's basket we be shown;
I'th' market then my price may be the higher,
Even when I am nearest to the cook and fire.'
So, to great men, the moral may be stretched: 140
Men oft are valued high, when th'are most wretched.
But come; whither you please: I am arm'd 'gainst misery;
Bent to all sways of the oppressor's will.
There's no deep valley, but near some great hill.   *Exeunt.*

---

140. stretched] *Q, Scott;* stretch'd *Dyce ii.*   141.] *italicized this ed.;*
„Men . . . *Q.*   wretched] *Q4;* wretch'd *Q, Dyce ii.*   144.] *italicized Q.*

143–4.] Cf. the proverb, 'There is no hill without its valley' (Tilley H467).

The last of these two lines is ambiguous: it might be a counsel of 'safety-first' (cf. *W.D.,* IV. i. 23–5) or yielding acceptance; but cf. the *Character* of 'A Noble . . . Housekeeper': 'His *thoughts haue a high aime,* though their dwelling bee in the Vale of an *humble heart*; whence, as by an Engin (that raises water to fall, that it may rise the higher) he is *heightned in his humility*' (italics ed.). An impression of pride is ensured in the play by l. 141, above, and by the duchess taking her own time (stopping to tell a tale and leaving before she is commanded to do so); humility is suggested by 'silly smelts . . . market . . . cook', and 'Bent to all sways'. So the last line of Act III prepares for Bosola's first speech in the following scene (especially l. 6).

Act IV

Enter FERDINAND *and* BOSOLA.

Ferd. How doth our sister duchess bear herself
 In her imprisonment?
Bos.   Nobly; I'll describe her:
 She's sad, as one long us'd to't; and she seems
 Rather to welcome the end of misery
 Than shun it:—a behaviour so noble   5
 As gives a majesty to adversity;
 You may discern the shape of loveliness
 More perfect in her tears, than in her smiles;
 She will muse four hours together, and her silence,
 Methinks, expresseth more than if she spake.   10
Ferd. Her melancholy seems to be fortify'd

IV. i. 0.1.] *Q4 subs.; Ferdinand, Bosola, Dutchesse, Cariola, Seruants Q.*
9. four] *Q; for conj. Collier, Haz.*

 IV. i.] Bosola's promise to convey the duchess to her 'palace' (III. v. 107)
and talk of her 'chamber' and 'lodging' (IV. i. 26 and 128, and IV. ii. 3)
could imply that he has done so (cf. 'lodgings', II. iii. 3). Thus 'imprisonment' (l. 2) could mean 'house-arrest'.

 But (1) Webster makes no dramatic point of such a return, (2) '*This* is a
prison?' (IV. ii. 11) can hardly refer to familiar surroundings.

 Perhaps the duchess was right to assume that she was to be taken to some
unknown prison (III. v. 106).

 3–8.] from *Arcadia*: 'But Erona sadde indeede, yet like one rather used,
then new fallen to sadnesse . . . seemed rather to welcome then to shunne
that ende of miserie' (II. xxix; *Wks*, I. 332); 'a behaviour so noble, as gave
a majestie to adversitie' (I. ii; *Wks*, I. 16); of Erona's sadness, in which
Plangus may 'perceyve the shape of lovelinesse more perfectly in wo, then
in joyfulnesse' (II. xxix; *Wks*, I. 333).

 shape = 'image, picture'.

 11–12. *Her . . . disdain*] from Alexander, *Croesus*, IV. i. 1431–2: '. . . with

With a strange disdain.

Bos.   'Tis so: and this restraint
    (Like English mastiffs, that grow fierce with tying)
    Makes her too passionately apprehend
    Those pleasures she's kept from.

Ferd.   Curse upon her!   15
    I will no longer study in the book
    Of another's heart: inform her what I told you.   *Exit.*

Enter Duchess.

Bos. All comfort to your grace!

Duch.   I will have none:—
    Pray thee, why dost thou wrap thy poison'd pills
    In gold and sugar?   20

Bos. Your elder brother, the Lord Ferdinand,
    Is come to visit you: and sends you word,
    'Cause once he rashly made a solemn vow
    Never to see you more, he comes i'th' night;
    And prays you, gently, neither torch nor taper   25
    Shine in your chamber: he will kiss your hand,
    And reconcile himself; but, for his vow,
    He dares not see you:—

Duch.   At his pleasure;

17.1.] *so Q4; at l. o.1 Q; . . . and Attendants Samp.*

---

a silent pittie-pleading looke, / Which shewes with sorrow mixt a high disdaine.'

   12–15. *restraint . . . from*] Cf. *Arcadia*, I. iv (*Wks*, I. 25): 'Leave womens minds, the most untamed that way of any: see whether . . . a dogge growe not fiercer with tying? what dooth jelousie [of a father for his daughters], but stirre up the mind to thinke, what it is from which they are restrayned?' See, also, *W.D.*, I. ii. 198–201, and note.

   16–17. *I . . . heart*] from P. Matthieu's supplement to de Serres, *General Inventory* (tr. 1607), p. 1033: 'the King of Spaine resolued not to studie any more in the Bookes of an others heart, hauing so good Intelligence with the King of France, as he desired not to vnderstand his affaires by any other Instrument then his Ambassadors.'

   19–20.] Cf. *W.D.*, III. ii. 190–1: 'I discern poison, / Under your gilded pills'; the notion was proverbial (see Tilley P325: 'To sugar [gild] the pill').

Take hence the lights: [*Bosola removes lights.*]

[*Enter* FERDINAND.]

he's come.

Ferd.   Where are you?

Duch.   Here sir:—

Ferd. This darkness suits you well.   30

Duch. I would ask you pardon:—

Ferd.   You have it;
    For I account it the honourabl'st revenge,
    Where I may kill, to pardon:—where are your cubs?

Duch. Whom?

Ferd. Call them your children;   35
    For though our national law distinguish bastards
    From true legitimate issue, compassionate nature
    Makes them all equal.

Duch.   Do you visit me for this?
    You violate a sacrament o'th' church
    Shall make you howl in hell for't.

Ferd.   It had been well   40
    Could you have liv'd thus always; for indeed

---

29. *Bosola . . . lights*] *This ed.; Exeunt Attendants with . . . Samp.*   *Enter*
Ferdinand] *Q4 subs. (after* come).

---

29. *Take . . . lights*] See Intro., pp. xxiii f.

30. *This . . . well*] See III. ii. 141, note; esp. quotation from *King and No King*.

32-3. *I . . . pardon*] Cf. the proverb, 'To pardon is divine revenge' (Tilley R92) and Hall, *Characters* (1608), 'Valiant Man': 'he holds it the noblest reuenge, that he might hurt and doth not.'

33. *cubs*] Cf. IV. ii. 259. Dent suggested an allusion to Raleigh's 1603 trial, in which the conspirators were charged with saying: 'there would never be a good world in England, till the King and his Cubs (meaning his Royall issue) were taken away.'

36-8. *though . . . equal*] Cf. Matthieu's de Serres, *General Inventory* (tr. 1607), p. 1027: 'A father . . . cannot think too soone nor to often, to breed vp the youth of his child in vertue, nor to assure his fortune: I say a child without distinction, for although the Law doth distinguish Bastards from them that are lawfully begotten, yet nature makes no difference.' Cf. *D.L.C.*, IV. ii. 278-80.

You were too much i' th' light:—but no more—
I come to seal my peace with you: here's a hand
                    Gives her a dead man's hand.
To which you have vow'd much love; the ring upon't
You gave.
Duch.   I affectionately kiss it.   45
Ferd. Pray do: and bury the print of it in your heart:
I will leave this ring with you for a love-token;
And the hand, as sure as the ring; and do not doubt
But you shall have the heart too; when you need a friend
Send it to him that ow'd it; you shall see   50
Whether he can aid you.
Duch.   You are very cold.
I fear you are not well after your travel:—
Hah! lights!—O, horrible!
Ferd.   Let her have lights enough.   *Exit.*
Duch. What witchcraft doth he practise that he hath left
A dead man's hand here?—   55

Here is discovered, behind a traverse, the artificial figures of Antonio
and his children, appearing as if they were dead.

43.1.] *so Q4; to right of ll. 43–5, approx. Q.   53. Exit] Q; Ex. | Enter*
Bosola Q4; Exit. Re-enter Seruants with lights Luc i.   55.2. children] Q;
child conj. Luc ii.

42. *too . . . light*] i.e., too exposed, not sufficiently sheltered; but *too much*
suggests also a very common quibble, as in *Mer.V.*, v. i. 129–30: 'Let me
give light, but let me not be light [i.e., wanton]; / For a light wife doth make
a heavy husband'. Webster varied the word-play in *D.L.C.*, I. ii. 51–2.

43.1.] For the source of this incident, see Intro., p. xxxiii.

50. *ow'd*] owned.

55.1. *Here . . . traverse*] 'discover' was often used in 17th-century stage-
directions for indicating the opening of some curtained acting area:
'traverse' was used of curtains or screens across a room, hall, or stage. See
W.D., v. iv. 64 and 65.1–3.

55.2. *children*] Lucas (2nd ed.) argued that only the elder son who rode
off with Antonio should be shown: the duchess would not leave instructions for their care (IV. ii. 203–5) if she thought they were dead, and 'why
should an avaricious Duke go to the cost and trouble of wax corpses for two
children who were in a few minutes to be real ones?'. But common sense
is not a true measure for such a scene in a play (or in life); the stage-direction
is probably authorial (see Intro., p. lxv) and we may suppose that Webster

Bos. Look you: here's the piece from which 'twas ta'en:
　　He doth present you this sad spectacle
　　That now you know directly they are dead—
　　Hereafter you may wisely cease to grieve
　　For that which cannot be recovered.　　　　　　　60
Duch. There is not between heaven and earth one wish
　　I stay for after this: it wastes me more
　　Than were't my picture, fashion'd out of wax,
　　Stuck with a magical needle and then buried
　　In some foul dunghill; and yon's an excellent property　65
　　For a tyrant, which I would account mercy.
Bos. What's that?
Duch. If they would bind me to that lifeless trunk,
　　And let me freeze to death.
Bos. 　　　　　　　　　　　Come, you must live.
Duch. That's the greatest torture souls feel in hell—　　70
　　In hell: that they must live, and cannot die.
　　Portia, I'll new-kindle thy coals again,

58. That] *Q; That, Dyce i.*　　　dead—] *This ed.; dead, Q, Dyce i.*

---

aimed at a maximum horror and cruelty. There may be dramatic point in the duchess reacting only to 'it' (ll. 62–3) and 'that . . . trunk' (l. 68) as if she saw Antonio only; and there may be more pathos if she forgets that she has seen her children dead when she remembers them before her own death.

58. *directly*] 'plainly' or 'immediately'.

59–60.] Dent compared Petrarch, *Physic against Fortune* (tr. 1579), Kk3ᵛ: 'Admit death be euyll, whiche the learned denye, truely no man wyl denie but that weepyng is in vayne, for that which cannot be recouered.'

62–5. *wastes . . . dunghill*] Dekker's *Whore of Babylon*, II. ii. 168–80 illustrates this superstition: 'This virgin waxe, / Burie I will in slimie putred ground, / Where it may peece-meale rot: As this consumes, / So shall shee pine, and (after languor) die. / These pinnes shall sticke like daggers to her heart, / And eating through her breast, turne there to gripings, / Cramp-like Convulsions, shrinking vp her nerues, / As into this they eate. / —. . . Where wilt thou burie it ?—On this dunghill' (so Dent).

68–9. *bind . . . death*] Anderson (*ap.* Dent) noted that this punishment is illustrated in emblem books (e.g. Whitney (1586), p. 99) to symbolize ill-matched marriages.

72. *Portia*] Plutarch told how, after the death of Brutus (not before as in *Caes.*, IV. iii. 152–6), Portia 'determining to kill herself . . . , took hot burning coals and cast them into her mouth, and kept her mouth so close that she choked herself' (tr. North, 1579, etc.; ed. Skeat (1875), p. 151).

> And revive the rare and almost dead example
> Of a loving wife.
>
> *Bos.*   O fie! despair? remember
> You are a Christian.
>
> *Duch.*   The church enjoins fasting: 75
> I'll starve myself to death.
>
> *Bos.*   Leave this vain sorrow:
> Things being at the worst begin to mend;
> The bee when he hath shot his sting into your hand
> May then play with your eyelid.
>
> *Duch.* Good comfortable fellow   80
> Persuade a wretch that's broke upon the wheel
> To have all his bones new set; entreat him live
> To be executed again:—who must despatch me?
> I account this world a tedious theatre,
> For I do play a part in't 'gainst my will.   85
>
> *Bos.* Come, be of comfort, I will save your life.
>
> *Duch.* Indeed I have not leisure to tend so small a business.
>
> *Bos.* Now, by my life, I pity you.
>
> *Duch.*   Thou art a fool then,
> To waste thy pity on a thing so wretch'd
> As cannot pity itself:—I am full of daggers: 90

77–8.] *so Q;* . . . bee / When . . . *Dyce i.*   87.] *so Q;* . . . tend / So . . .
Dyce i.   90. itself] *Q4 subs.;* it *Q.*

---

76. *starve . . . death*] Lucas noted that the legitimacy of this kind of
suicide is discussed in Donne, *Biathanatos*, II. 6.5.

77–9.] The common proverb and the image are found together in Whetstone, *Heptameron* (1582), U3: 'let this comfort you: that thinges when they
are at the worst, begin againe to amend. . . The Bee, when he hath lefte his
stinge in your hande without dainger may playe with your eye lidde.'

81. *wheel*] an instrument of torture.

84–90. *I . . . itself*] from *Arcadia*, II. xxix (*Wks*, I. 333), and, like the
borrowings at ll. 3–8 above, about Erona: 'But she (as if he had spoken of
a small matter, when he mencioned her life, to which she had not leisure
to attend) desired him if he loved her, to shew it, in finding some way to
save Antiphilus. For her, she found the world but a wearisom stage unto
her, where she played a part against her will: and therefore besought him,
not to cast his love in so unfruitfull a place, as could not love it selfe.'

90. *daggers*] The first record in *O.E.D.* of this figurative use (= 'mental

Puff: let me blow these vipers from me.

Enter Servant.

What are you?

Serv.   One that wishes you long life.

Duch. I would thou wert hang'd for the horrible curse

Thou hast given me: [*Exit Servant.*]

I shall shortly grow one

Of the miracles of pity:—I'll go pray: no,   95

I'll go curse:—

---

91. vipers] *Q;* vapours *conj. this ed.*   91.1.] *so Q4; at l. o.1 Q* (*Seruants*).
94. S.D.] *Samp.*   95–6. Of . . . curse] *so Q; . . .* pray; / No . . . *Dyce i.*

---

pain or affliction') is *Mer.V.*, III. i. 115: 'Thou stickest a dagger in me'; see also *Ham.*, III. iv. 95.

91.] The sense is obscure. Jacobean writers usually alluded to the poison of *vipers*, or to the belief that their young gnawed their way out of the womb, so killing the mother; they also echoed the biblical usage = 'wicked men' (see, e.g., *Matthew*, xxiii. 33). Along these lines, Webster might imply that the duchess wished to loose the stings within her and without her (cf. 'daggers', l. 90).

But '*Puff:* let me *blow*' is also strange with reference to '*vipers*'. Of course, the duchess is under strain that would lead to irrationality and fantasy, but Webster is normally exact in his use of natural history and fable (see notes at II. v. 38–9, v. v. 45, etc.), and in 'distracted' scenes in *W.D.* (v. iii. 82–126 and v. iv. 82–90) he maintains an exact 'reason in madness', not least in allusions to fables and natural history.

The text may be corrupt here, *vipers* being printed in error for 'vapours'; if the MS. from which Crane worked read 'vapors' (a common 17th-century spelling), the corruption could easily occur through misreading. Here 'vapours' would be a variation of 'mist' (cf. *O.E.D.*, *vapour*, 2b), a word Webster used of perplexities at the time of death (see IV. ii. 188 and note). He used 'vapours' = 'insubstantial things' (cf. *O.E.D.*, 2c) in *A Monumental Column* (1613), a poem with many echoes of *D.M.*: '. . . while men rotten vapours do persue, / They could not be thy friends, and flatterers too.'

92–4. *What . . . me*] from *Arcadia*, III. xxiii (*Wks*, I. 485): 'he heard one stirre in his chamber, by the motion of garments; and he with an angry voice asked, Who was there? A poore Gentlewoman (answered the partie) that wish long life unto you. And I soone death to you (said he) for the horrible curse you have given me.'

94.] The servant probably slips away when least noticeable. In this Act and the next several entrances are without the 'realistic' motivation that Webster usually contrived, and thus occur as if timed by 'Fate': so this servant enters at l. 91, and Bosola at IV. ii. 114; other examples are at v. i. 25 and v. iv. 33 and 41.

Bos.   O fie!

Duch.   I could curse the stars.

Bos.   O fearful!

Duch. And those three smiling seasons of the year
    Into a Russian winter, nay the world
    To its first chaos.

Bos. Look you, the stars shine still:—

Duch.   O, but you must   100
    Remember, my curse hath a great way to go.—
    Plagues, that make lanes through largest families,
    Consume them!—

Bos.   Fie lady!

Duch.   Let them, like tyrants,
    Never be remember'd, but for the ill they have done;
    Let all the zealous prayers of mortified   105
    Churchmen forget them!—

Bos.   O, uncharitable!

Duch. Let heaven, a little while, cease crowning martyrs,
    To punish them!
    Go howl them this: and say I long to bleed:
    It is some mercy, when men kill with speed.   *Exit.*   110

[*Enter* FERDINAND.]

Ferd. Excellent: as I would wish; she's plagu'd in art.
    These presentations are but fram'd in wax,

100–1. O . . . go] *so Dyce i; one line Q.*   108–9.] *so Dyce i; one line Q.*
110.] *italicized this ed.;* ,,It . . . *Q.*   Exit] *Q; Exit, with Servants Luc i.*
110.1.] *Q4.*

102–3. *Plagues . . . them*] probably from Chapman, writing of cannon
shot, *Penitential Psalms*, 'A Fragment', l. 44: 'Wars that make lanes thro
whole posterities', and *Bussy*, III. ii. 382: 'a murdering piece, making lanes
in armies' (so Lucas).

110.] Cf. *W.D.*, I. i. 56–8: 'I thank them, / And would account them
nobly merciful / Would they dispatch me quickly.' This was a Senecan
commonplace; *De Beneficiis*, ii. 5.3: '*Misericordiae genus est cito occidere.*'

112–14. *These . . . Lauriola*] Wax effigies of the dead were familiar to
Webster's audience, being placed on coffins in funeral processions of the
great; there was a collection of them in Westminster Abbey (so Lucas).

By the curious master in that quality,
Vincentio Lauriola, and she takes them
For true substantial bodies.   115

Bos. Why do you do this?
Ferd.   To bring her to despair.
Bos. Faith, end here:
And go no farther in your cruelty—
Send her a penitential garment to put on
Next to her delicate skin, and furnish her   120
With beads and prayer-books.
Ferd.   Damn her! that body of hers,
While that my blood ran pure in't, was more worth
Than that which thou wouldst comfort, call'd a soul—
I will send her masques of common courtesans,
Have her meat serv'd up by bawds and ruffians,   125
And, 'cause she'll needs be mad, I am resolv'd
To remove forth the common hospital
All the mad-folk, and place them near her lodging;
There let them practise together, sing, and dance,
And act their gambols to the full o'th' moon: 130
If she can sleep the better for it, let her—
Your work is almost ended.
Bos. Must I see her again?
Ferd.   Yes.
Bos.   Never.
Ferd.   You must.
Bos. Never in mine own shape,
That's forfeited by my intelligence,   135

---

curious = 'expert, ingenious, scrupulous'. *quality* = 'craft'.
Vincentio Lauriola seems to be a name invented by Webster.
129–30.] This continues the line of reaction from 'delicate skin. . . Damn
her! that body of hers . . . common courtesans . . . bawds and ruffians.'
Bedlam's representation in plays was usually bawdy or obscene (cf. *N.Ho.*,
IV. iii and Fletcher's *Pilgrim* (1621), III. vi). The sexual connotation is
obvious in *practise together* (cf. *W.D.*, II. i. 110), *act*, *gambols*, and *moon*.

130. *full o'th' moon*] Ferdinand alludes to the popular superstition that
madness was influenced by the moon, its effect being strongest when it was
full.

And this last cruel lie: when you send me next,
The business shall be comfort.

Ferd.   Very likely—
Thy pity is nothing of kin to thee:—Antonio
Lurks about Milan; thou shalt shortly thither
To feed a fire, as great as my revenge,   140
Which ne'er will slack, till it have spent his fuel:
Intemperate agues make physicians cruel.   *Exeunt.*

SCENA II.

Enter Duchess *and* CARIOLA.

Duch. What hideous noise was that?
Cari.   'Tis the wild consort
Of madmen, lady, which your tyrant brother
Hath plac'd about your lodging:—this tyranny,
I think, was never practis'd till this hour.
Duch. Indeed I thank him: nothing but noise and folly   5
Can keep me in my right wits, whereas reason
And silence make me stark mad:—sit down;
Discourse to me some dismal tragedy.
Cari. O, 'twill increase your melancholy.
Duch.   Thou art deceiv'd,
To hear of greater grief would lessen mine—   10
This is a prison?
Cari.   Yes, but you shall live
To shake this durance off.

142.] *italicized Q4;* "Intemperate . . . Q.

IV. ii. 0.1.] *Q4 subs.; Duchesse, Cariola, Seruant, Mad-men, Bosola, Executioners, Ferdinand Q.*

142.] 'Crudelem medicum intemperans aeger facit'; a Latin proverb of
some currency in English (see Dent).

IV. ii. 1. *consort*] company; but there might be an ironical quibble on
consort = 'group of musicians', for 'noise' of the same line was often used
for 'music' or 'band of musicians'.

8–10.] from Alexander, *Croesus*, III. i. 853–4: 'Tell on at length th'
originall of all, / To heare of greater griefe, 'twill make mine lesse.'

Duch.   Thou art a fool;
    The robin-redbreast, and the nightingale,
    Never live long in cages.
Cari.   Pray dry your eyes.
    What think you of, madam?
Duch.   Of nothing: 15
    When I muse thus, I sleep.
Cari. Like a madman, with your eyes open?
Duch. Dost thou think we shall know one another,
    In th'other world?
Cari.   Yes, out of question.
Duch. O that it were possible we might   '   20
    But hold some two days' conference with the dead,
    From them I should learn somewhat, I am sure
    I never shall know here:—I'll tell thee a miracle—
    I am not mad yet, to my cause of sorrow.
    Th' heaven o'er my head seems made of molten brass,   25
    The earth of flaming sulphur, yet I am not mad:
    I am acquainted with sad misery,

---

22. sure] *Q;* sure, *Dyce i.*

13–14. *robin . . . cages*] Cf. Ariosto, *Satires* (tr. 1608), III: 'The cage is to
the Nightingale a hell, / The Thrush and Black-bird both do loue it well, /
The Robin red-brest rob'd of libertie, / Growes sad and dies with inward
melancholy.'

18–19. *Dost . . . world*] Cf. Marston, *Dutch Courtezan* (1605), IV. iv. 72–5:
'—shall we know one another in the other world? . . . I would fain see him
again! O my tortured mind!' The duchess betrays no such doubts at
ll. 210–12, below.

24.] Cf. *John*, III. iv. 48–9 and 59–60: 'I am not mad: / I would to heaven
I were! / For then, 'tis like I should forget myself: / . . . / . . . too well, too
well I feel / The different plague of each calamity.'

25–6. *Th' heaven . . . sulphur*] Cf. one of the curses in *Deut.*, upon
those who 'will not hearken unto the voice of the Lord thy God': 'the
heaven that is over thy head shall be brass, and the earth that is under thee
shall be iron' (so Bradbrook, *M.L.R.*, 1947). Dekker or Webster associated
sulphur with God's judgement in *N.Ho*, I. iii. 100–4: 'if euer I had thought
vncleane, / . . . / Let Sulpher drop from Heauen, and naile my body / Dead
to this earth.'

27–30. *I . . . easy*] from Matthieu's continuation of de Serres, *Inventory*,
p. 817: 'I am inured to my afflictions, as a Galley slaue to his oare. Necessity
teacheth me to suffer constantly, and custome makes my suffrance easie';

As the tann'd galley-slave is with his oar;
Necessity makes me suffer constantly,
And custom makes it easy—who do I look like now?   30

Cari. Like to your picture in the gallery,
A deal of life in show, but none in practice;
Or rather like some reverend monument
Whose ruins are even pitied.

Duch.   Very proper:
And Fortune seems only to have her eyesight   35
To behold my tragedy:—How now!
What noise is that?

Enter Servant.

Serv.   I am come to tell you
Your brother hath intended you some sport:
A great physician, when the Pope was sick
Of a deep melancholy, presented him   40
With several sorts of madmen, which wild object,
Being full of change and sport, forc'd him to laugh,
And so th' imposthume broke: the self-same cure
The duke intends on you.

Duch.   Let them come in.

Serv. There's a mad lawyer, and a secular priest,   45
A doctor that hath forfeited his wits
By jealousy; an astrologian
That in his works said such a day o'th' month

30. who] *Q*; Whom *Haz.*   37. S.D.] *so Q4; at l. o.1 Q.*

so Dent, who also quoted Seneca, *De Tranquil.*, x. 1. 'To tan' was not yet
used = 'to thrash'.

31–2.] from *Arcadia*, I. xiii (*Wks*, I. 90): he 'stood like a well wrought
image, with some life in shew, but none in practise.'

35–6. *Fortune . . . tragedy*] In Act I she had spoken of 'blind' Fortune
(I. i. 494–5); this idea is possibly from *Arcadia*, II. xxix (*Wks*, I. 331) of
Antiphilus in prosperity: 'as if fortune had only gotten eies to cherish him.'

39–43. *A . . . broke*] Lucas compared Donne, *Of the Progress of the Soul*,
ll. 477–9: 'When no Physitian of redresse can speake, / A joyfull casuall
violence may breake / A dangerous Apostem in thy breast'. *imposthume* =
'abscess'.

45. *secular*] 'living "in the world", not in monastic seclusion'.

Should be the day of doom, and failing of 't,
Ran mad; an English tailor, craz'd i'th' brain   50
With the study of new fashion; a gentleman usher
Quite beside himself, with care to keep in mind
The number of his lady's salutations,
Or 'How do you', she employ'd him in each morning;
A farmer too, an excellent knave in grain,   55
Mad 'cause he was hinder'd transportation:
And let one broker that's mad loose to these,
You'd think the devil were among them.

Duch. Sit Cariola: let them loose when you please,
For I am chain'd to endure all your tyranny.   60

Enter Madmen.

Here, by a Madman, *this song is sung, to a dismal kind of music.*

O, let us howl, some heavy note,
    Some deadly dogged howl,
    Sounding as from the threat'ning throat

---

51. fashion] *Q;* fashions *Q2.*   60.1.] *so Dyce ii; at l. 0.1 Q; after l. 44 Q4.*
61–72.] *italicized Q.*

50–1. *English . . . fashion*] a common jibe: cf. Nashe, *Unfortunate Travel-ler*; *Wks*, II. 281: 'I, being a youth of the English cut, . . . imitated foure or fiue sundry nations in my attire at once', and *Fair Maid of the Inn*, IV. ii, where the man in the moon is said to be 'an Englishman that stands there starke naked, with a paire of sheires in one hand, and a great bundle of broad cloath in the other . . . cutting out of new fashions' (ll. 152–5).

55. *knave in grain*] a common phrase for a thorough rogue (*in grain* = 'dyed fast'); with a quibble on *grain* = 'corn'.

56. *hinder'd transportation*] probably an allusion to regulations allowing the export of grain when its price fell below a certain level; on 18 Jan. 1613, there was a special proclamation against export (*transportation*) of grain because of a peculiar shortage (so Lucas, quoting *Cal. State Papers, Dom.* (*1611–18*), p. 168). Cf. *Characters* (1615), 'An Ingrosser of Corne'.

57. *broker*] used of a variety of trades, as pedlar, dealer, pawnbroker, agent, procurer.

60. *chain'd*] in apposition to 'loose' of the previous line: madmen were frequently controlled by being bound (cf. *N.Ho*, IV. iii. 164 ff.), and the most violent *chain'd*.

60.1.] For the masque-like elements of this incident, see Intro., pp. xxxvi–xxxvii.

60.2.] For the setting of this song, see App. II.

> *Of beasts, and fatal fowl !*
> *As ravens, screech-owls, bulls, and bears,*   65
>   *We'll bill and bawl our parts,*
> *Till irksome noise have cloy'd your ears*
>   *And corrosiv'd your hearts.*
> *At last when as our choir wants breath,*
>   *Our bodies being blest,*   70
> *We'll sing like swans, to welcome death,*
>   *And die in love and rest.*

1st. Madman. Doomsday not come yet ? I'll draw it nearer
   by a perspective, or make a glass that shall set all the
   world on fire upon an instant: I cannot sleep; my pillow   75
   is stuffed with a litter of porcupines.

2nd. Madman. Hell is a mere glass-house, where the devils

66. bill] *Q; bell Q2.*

---

66. bill] Q2's '*bell*' = 'to bellow', and is an attractive reading; but, like
'bawl', it is appropriate to animals rather than birds. *bill* may be a nonce-
usage, meaning 'to utter through the bill or beak' (on the analogy of 'to
mouth' = 'to declaim'); so the repeated opposition between birds and
beasts would be suitably sustained in the words of the song.

68. corrosiv'd] corroded, fretted, vexed.

71. swans . . . death] For the wide currency of this idea, see Tilley S1028.

73. 1st. Madman] His first speech characterizes him as the Astrologer,
but at l. 93 he sounds like the Lawyer, and at l. 100 he might be any of the
eight. The 2nd Madman is nowhere clearly characterized; the 3rd is the
Priest for his first three or four speeches; and the 4th is consistently the
Doctor. Probably Webster numbered the speeches 1 to 4 in order to show
where they begin and end, expecting the uncharacterized speeches to be
allocated among the eight Madmen as the scene was elaborated in re-
hearsals. Or Crane may have tried to simplify Webster's arrangement when
he prepared the printer's copy.

74. *perspective*] optical instrument, magnifying glass.

75–6. *my pillow . . .*] Camillo's pillow was said to be stuffed with 'horn-
shavings', appropriate to a cuckold (*W.D.*, I. ii. 76–7), and a sleepless 'Law-
bound' man's with 'Lawyers penknifes' (*Characters*, 'Franklin', ll. 11–13).

77–9.] Cf. Dekker, *A Knight's Conjuring* (1607), C4ᵛ, of hell: 'for like the
Glasse-house Furnace in Blacke-friers, the bone fires that are kept there,
neuer goe out.' Blown glass interested Webster, with a Bosch-like fascina-
tion: at II. ii. 6–12, its shape is likened to a woman's pregnant belly and in
W.D., I. ii. 136–9, the fire of a glass-factory is associated with lust. In the
present passage he probably imagined a soul as a naked body, as in pic-
torial representations of hell.

are continually blowing up women's souls, on hollow
irons, and the fire never goes out.

3rd. Madman. I will lie with every woman in my parish the   80
tenth night: I will tythe them over, like hay-cocks.

4th. Madman. Shall my pothecary outgo me, because I am a
cuckold? I have found out his roguery: he makes alum
of his wife's urine, and sells it to puritans that have sore
throats with over-straining.   85

1st. Madman. I have skill in heraldry.

2nd. Madman. Hast?

1st. Madman. You do give for your crest a woodcock's head,
with the brains picked out on't—you are a very ancient
gentleman.   90

3rd. Madman. Greek is turned Turk; we are only to be saved
by the Helvetian translation.

1st. Madman. Come on sir, I will lay the law to you.

2nd. Madman. O, rather lay a corrosive; the law will eat to
the bone.   95

3rd. Madman. He that drinks but to satisfy nature is
damned.

4th. Madman. If I had my glass here, I would show a sight

88–90.] For the granting of arms, see III. ii. 298, note: *ancient* implies
that there was no need to invent the coat of arms. Sogliardo's crest in
Every Man Out is 'your boar without head, rampant'.

woodcock was often used of a fool or dupe; the bird is reputed to be easily
caught in snares or nets.

91–2.] The Geneva, or 'Breeches', Bible of 1560 had a strong Puritan
bias in the translation and notes; the Authorized Version of 1611 aimed at
greater accuracy and eradication of 'seditious' material.

The title-page of the Geneva New Testament had *Exodus*, xiv. 13, as a
prominent motto: 'Feare ye not, stand stil, and behold the saluacion of the
Lord, which he wil shewe to you this day:' cf. *only . . . saved* (l. 91).

93. *lay*] expound.

94. *corrosive*] corrosive, or caustic, medicine; often used figuratively, =
'grief, annoyance', or 'sharp remedy'.

98. *glass*] either a glass vessel used for alchemical or medicinal experi-
ments (so in *A.Q.L.*, I. i. 332), or a perspective glass, like the 'spectacles'
Flamineo describes to Camillo (*W.D.*, I. ii. 100–6), in which the mad
Doctor would show some indecent illusion. Or perhaps the Astrologer is
speaking (cf. 'perspective', l. 74).

should make all the women here call me mad doctor.

1st. Madman. What's he, a rope-maker ? [*Points at 3rd. Madman.*]

2nd. Madman. No, no, no, a snuffling knave, that while he   101
shows the tombs, will have his hand in a wench's
placket.

3rd. Madman. Woe to the caroche, that brought home my
wife from the masque, at three o'clock in the morning!   105
it had a large featherbed in it.

4th. Madman. I have pared the devil's nails forty times,
roasted them in raven's eggs, and cured agues with
them.

3rd. Madman. Get me three hundred milch-bats to make   110
possets, to procure sleep.

4th. Madman. All the college may throw their caps at me, I
have made a soap-boiler costive—it was my masterpiece:—

Here the dance, consisting of 8 Madmen, *with music answerable there-
unto; after which* BOSOLA, *like an old man, enters* [*and the* Madmen
leave].

Duch. Is he mad too ?

100. S.D.] *Luc i subs.*   114.2. *man*] *Q; Bell-Man Q4.*   114.2–3. *and
. . . leave*] *This ed.*

---

100. *rope-maker*] a trade closely allied to the hangman's in *Characters,*
'Sexton', ll. 14–17.

103. *placket*] petticoat, or, possibly, 'opening in a skirt'; cf. *Lr,* III. iv.
99–100: 'keep thy foot out of brothels, thy hand out of plackets . . .'

106. *featherbed*] fantasy mixed with the fact that coaches were sometimes luxuriously equipped: cf. *Fair Maid of the Inn,* IV. ii. 27–31: 'we
shall haue em come hurrying hither in Fetherbeds . . . that moue vpon
4 wheeles, in Spanish caroches'.

107. *pared . . . nails*] a proverbial saying, similar to 'clipping his wings'
(cf. Tilley N12).

111. *possets*] drinks of hot milk curdled with ale or wine, sugar, spices,
etc.

112. *throw . . . me*] a common phrase (cf. Tilley C62) = 'give pursuit, or
emulate'.

113. *made . . . costive*] making a soap-maker (*soap-boiler*) constipated was
a difficult feat, for diarrhoea was an occupational hazard: cf. *A.Q.L.,*
v. i. 64: 'I may turn Soap-boyler, I haue a loose body.'

Serv.   Pray question him: I'll leave you.   [*Exit.*]

Bos. I am come to make thy tomb.

Duch.   Hah, my tomb!   116

    Thou speak'st as if I lay upon my death-bed,

    Gasping for breath: dost thou perceive me sick?

Bos. Yes, and the more dangerously, since thy sickness is

    insensible.   120

Duch. Thou art not mad, sure—dost know me?

Bos. Yes.

Duch. Who am I?

Bos. Thou art a box of worm-seed, at best, but a salvatory of

    green mummy:—what's this flesh? a little crudded   125

    milk, fantastical puff-paste; our bodies are weaker than

    those paper prisons boys use to keep flies in; more con-

    temptible, since ours is to preserve earth-worms. Didst

    thou ever see a lark in a cage? such is the soul in the

    body: this world is like her little turf of grass, and the   130

    heaven o'er our heads, like her looking-glass, only gives

    us a miserable knowledge of the small compass of our

    prison.

---

115. *Exit*] *This ed.; Exeunt Servant and Madmen Dyce i.*   124. best,]
Q; best *Dyce i.*

118–20. *dost . . .*] Cf. Florio, II. xxv: 'Let us not seeke our euell out of us;
it is within us, it is rooted in our entrailes. And onely because we perceiue
not to be sicke, makes our recouerie to proue more difficult.'

124. *worm-seed*] The dried flower heads of this plant were a medicine
used against intestinal worms. There is a quibble on *seed* = 'origin, germ'.
salvatory] box for holding ointment.

125. *green mummy*] a medicine was prepared from mummies; *green* is
presumably a quibble to suggest a 'living' corpse, or flesh that is not 'ripe'
enough to be mummy.

125–6. *crudded milk*] Crawford compared Donne, *Of the Progress of the
Soul*, ll. 165–6: 'This curded milke, this poore unlittered whelpe, / My
body.' The ultimate source is probably *Job*, x. 9–10.

126. *fantastical*] eccentric, grotesque; *O.E.D.* first records 'puff-paste'
in Marston, *Antonio and Mellida* (1602), III, used figuratively of a dandy
(Cotgrave's *Dictionary* (1611) is its first literal usage).

127. *prisons*] 'The body is the prison of the soul' was a common proverb
(Tilley B497); see, e.g., *A.V.*, IV. ii. 89–91: 'My mighty soule might rush
out of this prison . . .'

Duch. Am not I thy duchess ?

Bos. Thou art some great woman, sure, for riot begins to sit   135
   on thy forehead, clad in gray hairs, twenty years sooner
   than on a merry milkmaid's. Thou sleepest worse than if
   a mouse should be forced to take up her lodging in a cat's
   ear : a little infant that breeds its teeth, should it lie with
   thee, would cry out, as if thou wert the more unquiet   140
   bedfellow.

Duch. I am Duchess of Malfi still.

Bos. That makes thy sleeps so broken :
   Glories, like glow-worms, afar off shine bright,
   But look'd to near, have neither heat, nor light.   145

Duch. Thou art very plain.

Bos. My trade is to flatter the dead, not the living—I am a
   tomb-maker.

Duch. And thou comest to make my tomb ?

Bos. Yes.   150

Duch. Let me be a little merry—of what stuff wilt thou make
   it ?

Bos. Nay, resolve me first, of what fashion ?

Duch. Why, do we grow fantastical in our death-bed ? do we
   affect fashion in the grave ?   155

Bos. Most ambitiously : princes' images on their tombs do

144–5.] *italicized this ed.;* "Glories . . . *Q.*   147–8.] *so Dyce i;* . . . liuing /
I . . . *Q.*   151–2.] *so Dyce i;* : . . merry, / Of . . . *Q.*   154–62.] *so Dyce i;*
. . . bed ? / Do . . . graue ? / *Bos.* . . . tombes, / Do . . . pray, / Vp . . .
cheekes, / (As . . . carued / With . . . their / Mindes . . . world, / The . . . *Q.*

---

137. *merry milkmaid's*] proverbially fair, innocent, and carefree; cf.
Characters, 'A Fair and Happy Milkmaid'.

138–9. *mouse . . . ear*] Cf. the proverb, 'It is a bold mouse that breeds
(nestles) in a cat's ear' (Tilley M1231).

140–1. *thou . . .*] an echo of III. ii. 11–14.

144–5.] repeated from *W.D.*, v. i. 41–2; taken from *A.T.*, v. iii. 3428–9:
'Some things afarre doe like the Glow-worme shine, / Which look't too
neere, have of that light no signe.'

156–62.] This fashion in tomb-making had started in England by the
1560s (cf. tomb of the Hoby's, illustrated in E. Mercer, *English Art, 1553–
1625* (1962), plate 83b); but a full freedom in the choice of pose dates from
the early 17th century (cf. *op. cit.,* pp. 239–52).

not lie, as they were wont, seeming to pray up to heaven,
but with their hands under their cheeks, as if they died of
the tooth-ache; they are not carved with their eyes fixed
upon the stars, but as their minds were wholly bent upon   160
the world, the selfsame way they seem to turn their
faces.

Duch. Let me know fully therefore the effect
Of this thy dismal preparation,
This talk fit for a charnel.

Bos.   Now I shall: 165

    Enter Executioners[, *with*] *a coffin, cords and a bell.*

Here is a present from your princely brothers,
And may it arrive welcome, for it brings
Last benefit, last sorrow.

Duch.   Let me see it—
I have so much obedience in my blood,
I wish it in their veins, to do them good.   170

Bos. This is your last presence-chamber.

Cari. O my sweet lady!

Duch.   Peace, it affrights not me.

Bos. I am the common bellman

165.1. *Enter Executioners*] so Dyce i; at l. 0.1 Q; after l. 166 Q4.   *with*
. . . *bell*] Dyce i; *A Coffin . . . Bell* (*to right of ll. 166–8*) Q; *A Coffin, brought
in* (*after l. 166*) Q4.

---

163. *effect*] purpose.

165.1. *cords*] These may represent, as symbols in a masque (see Intro.,
p. xxxvi), both a wedding ring (cf. l. 249, below and I. i. 88, note) and 'love
knot' (cf. *W.D.*, v. iii. 174–5, as Bracciano is strangled: 'This is a true-love
knot / Sent from the Duke of Florence.')

173. *common bellman*] In 1605, a charity was presented to the church of
St Sepulchre near Newgate prison, to provide a *bellman* to make a speech
outside the dungeon of condemned prisoners the night before their execution, and another the next morning as the cart conveying them to Tyburn
was stayed outside the church; this was to 'put them in minde of their
mortalitie' and so 'to awake their sleepie senses from securitie, to saue
their soules from perishing' (*London's Dove* (1612), C4ᵛ). The words of
both speeches were prescribed and a refrain, 'Our Lord Take Mercy Upon
You All', which was to be accompanied by a tolling handbell.

One of the signatories to this gift of Robert Dove, Merchant Tailor, was

That usually is sent to condemn'd persons
The night before they suffer:—

Duch.   Even now thou said'st   175
Thou wast a tomb-maker.

Bos.   'Twas to bring you
By degrees to mortification. Listen:
    Hark, now everything is still,
    The screech-owl, and the whistler shrill
    Call upon our dame, aloud,   180
    And bid her quickly don her shroud.
    Much you had of land and rent,
    Your length in clay's now competent.
    A long war disturb'd your mind
    Here your perfect peace is sign'd.   185
    Of what is't fools make such vain keeping ?

---

177. Listen] *Q; Listen. | Rings his Bell Q4; Listen: (dirge Haz.*   178–
95.] *italicized Q.*

---

a 'John Webster', a member of the 'common Council' of the Tailors; but 'the name is too common for us to be sure that he is the dramatist' (F. P. Wilson, *Elizabethan and Jacobean* (1945), p. 106).

   177. *mortification*] in Webster's day, often applied to the state of torpor and insensibility preceding death.

   Listen] Twelve 'solemn towles by double strokes' preceded the speech of Mr Dove's bellman: Bosola probably sounds his bell here, and possibly before new sentences in his dirge. Something of the stage-effect desired by Webster may be gathered from *D.L.C.*, II. iii, where a 'dismall' sounding bell is heard and then two bell-men enter asking for prayers for the newly dead.

   179.] A catalogue of 'fatal birds' in *The Faerie Queene* (II. xii. 36) includes: 'The ruefull strich, still waiting on the bere. / The whistler shrill, that who so heares doth dy.'

   whistler was applied to various species, as the widgeon, ring ouzel, and lapwing.

   At this point the dirge is antithetical to an epithalamium, which customarily bade such creatures be silent on the wedding night: cf. *Two Noble Kinsmen*, I. i and Spenser, *Epith.*, ll. 345–6 (so Ekeblad, *R.E.S.*, n.s., ix (1958), pp. 253–67).

   183. competent] appropriate, sufficient.

   186–9.] traditional sentiments and largely conventional expression: cf. *Misfortunes of Arthur*, Epilogus, 13–15: 'Whereof (alas) should wretched man be proude, / Whose first conception is but Sinne, whose birth / But paine, whose life but toyle, and needes must dye ?' (so Dent).

> *Sin their conception, their birth weeping;*
> *Their life a general mist of error,*
> *Their death a hideous storm of terror.*
> *Strew your hair with powders sweet,*   190
> *Don clean linen, bathe your feet,*
> *And (the foul fiend more to check)*
> *A crucifix let bless your neck.*
> *'Tis now full tide, 'tween night and day:*
> *End your groan, and come away.*   195

Cari. Hence villains, tyrants, murderers! alas!
     What will you do with my lady? call for help.
Duch. To whom? to our next neighbours? they are mad-folks.
Bos. Remove that noise.
Duch.   Farewell Cariola:
     In my last will I have not much to give;   200
     A many hungry guests have fed upon me,
     Thine will be a poor reversion.
Cari.   I will die with her.
Duch. I pray thee, look thou giv'st my little boy
     Some syrup for his cold, and let the girl
     Say her prayers, ere she sleep.

               [*Executioners force* CARIOLA *off.*]
                         Now what you please—   205
     What death?

205. S.D.] *Q4 subs. (after l. 204).*

---

188. mist] often used by Webster for 'uncertainty' or 'confused knowledge', as v. vi. 94: 'In a mist: I know not how— / Such a *mis*take . . .', and *W.D.*, v. vi. 259–60: 'we confound / Knowledge with knowledge. O I am in a mist.'

190.] In requiring the duchess to prepare herself to be laid out, the dirge echoes epithalamiums, for a bride might strew her flowing hair with powder (so Ekeblad, who quoted Donne's *Epithalamium* for the Earl of Somerset in 1613, iv: see also Jonson, *Hymenaei* (1606), ll. 57 and 184).

The powdered 'hair' is another echo of earlier scenes, here of III. ii. 58–60.

194–5.] This 'strongly suggests the traditional exhortation at the end of the epithalamium, referring to the impatiently awaited night of the bridal bed. . . And so the Duchess goes, not to ardent bridegroom, but to "violent death"' (Ekeblad, *op. cit.*).

Bos.   Strangling: here are your executioners.

Duch. I forgive them:

The apoplexy, catarrh, or cough o'th' lungs

Would do as much as they do.

Bos. Doth not death fright you?

Duch.   Who would be afraid on't?   210

Knowing to meet such excellent company

In th' other world.

Bos. Yet, methinks,

The manner of your death should much afflict you,

This cord should terrify you?

Duch.   Not a whit: 215

What would it pleasure me to have my throat cut

With diamonds? or to be smothered

With cassia? or to be shot to death with pearls?

I know death hath ten thousand several doors

For men to take their exits; and 'tis found   220

They go on such strange geometrical hinges,

You may open them both ways:—any way, for heaven-sake,

So I were out of your whispering:—tell my brothers

That I perceive death, now I am well awake,

Best gift is they can give, or I can take.   225

210. on't?] *Q;* on't, *Q3.*   215. you?] *Q;* you. *Dyce i.*

---

208. *catarrh*] formerly a name for cerebral haemorrhage.

210–15.] Cf. *W.D.*, v. vi. 219–26: 'Are you so brave? . . . Methinks fear should dissolve thee into air . . .', and Florio, I. xxv: 'So many thousands of men, lowe-layde in their graves afore-vs, may encourage-vs, not to fear, or be dismayed to goe meete so good company in the other world . . .'. Ll. 211–12 echo III. v. 71–2.

219–20. *I . . . exits*] a Senecan commonplace; Tilley (D140) quoted from Greville, Marston, Florio, Fletcher, etc.

221–2. *go . . . ways*] obscure: perhaps, 'lead to heaven or hell', or 'open by an act of will (i.e. suicide) or of acceptance (i.e., of murder or accident)'. C. Leech suggests that *geometrical* gives a nightmarish impression of swinging doors; cf. I. i. 59–66 (*Webster: The Duchess of Malfi* (1963), pp. 43–6).

225.] In Alexander, *A.T.*, IV. ii. 2163–4, a queen grieving over her murdered husband welcomes a sword, cord, and poison given to aid her own suicide: 'Fit gifts for her to giue, for me to take, / Since she exceeds in hate, and I in griefe.'

I would fain put off my last woman's fault,
  I'd not be tedious to you.
Execut.   We are ready.
Duch. Dispose my breath how please you, but my body
  Bestow upon my women, will you?
Execut.   Yes.
Duch. Pull, and pull strongly, for your able strength   230
  Must pull down heaven upon me:—
  Yet stay; heaven-gates are not so highly arch'd
  As princes' palaces, they that enter there
  Must go upon their knees.—[*Kneels.*] Come violent death,
  Serve for mandragora to make me sleep!   235
  Go tell my brothers, when I am laid out,
  They then may feed in quiet.   *They strangle her.*
Bos. Where's the waiting woman?
  Fetch her: some other strangle the children.

[Executioners *fetch* CARIOLA, *and one goes to strangle the children.*]

  Look you, there sleeps your mistress.

234. *Kneels*] *Dyce ii; after l. 233 Q4.*   237. *S.D.*] *so Q4; to right of ll.*
236–7 Q.   239.1.] *This ed.; Enter Cariola Q4 (after* mistress, *l. 240);*
Cariola and Children are brought in by the Executioners; who presently
strangle the Children Dyce ii.

226–7. *I . . . you*] Cf. the proverbs that a woman's tongue 'is the last thing
about her that dies' and 'is always in motion' (Tilley W676–7).
  232–4. *heaven . . . knees*] a commonplace: Webster might have derived
it from *Cymbeline* (III. iii. 2–7), for Belarius speaks of 'the gates of mon-
archs . . . arch'd so high' (so Lucas).
  235. *mandragora*] mandrake; this is the only occasion Webster used this
form or alluded to the plant's narcotic properties; possibly he was influenced, as other writers have been, by *Oth.*, III. iii. 330.
  236–7.] Vittoria's heightened consciousness at her death was shown by
word-play (*W.D.*, v. vi. 224 and 240–1), and so may the duchess': *laid
out* = (1) 'prepared for burial', and (2) 'spent, expended' (usually of
money; but cf. *Tw.N.*, III. iv. 222); and, in view of *feed*, there may be a
further pun on '*lay*ing a table'. *feed in quiet* may allude to the proverbs
'A little with quiet is the only diet', and 'Better enjoy a little with quietness
than possess much with trouble' (Tilley L361 and L350).
  239.1] Probably the children are strangled off-stage: cf. 'this' of l. 256
below, and Q's S.D. two lines later.

Cari.   O, you are damn'd   240
   Perpetually for this:—my turn is next,
   Is't not so order'd?
Bos.   Yes, and I am glad
   You are so well prepar'd for't.
Cari.   You are deceiv'd sir,
   I am not prepar'd for't, I will not die;
   I will first come to my answer, and know   245
   How I have offended.
Bos.   Come, despatch her:—
   You kept her counsel, now you shall keep ours.
Cari. I will not die, I must not, I am contracted
   To a young gentleman.
Execut.   Here's your wedding ring.
Cari. Let me but speak with the duke: I'll discover   250
   Treason to his person.
Bos.   Delays:—throttle her.
Execut. She bites, and scratches:—
Cari.   If you kill me now
   I am damn'd: I have not been at confession
   This two years:—
Bos.   When?
Cari.   I am quick with child.
Bos.   Why then,
   Your credit's sav'd:—   [*The Executioners strangle Cariola.*]
           bear her into th' next room;   255
   Let this lie still.

        [*Exeunt* Executioners *with the body of Cariola.*]

          Enter FERDINAND.

Ferd.   Is she dead?

255. S.D.] *Dyce ii.*   256. this] *Q;* these *Dyce ii.*   256. *Exeunt . . .
Cariola*] *Dyce ii.*   *Enter Ferdinand*] *Q4 (after l. 255); at l. 0.1 Q.*

---

  245. *come . . . answer*] make a legal defence.
  249. *Here's . . . ring*] Cf. Painter; App. I, p. 203: 'in stead of a carcanet
placed a roape . . .'

Bos.   She is what
    You'd have her: but here begin your pity—
                              Shows the Children strangled.
    Alas, how have these offended?
Ferd.   The death
    Of young wolves is never to be pitied.
Bos. Fix your eye here:—
Ferd.   Constantly.
Bos.   Do you not weep?   260
    Other sins only speak; murder shrieks out:
    The element of water moistens the earth,
    But blood flies upwards, and bedews the heavens.
Ferd. Cover her face: mine eyes dazzle: she died young.
Bos. I think not so: her infelicity   265
    Seem'd to have years too many.
Ferd. She and I were twins:
    And should I die this instant, I had liv'd
    Her time to a minute.
Bos.   It seems she was born first:
    You have bloodily approv'd the ancient truth,   270

257.1.] *so Dyce i; to right of ll. 257–8 Q.*

258–9. *The . . .*] Cf. the proverbs, 'The death of a young wolf does never
come too soon', and 'The death of wolves is the safety of the sheep' (Tilley
D145 and D146).

261.] Cf. Hall, *Epistles*, VI. viii: 'Other sinnes speake, this crieth, and will
neuer be silent, till it be answered with it selfe.'

262–3.] probably from Nashe, *Unfortunate Traveller* (*Wks*, II. 320):
'water powred forth sinkes downe quietly into the earth, but bloud spilt on
the ground sprinkles vp to the firmament;' see also *Genesis*, iv. 10: 'the
voice of thy brother's blood crieth unto me from the ground'.

264. *she . . . young*] There may be an allusion to the well-known proverb,
'The good die young' (Tilley G251); so Ferdinand's reaction to her death
would include a response to her 'innocence' (l. 278) from the very beginning
(see also 'good cause', l. 276). The other form of the proverb, 'Those that
God loves do not live long', suggests an acceptance of Fate, or Providence;
but this idea is not reflected elsewhere in the scene. Possibly both reactions
are implied in Ferdinand's three words: they are mingled, for example, in
Nashe's 'Beauty is but a flowre, / . . . / Queenes haue *died yong* and faire, /
Dust hath closde Helens eye. / I am sick, I must dye: / Lord, haue mercy
on vs' (*Summer's Last Will*, ll. 1588–94).

270–2. *You . . . strangers*] Cf. More, *Richard III*; *Works* (1557), p. 50:

    That kindred commonly do worse agree
    Than remote strangers.
Ferd.   Let me see her face again:—
    Why didst not thou pity her ? what an excellent
    Honest man mightst thou have been
    If thou hadst borne her to some sanctuary!   275
    Or, bold in a good cause, oppos'd thyself
    With thy advanced sword above thy head,
    Between her innocence and my revenge!
    I bade thee, when I was distracted of my wits,
    Go kill my dearest friend, and thou hast done 't.   280
    For let me but examine well the cause:
    What was the meanness of her match to me ?
    Only I must confess, I had a hope,
    Had she continu'd widow, to have gain'd
    An infinite mass of treasure by her death: 285
    And that was the main cause: . . . her marriage!—
    That drew a stream of gall, quite through my heart.
    For thee, (as we observe in tragedies
    That a good actor many times is curs'd
    For playing a villain's part) I hate thee for 't: 290
    And for my sake say thou hast done much ill well.
Bos. Let me quicken your memory; for I perceive

272–4. Let . . .] *so Q;* . . . face / Again . . . what / An . . . *Dyce i.*   285.
death:] *Q.*   286. that] *Q;* what *Q2, Q3.*   cause: . . . her marriage!—]
This ed.; cause; her Marriage, *Q;* cause ? her Marriage, *Q3;* cause, her
marriage, *Haz;* cause; her Marriage— *Luc i.*

'As though . . . children could not play but w[t] their kyndred, wit whom for
the more part they agree much worse then wyth straungers' (so Dent).
   281–7.] A break in sense (and the actor's delivery) seems inevitable before
and after *her marriage*; the alternative is emendation. (For comparable
abrupt changes in the course of a speech, cf. *W.D.*, II. i. 78, note). The hope
of 'infinite' treasure is a spurious explanation: it is designed to deceive
Bosola (cf. *Rom.*, v. iii. 28–32, where Romeo deceives Balthasar) or, rather,
it is an instinctive attempt to 'cover up' the deep feeling exposed by
'dearest friend' of l. 280, or even deeper feelings of guilt. (The speech does
not read like self-questioning; the context is too impassioned.) After
the confession of l. 287, Ferdinand again veers, to attack the only man
he can.

You are falling into ingratitude: I challenge
The reward due to my service.

Ferd.   I'll tell thee
What I'll give thee—

Bos.   Do:—

Ferd.   I'll give thee a pardon   295
For this murder:—

Bos.   Hah?

Ferd.   Yes: and 'tis
The largest bounty I can study to do thee.
By what authority didst thou execute
This bloody sentence?

Bos.   By yours—

Ferd.   Mine? was I her judge?
Did any ceremonial form of law   300
Doom her to not-being? did a complete jury
Deliver her conviction up i'th' court?
Where shalt thou find this judgement register'd
Unless in hell? See: like a bloody fool
Th' hast forfeited thy life, and thou shalt die for't.   305

Bos. The office of justice is perverted quite
When one thief hangs another:—who shall dare
To reveal this?

Ferd.   O, I'll tell thee:
The wolf shall find her grave, and scrape it up:
Not to devour the corpse, but to discover   310
The horrid murder.

Bos.   You, not I, shall quake for't.

Ferd. Leave me:—

---

299. Mine?] *Q; Mine!* Dyce i.

306–7. *The . . . another*] perhaps from Guevara, *Dial of Princes* (1557),
III. ix; H6ᵛ: 'For much is the office of iustice peruerted, when one thiefe
hangeth another on the galouse' (so Dent, noting that this book is echoed
several times in *A.V.*).

309–11. *The . . . murder*] The superstitious believed that wolves un-
covered the bodies of murdered men and left them exposed; cf. *W.D.*,
v. iv. 103–4.

Bos.   I will first receive my pension.

Ferd. You are a villain:—

Bos.   When your ingratitude
   Is judge, I am so.

Ferd.   O horror!
   That not the fear of him which binds the devils   315
   Can prescribe man obedience!
   Never look upon me more.

Bos.   Why fare thee well:
   Your brother and yourself are worthy men;
   You have a pair of hearts are hollow graves,
   Rotten, and rotting others: and your vengeance,   320
   Like two chain'd bullets, still goes arm in arm—
   You may be brothers; for treason, like the plague,
   Doth take much in a blood. I stand like one
   That long hath ta'en a sweet and golden dream:
   I am angry with myself, now that I wake.   325

Ferd. Get thee into some unknown part o'th' world
   That I may never see thee.

Bos.   Let me know
   Wherefore I should be thus neglected? sir,
   I serv'd your tyranny; and rather strove
   To satisfy yourself, than all the world;   330
   And though I loath'd the evil, yet I lov'd
   You that did counsel it; and rather sought
   To appear a true servant, than an honest man.

Ferd. I'll go hunt the badger, by owl-light:

321.] Cf. Chapman, *Revenge*, v. i. 7–9: '. . . who in th' act itself /Includes th' infliction, which like chained shot / Batter together still.' *chain'd bullets* = cannon balls (or half-balls) linked by a chain, and used chiefly in naval warfare for destroying masts, rigging, etc.

323. *take . . . blood*] catch a strong hold on a family; see *O.E.D.*, *take*, 7 f.

329–33.] from *Arcadia*, II. x (*Wks*, I. 211–2), of a villain's assistants who 'willingly held out the course, rather to satisfie him, then al the world; and rather to be good friendes, then good men: so as though they did not like the evill he did, yet they liked him that did the evill; and though not councellors of the offence, yet protectors of the offender.'

334–5.] A *badger* 'is hardlie taken, but by devises and ginnes' (Topsell,

    'Tis a deed of darkness.   *Exit.* 335

Bos. He's much distracted:—off my painted honour:
    While with vain hopes our faculties we tire,
    We seem to sweat in ice, and freeze in fire.
    What would I do, were this to do again?
    I would not change my peace of conscience   340
    For all the wealth of Europe:—she stirs; here's life:
    Return, fair soul, from darkness, and lead mine
    Out of this sensible hell:—she's warm, she breathes:—
    Upon thy pale lips I will melt my heart
    To store them with fresh colour:—who's there?   345
    Some cordial drink!—Alas! I dare not call:
    So pity would destroy pity:—her eye opes,
    And heaven in it seems to ope, that late was shut,
    To take me up to mercy.

Duch. Antonio!

Bos.   Yes, madam, he is living—   350
    The dead bodies you saw were but feign'd statues;
    He's reconcil'd to your brothers; the Pope hath wrought
    The atonement.

Duch.   Mercy!   *She dies.*

Bos. O, she's gone again: there the cords of life broke.
    O sacred innocence, that sweetly sleeps   355
    On turtles' feathers, whilst a guilty conscience
    Is a black register, wherein is writ

Four-Footed Beasts (1607), p. 34); Turberville's *Book of Hunting* (1576) recommends 'a fayre mooneshine night' (ed. 1908, p. 190).

    The *Character* of the 'Franklin' (ll. 15–16) may show something of the associations in Webster's mind: 'He neuer sits vp late, but when he hunts the Badger, the vowed foe of his Lambs'.

    owl-light was a fairly common phrase for twilight or evening.

    336. *painted*] false, specious; cf. III. ii. 279.

    347. *pity . . . pity*] i.e., calling for help would bring back Ferdinand.

    353. *atonement*] reconciliation.

    354. *cords of life*] sinews or nerves. 'Heart-strings' were often spoken of as if they were tangible; cf. *John*, v. vii. 52–5, and *Lr*, v. iii. 216–17: 'the strings of life / Began to crack'.

    356–8. *guilty . . . bad*] a variation of the more usual idea that *bad* deeds are recorded.

All our good deeds and bad, a perspective
That shows us hell! That we cannot be suffer'd
To do good when we have a mind to it!   360
This is manly sorrow:
These tears, I am very certain, never grew
In my mother's milk. My estate is sunk
Below the degree of fear: where were
These penitent fountains while she was living?   365
O, they were frozen up! Here is a sight
As direful to my soul as is the sword
Unto a wretch hath slain his father. Come,
I'll bear thee hence:
And execute thy last will; that's deliver   370
Thy body to the reverent dispose
Of some good women: that the cruel tyrant
Shall not deny me. Then I'll post to Milan
Where somewhat I will speedily enact
Worth my dejection.   *Exit[, with the body of the* Duchess].

364–5.] *so Q;* . . . fountaines, / While . . . *Luc i.*   368–9.] *so Dyce i; one
line Q;* . . . Father: / Come . . . *Q4.*   375. *with* . . . *Duchess] Q4 subs.*

---

358. *perspective*] 'optical glass', or 'aspect'.
363–4. *My* . . . *fear*] i.e., I am past fear; from *Arcadia*, II. x (*Wks*, I. 208):
'our state is soncke below the degree of feare.'
estate = 'condition' (moral, bodily or mental), 'fortune', and 'status'.
371. *dispose*] This was the usual form; 'disposal' is first recorded by
O.E.D. in 1630.
375. *dejection*] 'overthrow, humiliation', the usual senses in Webster's
day.

Act V

ACTUS V, SCENA I.

     Enter ANTONIO *and* DELIO.

Ant. What think you of my hope of reconcilement
  To the Arragonian brethren?
Delio.   I misdoubt it,
  For though they have sent their letters of safe conduct
  For your repair to Milan, they appear
  But nets to entrap you: the Marquis of Pescara,   5
  Under whom you hold certain land in cheat,
  Much 'gainst his noble nature, hath been mov'd
  To seize those lands, and some of his dependants
  Are at this instant making it their suit
  To be invested in your revenues.   10
  I cannot think they mean well to your life
  That do deprive you of your means of life,
  Your living.
Ant.   You are still an heretic
  To any safety I can shape myself.

      Enter PESCARA.

Delio. Here comes the Marquis: I will make myself 15
  Petitioner for some part of your land,

---

v. i. 0.1.] *Q4; Antonio, Delio, Pescara, Iulia Q.* 14.1.] *so this ed.; at*
l. 0.1 Q; after l. 17 Q4.

---

v. i. 6. *in cheat*] 'subject to escheat'; Antonio possessed land on condition
that if he died intestate without heirs or committed treason, felony, etc.,
it would revert to Pescara.
 11–13. *I . . . living*] Cf. *Mer.V.*, IV. i. 374–7: '. . . you take my life / When
you do take the means whereby I live', and *Ecclesiasticus*, XXXIV. 22: 'He
that taketh away his neighbour's living, slayeth him.'

      To know whither it is flying.

Ant.   I pray do.   *[He retires.]*

Delio. Sir, I have a suit to you.

Pes.   To me?

Delio.   An easy one:

      There is the Citadel of Saint Bennet,

      With some demesnes, of late in the possession   20

      Of Antonio Bologna—please you bestow them on me?

Pes. You are my friend: but this is such a suit,

      Nor fit for me to give, nor you to take.

Delio. No sir?

Pes.   I will give you ample reason for 't

      Soon in private:—

Enter JULIA.

                    here's the cardinal's mistress.   25

Julia. My lord, I am grown your poor petitioner,

      And should be an ill beggar, had I not

      A great man's letter here, the cardinal's,

      To court you in my favour.   *[Gives letter.]*

Pes.   He entreats for you

      The Citadel of Saint Bennet, that belong'd   30

      To the banish'd Bologna.

Julia.   Yes.

Pes. I could not have thought of a friend I could

      Rather pleasure with it: 'tis yours.

Julia.   Sir, I thank you:

      And he shall know how doubly I am engag'd

      Both in your gift, and speediness of giving,   35

      Which makes your grant the greater.   *Exit.*

17. S.D.] *Samp subs.*   25. S.D.] *so this ed.; at l. 0.1 Q; at end of line Q4.*
29. S.D.] *Dyce ii.*   32–3. I . . . yours] *so Q; . . . rather / Pleasure . . .
Dyce i.*   32. could] *Q;* would *Q4.*

19. *Bennet*] Benedict.

23.] Cf. the passages from *A.T.* quoted at I. i. 264–6 and IV. ii. 225, above.

34–6. *how . . . greater*] Cf. the old and common proverb, 'He that gives quickly gives twice' (Tilley G125).

Ant. [*Aside*]   How they fortify
    Themselves with my ruin!

Delio.   Sir, I am
    Little bound to you.

Pes.   Why?

Delio. Because you deny'd this suit to me, and gave 't
    To such a creature.

Pes.   Do you know what it was?   40
    It was Antonio's land: not forfeited
    By course of law, but ravish'd from his throat
    By the cardinal's entreaty: it were not fit
    I should bestow so main a piece of wrong
    Upon my friend; 'tis a gratification   45
    Only due to a strumpet, for it is injustice.
    Shall I sprinkle the pure blood of innocents
    To make those followers I call my friends
    Look ruddier upon me? I am glad
    This land, ta'en from the owner by such wrong,   50
    Returns again unto so foul an use
    As salary for his lust. Learn, good Delio,
    To ask noble things of me, and you shall find
    I'll be a noble giver.

Delio.   You instruct me well.

Ant. [*Aside*] Why, here's a man now, would fright impudence   55
    From sauciest beggars.

Pes. Prince Ferdinand's come to Milan
    Sick, as they give out, of an apoplexy;
    But some say 'tis a frenzy: I am going

36. *Aside*] *Samp.*   55. *Aside*] *Samp.*

43–6. *it . . . injustice*] The whole episode, as well as these words, may
derive from Florio, I. xxix: 'Epaminondas had caused a dissolute yoong
man to be imprisoned: Pelopidas entreated him, that for his sake he would
set-him at libertie, but he refused him, and yeelded to free-him at the
request of an harlot of his, which likewise sued for his enlargement; saying,
it was a gratification due unto a Courtizan, and not to a Captaine.'

59. *frenzy*] Frenzy was said to be an inflammation of the brain due to an
invasion of choler: its symptoms were like those of melancholic madness,
but continuous rather than cyclic. Men so afflicted 'swarue from al sense,

To visit him.   *Exit.*

Ant.   'Tis a noble old fellow.   [*He advances.*] 60

Delio. What course do you mean to take, Antonio?

Ant. This night I mean to venture all my fortune
(Which is no more than a poor ling'ring life)
To the cardinal's worst of malice: I have got
Private access to his chamber, and intend   65
To visit him, about the mid of night,
As once his brother did our noble duchess.
It may be that the sudden apprehension
Of danger—for I'll go in mine own shape—
When he shall see it fraught with love and duty,   70
May draw the poison out of him, and work
A friendly reconcilement: if it fail,
Yet it shall rid me of this infamous calling;
For better fall once, than be ever falling.

Delio. I'll second you in all danger: and how e'er,   75
My life keeps rank with yours.

Ant. You are still my lov'd, and best friend.   *Exeunt.*

SCENA II.

Enter PESCARA *and a* Doctor.

Pes. Now doctor, may I visit your patient?

Doc. If't please your lordship: but he's instantly

60. *He advances*] McIl subs.

v. ii. 0.1.] *Q4 subs.; Pescara, a Doctor, Ferdinand, Cardinall, Malateste, Bosola, Iulia Q.*

---

in any thing they vtter, being inconstant, and so intricating themselues, that another Sphinx should haue work enough to explane their conceits, & Oedipus himself would sweate, to apprehend the meaning of their words . . .' (T. Garzoni, *Incurable Fools* (1600), C1ᵛ).

73. *calling*] position in life, means of livelihood.

74.] Cf. Florio, I. xxxii: 'There is no man so base-minded, that loveth not rather to fall once, than ever to remaine in feare of falling;' this derives from Seneca, *Epistles*, xxii. 3.

75. *how e'er*] whatever happens.

　　　To take the air here in the gallery,
　　　By my direction.
Pes.　　　　　　　　Pray thee, what's his disease?
Doc.　A very pestilent disease, my lord,　　　　　　　5
　　　They call lycanthropia.
Pes.　　　　　　　　What's that?
　　　I need a dictionary to't.
Doc.　　　　　　　I'll tell you:
　　　In those that are possess'd with't there o'erflows
　　　Such melancholy humour, they imagine
　　　Themselves to be transformed into wolves,　　　　10
　　　Steal forth to churchyards in the dead of night,
　　　And dig dead bodies up: as two nights since
　　　One met the duke, 'bout midnight in a lane
　　　Behind Saint Mark's church, with the leg of a man
　　　Upon his shoulder; and he howl'd fearfully;　　　15
　　　Said he was a wolf, only the difference
　　　Was, a wolf's skin was hairy on the outside,
　　　His on the inside; bade them take their swords,
　　　Rip up his flesh, and try: straight I was sent for,
　　　And having minister'd to him, found his grace　　20
　　　Very well recovered.
Pes.　　　　　　　　I am glad on't.

6. call] *Q;* call it *conj. Samp.*

3–4. *take . . . direction*] Doctors recommended that melancholic patients
should expose themselves only to warm, moist air, and take only moderate
exercise (cf. L. Babb, *Eliz. Malady* (1951), p. 39).

5–19. *A . . . try*] from Goulart, *Admirable and Memorable Histories* (tr.
1607), pp. 386–7: 'For there be Licanthropes in whom the melancholike
humor doth so rule, as they imagine themselues to be transformed into
Wolues . . . and all night doe nothing but runne into Church-yardes, and
about graues. . . One of these melancholike Licanthropes . . . carried then
vpon his shoulders the whole thigh and legge of a dead man. . . A Countri-
man neere vnto Pauia, in the yeare 1541 . . . did constantlye affirme that hee
was a Wolfe, and that there was no other difference, but that Wolues were
commonlie hayrie without, and hee was betwixt the skinne and the flesh.
Some (too barbarous and cruell Wolues in effect) desiring to trie the truth
thereof, gaue him manie wounds vpon the armes and legges [from which
the man died]'.
Burton discusses the disease in his *Anatomy*, I. i. I. iv.

Doc. Yet not without some fear
    Of a relapse. If he grow to his fit again
    I'll go a nearer way to work with him
    Than ever Paracelsus dream'd of: if   25
    They'll give me leave I'll buffet his madness out of him.

      Enter FERDINAND, MALATESTE, *and* Cardinal*;* BOSOLA
           [*follows and watches, apart*].

    Stand aside: he comes.
Ferd. Leave me.
Mal. Why doth your lordship love this solitariness ?
Ferd. Eagles commonly fly alone: they are crows, daws, and   30
    starlings that flock together:—look, what's that follows
    me ?
Mal. Nothing, my lord.
Ferd. Yes:—
Mal. 'Tis your shadow.   35
Ferd. Stay it, let it not haunt me.
Mal. Impossible: if you move, and the sun shine:—
Ferd. I will throttle it.   [*Throws himself down on his shadow.*]

26.1.] *so Q4; at l. 0.1 Q; after l. 27 Dyce i; . . . Ferdinand, with Attendants at
a distance, Malateste . . . conj. this ed.*   26.2.] *This ed.*   30–2.] *so Dyce i;
. . . and* / *Sterlings . . . that,* / *Followes . . . Q; . . . crows,* / *Daws, . . . Look,* /
What's . . . Haz.   38. S.D.] *Q4 subs.*

---

24. *nearer*] 'more direct', or, possibly, 'more intimate, familiar'.

25. *Paracelsus*] a noted physician-magician (1493–1541): he combined
the studies of chemistry and medicine, and classified animal and vegetable
bodies together; many strange stories were told of him.

26. *buffet*] Whipping was a usual and authoritatively recommended
remedy, as well as a means of control.

28–9.] Pleasant company was recommended by doctors as a cure for
melancholy; *solitariness* was forbidden.

30–1. *Eagles . . . together*] from *Arcadia*, I. ix (*Wks*, I. 56): 'Eagles we see
fly alone; and they are but sheepe, which alwaies heard together': this is the
first occurrence of the proverb noted by Tilley (E7 and S314). See also
Troil., I. ii. 265–6: 'The eagles are gone: crows and daws, crows and
daws!'

31–41. *look . . . upon't*] 'To be afraid of one's own shadow' was a proverbial expression for causeless fear, and 'to fight with one's own shadow',
for a vain or useless act (Tilley S261–2).

Mal. O, my lord: you are angry with nothing.

Ferd. You are a fool: how is't possible I should catch my   40
    shadow unless I fall upon't? When I go to hell, I mean to
    carry a bribe; for look you, good gifts evermore make way
    for the worst persons.

Pes. Rise, good my lord.

Ferd. I am studying the art of patience.   45

Pes. 'Tis a noble virtue:—

Ferd. To drive six snails before me, from this town to Mos-
    cow; neither use goad nor whip to them, but let them take
    their own time:—the patientest man i'th' world match
    me for an experiment—and I'll crawl after like a sheep-   50
    biter.

Card. Force him up.   [*They raise him.*]

Ferd. Use me well, you were best: what I have done, I have
    done: I'll confess nothing.

Doc. Now let me come to him:—are you mad, my lord? are   55
    you out of your princely wits?

Ferd. What's he?

Pes. Your doctor.

Ferd. Let me have his beard sawed off, and his eyebrows filed
    more civil.   60

40–3.] *so Dyce i;* ... foole: / How ... shadow / Vnlesse ... Hell, / I ...
you / Good ... *Q.*   47–51.] *so Dyce i;* ... towne / To ... them, / But
... world / Match ... after / Like ... *Q.*   52. S.D.] *Dyce ii.*   53–4.]
so Dyce i; ... best: / What ... *Q.*   55–6.] *so Dyce i;* ... mad / (My ... *Q;*
... Lord? / Are ... *Samp.*   59–60.] *so Dyce i;* ... eye / Browes ... *Q;*
... off, / And ... *Haz;* ... browes / Fil'd ... *Samp.*

42–3. *good* ... *persons*] an allusion to the practice of bribing a gaoler in
the more usual kind of prison (so General Editor).

45–6.] Cf. the common proverb, 'Patience is a virtue' (Tilley P109).

47–9. *To* ... *time*] For the proverb, 'You drive a snail to Rome', Tilley
cited only one MS. collection before the date of *D.M.* (S582).

50–1. *sheep-biter*] dog that worries sheep.

53–4. *what* ... *done*] The common proverb was 'I know what I know'
(Tilley K173), although Shakespeare had come closer to Webster's usage,
for Iago in *Oth.*, v. ii. 303–4; the alteration of a commonplace is eloquent
of Ferdinand's state of mind.

60. *civil*] decent, becoming.

Doc. I must do mad tricks with him, for that's the only way
on't. I have brought your grace a salamander's skin, to
keep you from sun-burning.

Ferd. I have cruel sore eyes.

Doc. The white of a cockatrix's egg is present remedy.   65

Ferd. Let it be a new-laid one, you were best:—
Hide me from him; physicians are like kings,
They brook no contradiction.

Doc. Now he begins to fear me, now let me alone with him.

Card. How now, put off your gown!   70

Doc. Let me have some forty urinals filled with rose-water:
he and I'll go pelt one another with them—now he begins to fear me:—can you fetch a frisk, sir?—Let him
go, let him go upon my peril: I find by his eye, he
stands in awe of me; I'll make him as tame as a dor-   75
mouse.

Ferd. Can you fetch your frisks, sir?—I will stamp him into a

61–3.] *so Dyce i;* ... him, / For ... brought / Your ... you / From ... *Q.*
69.] *so Dyce i;* ... me, / Now ... *Q;* ... begins / To ... *Samp.*   him]
Q; him. | *puts off his four Cloaks one after another Q4.*   71–6.] *so Dyce i;*
... water: / He ... them, / Now ... sir? / Let ... perill: / I ... me, / I'll
... *Q.*   77–82.] *so Dyce i;* ... Cullice: / Flea ... Anotomies, / This ...
hall: / Hence ... sacrifice, / There's ... belly, / Flattery ... *Q.*

---

61. *mad tricks*] Burton disapproved of this treatment (II. ii. 6. ii); it is
enacted, however, by Corax in Ford's *Lover's Melancholy*, IV. ii.

62. *salamander's skin*] The skin of this lizard-like creature was supposed
to resist fire, as the *salamander* itself was said to live in it, or to quench it.

64. *I . . . eyes*] 'In the eyen is seene and knowne the disturbaunce and
gladnesse of the Soule. And also loue and wrath, and other passions'
(Bartholomeus, *De Prop. Rerum* (tr. 1582), v. v).

65–6.] See III. ii. 86–7, note. *Isaiah*, lix. 4–8, says that wicked and violent
men 'hatch cockatrice' eggs . . . : [and] he that eateth of their eggs dieth.'
present = 'instant, immediate'.

69.] The business with four gowns in Q4 is reminiscent of the many
waistcoats of the Gravedigger in *Hamlet* in the 18–19th centuries; but for
Shakespeare's play the business was not introduced until after Garrick's
death in 1779 (see A. C. Sprague, *Shakespeare and the Actors* (1944),
pp. 175–6 and note).

73. *fetch a frisk*] cut a caper.

77–8. *stamp . . . cullis*] The original use of *stamp* = 'pound, crush' (as in
a mortar) was still common, along with the primary mod. sense.
cullis = 'broth' (often made from pulverized ingredients).

  cullis, flay off his skin, to cover one of the anatomies this
  rogue hath set i'th' cold yonder, in Barber-Chirurgeons'
  Hall. Hence, hence, you are all of you like beasts for sacri- 80
  fice; there's nothing left of you, but tongue, and belly,
  flattery, and lechery.   [*Exit.*]
Pes. Doctor, he did not fear you throughly.
Doc. True, I was somewhat too forward.   [*Exit.*]
Bos. Mercy upon me, what a fatal judgement   85
  Hath fall'n upon this Ferdinand!
Pes.   Knows your grace
  What accident hath brought unto the prince
  This strange distraction?
Card. [*Aside*] I must feign somewhat:—[*To them*] Thus they say
   it grew:
  You have heard it rumour'd for these many years, 90
  None of our family dies, but there is seen

80–1. sacrifice] *Q; sacrifice. | Throws the Doctor down and beats him
Q4.* 82. *Exit*] *Q4; Exit, followed by Attendants conj. this ed.* 84.
Exit] *This ed.* 85. *Bos.*] *Q; Bos.* [*Aside*] *conj. this ed.* 89. *S.Ds.*]
Dyce ii subs.

  78–80. *one . . . Hall*] Dead bodies, especially of executed criminals, were
brought to the Barber-Surgeons' Hall, in Monkswell Street, near Cripple-
gate, London, to be dissected or preserved and displayed as specimens
(*anatomies*) in the museum of the Hall.
  80–2. *like . . .*] Cf. North's Plutarch, 'Phocion' (ed. 1612), p. 751:
'Demades . . . liued so insolently, and gouerned so lewdly . . . as Antipater
sayd of him, after he was very old: that there was nothing left of him, no
more then of a beast sacrificed, but the tongue and belly'; the idea was
fairly common, appearing for example in *Arcadia*, 2nd Eclogue (*Wks*, II.
230; so Dent).
  83. *throughly*] thoroughly.
  84. *Exit*] An immediate exit accentuates the laugh-line; in *W.D.*, the
lawyer's words imply an exit at a similar moment (III. ii. 50).
  90–4. *You . . . riches*] as ll. 5–19 above, from Goulart, *Histories* (tr. 1607),
p. 620: 'There is a Noble and ancient familie at Parma, called Tortelles,
hauing a Castell, in the which there is a great Hall, vnder the Chimney
wher-of there doth some-times appeare an ancient Woman, seeming to be
a 100. yeares old. This signifieth that some one of the familie shall dye soone
after. . . They say this old woman whose shadow appeares, was some-times
a riche Lady, who for her money was slaine by her Nephews, which cutte
her body in peeces, and cast it into the Priuies.'

> The shape of an old woman, which is given
> By tradition to us to have been murder'd
> By her nephews, for her riches; such a figure
> One night, as the prince sat up late at's book,   95
> Appear'd to him; when crying out for help,
> The gentlemen of's chamber found his grace
> All on a cold sweat, alter'd much in face
> And language; since which apparition,
> He hath grown worse and worse, and I much fear   100
> He cannot live.

Bos. Sir, I would speak with you.

Pes.   We'll leave your grace,
> Wishing to the sick prince, our noble lord,
> All health of mind and body.

Card.   You are most welcome.

> [*Exeunt all except* Cardinal *and* BOSOLA.]

> [*Aside*] Are you come? so:—this fellow must not know   105
> By any means I had intelligence
> In our duchess' death; for, though I counsell'd it,
> The full of all th' engagement seem'd to grow
> From Ferdinand. [*To him*] Now sir, how fares our sister?
> I do not think but sorrow makes her look   110
> Like to an oft-dy'd garment: she shall now
> Taste comfort from me—why do you look so wildly?
> O, the fortune of your master here, the prince,
> Dejects you—but be you of happy comfort:
> If you'll do one thing for me I'll entreat,   115
> Though he had a cold tomb-stone o'er his bones,
> I'd make you what you would be.

Bos.   Any thing—
> Give it me in a breath, and let me fly to 't:

104.1.] *Q4 subs.*   105. *Aside*] *This ed.; after* so *Dyce ii.*   109. *To him*]
Dyce ii subs.   117. I'd] *Q (I'll'd); I'll Luc i.*

92. *shape*] used of both spectral and imaginary forms.
111. *Like . . . garment*] Crawford compared Donne, *Anat. of the World*,
ll. 355–6: 'And colour is decai'd: summers robe growes / Duskie, and like
an oft dyed garment showes.'

They that think long, small expedition win,
For musing much o'th' end, cannot begin.   120

Enter JULIA.

Julia. Sir, will you come in to supper?
Card.   I am busy, leave me.
Julia. [*Aside*] What an excellent shape hath that fellow!   *Exit.*
Card. 'Tis thus: Antonio lurks here in Milan;
    Inquire him out, and kill him:—while he lives
    Our sister cannot marry, and I have thought   125
    Of an excellent match for her:—do this, and style me
    Thy advancement.
Bos. But by what means shall I find him out?
Card. There is a gentleman, call'd Delio,
    Here in the camp, that hath been long approv'd   130
    His loyal friend: set eye upon that fellow,
    Follow him to mass—may be Antonio,
    Although he do account religion
    But a school-name, for fashion of the world
    May accompany him; or else go inquire out   135
    Delio's confessor, and see if you can bribe
    Him to reveal it; there are a thousand ways
    A man might find to trace him; as to know
    What fellows haunt the Jews for taking up
    Great sums of money, for sure he's in want;   140
    Or else to go to th' picture-makers and learn

120.1.] *so Q4; at l. o.1 Q.*   122. *Aside*] *Dyce ii.*

119–20.] Cf. Alexander, *J.C.*, IV. i. 1803–4: 'Who muse of many things, resolue of none, / And thinking of the end, cannot beginne.'

126–7. *style* . . .] name your reward to me.

133–4. *he . . . name*] Cf. *Arcadia*, IV (*Wks*, II. 133): 'As for vertue, hee counted it but a schoole name.' *O.E.D.* first records *school-name* in this passage of *Arcadia*: the allusion is to the 'Schoolmen' of 9–14th centuries; according to Bacon (*Advancement*, I) they brought forth 'cobwebs of learning, admirable for the fineness of thread and work, but of no substance or profit'.

139. *haunt*] frequent, visit.

taking up] borrowing.

Who bought her picture lately—some of these
Happily may take—

Bos.   Well, I'll not freeze i'th' business;
I would see that wretched thing, Antonio,
Above all sights i'th' world.

Card.   Do, and be happy.   *Exit.* 145

Bos. This fellow doth breed basilisks in's eyes,
He's nothing else but murder: yet he seems
Not to have notice of the duchess' death—
'Tis his cunning: I must follow his example;
There cannot be a surer way to trace   150
Than that of an old fox.

[*Enter* JULIA *pointing a pistol at him.*]

Julia.   So, sir, you are well met.

Bos. How now?

Julia.   Nay, the doors are fast enough:—
Now sir, I will make you confess your treachery.

Bos. Treachery?

Julia.   Yes, confess to me
Which of my women 'twas you hir'd, to put   155
Love-powder into my drink?

Bos.   Love-powder!

Julia.   Yes,
When I was at Malfi—
Why should I fall in love with such a face else?
I have already suffer'd for thee so much pain,
The only remedy to do me good   160
Is to kill my longing.

Bos.   Sure your pistol holds

142. bought] *Dyce i,* brought *Q.*   151. S.D.] *conj. Samp, Luc i;* Enter
Julia *Q4.*   156–7. Yes . . .] *so McIl; one line Q.*

---

143. *freeze*] *O.E.D.* does not record a similar figurative use.
146. *basilisks*] Cf. III. ii. 86–7 and note.
150–1. *There . . . fox*] proverbial, although Tilley quoted only one MS.
source before *D.M.* (W164).
156. *Love-powder*] Cf. III. i. 63–77.

Nothing but perfumes, or kissing-comfits.
Excellent lady,
You have a pretty way on't to discover
Your longing: come, come, I'll disarm you,   165
And arm you thus—yet this is wondrous strange.

Julia. Compare thy form, and my eyes together,
You'll find my love no such great miracle.
Now you'll say
I am wanton: this nice modesty in ladies   170
Is but a troublesome familiar
That haunts them.

Bos. Know you me, I am a blunt soldier.

Julia.   The better—
Sure, there wants fire where there are no lively sparks
Of roughness.

Bos.   And I want compliment.

Julia.   Why ignorance   175
In courtship cannot make you do amiss,
If you have a heart to do well.

Bos.   You are very fair.

Julia. Nay, if you lay beauty to my charge,
I must plead unguilty.

162–3.] *so Dyce i; one line Q.*   168–9.] *so Dyce i; one line Q.*   173. me,]
Q; me? *Q3.*   175–6. Why . . .] *so Dyce i; one line Q.*

---

162. *kissing-comfits*] sweetmeats to perfume the breath.

166. *arm*] embrace (a sense first recorded by *O.E.D.* a few years before
D.M., in *Cym.*, IV. ii. 400).

167–8.] from *Arcadia*, V (*Wks*, II. 186): 'Let her beawtie be compared to
my yeares, and such effectes will be found no miracles'; Webster rephrased
this again in *D.L.C.*, II. i. 258–60: 'Compare her beauty and my youth
together, / And you will find the faire effects of loue / No myracle at all.'

170–2. *this* . . .] suggested by *Arcadia*, III (*Wks*, II. 31); see ll. 218–21,
note below. *nice* had a range of meanings, as 'shy, delicate, fastidious;
reluctant, trivial'; perhaps 'shy' is most appropriate here, giving a quibble
on 'familiar' (cf. l. 185, below). For *familiar*, see I. i. 259, note.

174–5. *Sure . . . roughness*] from *Arcadia*; see ll. 193–6, note below.

175–7. *Why . . . well*] from *Arcadia*, I. xvii (*Wks*, I. 106): '. . . doing all
things with so pretie grace, that it seemed ignorance could not make him
do amisse, because he had a hart to do well'; this is based on the common
proverb, 'Nothing is impossible to the willing heart' (Tilley N299).

Bos.   Your bright eyes
    Carry a quiver of darts in them, sharper   180
    Than sunbeams.
Julia.   You will mar me with commendation,
    Put yourself to the charge of courting me
    Whereas now I woo you.
Bos. [*Aside*] I have it, I will work upon this creature—
    [*To her*] Let us grow most amorously familiar: 185
    If the great cardinal now should see me thus,
    Would he not count me a villain?
Julia. No: he might count me a wanton,
    Not lay a scruple of offence on you;
    For if I see and steal a diamond,   190
    The fault is not i'th' stone, but in me the thief
    That purloins it:—I am sudden with you;
    We that are great women of pleasure use to cut off
    These uncertain wishes, and unquiet longings,
    And in an instant join the sweet delight   195
    And the pretty excuse together; had you been i'th' street,
    Under my chamber window, even there
    I should have courted you.
Bos.   O, you are an excellent lady.
Julia. Bid me do somewhat for you presently,
    To express I love you.
Bos.   I will, and if you love me,   200
    Fail not to effect it.
    The cardinal is grown wondrous melancholy;

---

184. *Aside*] Dyce ii.   185. *To her*] Dyce ii subs.   201–2.] *so* Dyce i; *one line* Q.

   179–81. *Your . . . sunbeams*] two commonplaces linked together; for the first part cf., e.g., *Arcadia*, I. xvii (*Wks*, I. 107): 'what a quiver of arrowes her eyes caried.'

   193–6. *We . . . together*] with ll. 174–5 above, from *Arcadia*, III. xvii (*Wks*, I. 452–3), of the pleasures of being raped: 'For what can be more agreable, then upon force to lay the fault of desire, and in one instant to joyne a deare delight with a just excuse? or rather the true cause is . . . we thinke there wants fire, where we find no sparkles at lest of furie.'

   199. *presently*] immediately.

Demand the cause; let him not put you off
With feign'd excuse, discover the main ground on't.

Julia. Why would you know this?

Bos.   I have depended on him,   205
And I hear that he is fall'n in some disgrace
With the Emperor—if he be, like the mice
That forsake falling houses, I would shift
To other dependance.

Julia. You shall not need follow the wars;   210
I'll be your maintenance.

Bos.   And I your loyal servant—
But I cannot leave my calling.

Julia.   Not leave
An ungrateful general, for the love of a sweet lady?
You are like some, cannot sleep in feather-beds,
But must have blocks for their pillows.

Bos.   Will you do this? 215

Julia. Cunningly.

Bos.   Tomorrow I'll expect th' intelligence.

Julia. Tomorrow? get you into my cabinet,
You shall have it with you: do not delay me,
No more than I do you; I am like one
That is condemn'd—I have my pardon promis'd,   220
But I would see it seal'd:—go, get you in,
You shall see me wind my tongue about his heart,
Like a skein of silk.   [*Exit* BOSOLA.]

210–12. You . . . calling] *so Q; . . .* need / Follow . . . maintenance /
Bos. . . . cannot / Leave . . . *Dyce i.*   212–13. Not . . .] *so Haz; . . .* an /
Vngratefull . . . *Q; . . .* ungrateful / General . . . *Dyce i.*   223. *Exit*
Bosola] *Q4.*

207–8. *mice . . . houses*] so Pliny, *et alii*; the saying became proverbial (see
Tilley M1243).

218–21. *do . . . seal'd*] from *Arcadia*, III (*Wks*, II. 31): 'But in deede this
direct promise of a short space [of time before her longing is satisfied],
joyned with the cumbersome familiar of womankinde, I meane modestie,
stayed so Gynecias minde, . . . not unlike to the condemned prisoner, whose
minde still running uppon the violent arrivall of his cruell death, heares
that his pardon is promised, but not yet signed.'

[*Enter* Cardinal, *followed by* Servants.]

Card. Where are you ?
Serv.   Here.
Card.   Let none upon your lives
    Have conference with the Prince Ferdinand,   225
    Unless I know it: [*Exeunt* Servants.]
           —[*Aside*] in this distraction
    He may reveal the murder.
    Yon's my ling'ring consumption:
    I am weary of her; and by any means
    Would be quit of.
Julia.   How now, my lord ?   230
    What ails you ?
Card.   Nothing.
Julia.   O, you are much alter'd:
    Come, I must be your secretary, and remove
    This lead from off your bosom—what's the matter ?
Card. I may not tell you.
Julia. Are you so far in love with sorrow,   235
    You cannot part with part of it ? or think you
    I cannot love your grace when you are sad,
    As well as merry ? or do you suspect
    I, that have been a secret to your heart
    These many winters, cannot be the same   240

223.1.] *Dyce i subs.; Enter Cardinal Q4.*   224–8.] *so Q;* . . . conference /
With . . . it:— / In . . . reveal / The . . . (*4 lines*) *Dyce i;* . . . lives / Have . . .
Ferdinand, / Unless . . . it:— / In . . . murder. / Yond's . . . *Haz.*   226.
Exeunt Servants] *so Haz; after l. 227 Dyce ii.   Aside*] *Dyce ii.*   230.
quit] *Q;* quite *conj. Luc i.   of*] *Dyce i;* off *Q, Luc i.*   230–1. How . . .
you] *so Q; one line Dyce i.*

---

    228. *ling'ring consumption*] Cf. Overbury, *Characters*, 'A Very Woman':
'She is Salomon's cruell creature and a man's walking-consumption.'
    230. *quit of*] rid of (see *O.E.D., v.,* 1 b).
    232. *secretary*] confidant (see *O.E.D.,* 1).
    235–41. *Are . . . tongue*] from *Arcadia,* II. v (*Wks,* I. 176): 'Do you love
your sorrowe so well, as to grudge me part of it ? Or doo you thinke I shall
not love a sadde Pamela, so well as a joyfull ? Or be my eares unwoorthie,
or my tongue suspected ?'

Unto your tongue?

Card.   Satisfy thy longing—
The only way to make thee keep my counsel
Is not to tell thee.

Julia.   Tell your echo this,
Or flatterers that like echoes still report
What they hear though most imperfect, and not me: 245
For, if that you be true unto yourself,
I'll know.

Card.   Will you rack me?

Julia.   No, judgement shall
Draw it from you: it is an equal fault
To tell one's secrets unto all, or none.

Card. The first argues folly.

Julia.   But the last tyranny.   250

Card. Very well—why imagine I have committed
Some secret deed, which I desire the world
May never hear of.

Julia.   Therefore may not I know it?
You have conceal'd for me as great a sin
As adultery:—sir, never was occasion   255
For perfect trial of my constancy
Till now: sir, I beseech you.

Card.   You'll repent it.

Julia.   Never.

Card. It hurries thee to ruin: I'll not tell thee—
Be well advis'd, and think what danger 'tis
To receive a prince's secrets: they that do,   260
Had need have their breasts hoop'd with adamant

242-3. *The . . . thee*] a proverbial charge against women (see Tilley
W649 and S196).

261. *breasts . . . adamant*] a common phrase; cf. Marston, *Antonio and
Mellida*, v. i: 'And 'twere not hoopt with steele, my brest wold break'
and Chapman, *Bussy*, III. ii. 213-14: 'if my heart were not hooped with
adamant, the conceit of this would have burst it.' *adamant*, usually = 'loadstone' or 'diamond', was used poetically (as in Latin) for the hardest iron or
steel.

To contain them: I pray thee yet be satisfy'd;
Examine thine own frailty; 'tis more easy
To tie knots, than unloose them:—'tis a secret
That, like a ling'ring poison, may chance lie   265
Spread in thy veins, and kill thee seven year hence.

Julia. Now you dally with me.

Card.   No more; thou shalt know it.
By my appointment, the great Duchess of Malfi,
And two of her young children, four nights since,
Were strangled.

Julia.   O heaven! sir, what have you done?   270

Card. How now? how settles this? think you your bosom
Will be a grave, dark and obscure enough,
For such a secret?

Julia.   You have undone yourself, sir.

Card. Why?

Julia.   It lies not in me to conceal it.

Card.   No?
Come, I will swear you to't upon this book.   275

Julia. Most religiously.

Card.   Kiss it.   [*She kisses the book.*]
Now you shall never utter it; thy curiosity
Hath undone thee: thou'rt poison'd with that book;
Because I knew thou couldst not keep my counsel,
I have bound thee to't by death.   280

[*Enter* BOSOLA.]

Bos. For pity-sake, hold!

Card.   Ha, Bosola!

271–2.] *so Dyce i;* . . . your / Bosome . . . *Q.*   274–5. No . . .] *so Dyce i;*
one line *Q.*   276. S.D.] *Dyce ii.*   280.1.] *Q4.*   281. Bosola!] *Dyce i;*
Bosola? *Q.*

263–4. '*tis . . . them*] This sounds proverbial, yet Dent reported he had
not found it except in *Arcadia*, II. xxvi (*Wks*, I. 318), of rebels who cannot
halt their rebellion: 'finding it far easier to tie th[a]n to loose knots.'

271. *settles*] either 'sinks deeply' (i.e., into the mind; see *O.E.D.*, 13b),
or 'settles down, becomes still'.

Julia.   I forgive you—
 This equal piece of justice you have done,
 For I betray'd your counsel to that fellow:
 He overheard it; that was the cause I said
 It lay not in me to conceal it.   285
Bos. O foolish woman,
 Couldst not thou have poison'd him?
Julia.   'Tis weakness,
 Too much to think what should have been done—I go,
 I know not whither.   [*Dies.*]
Card.   Wherefore com'st thou hither?
Bos. That I might find a great man, like yourself,   290
 Not out of his wits as the Lord Ferdinand,
 To remember my service.
Card.   I'll have thee hew'd in pieces.
Bos. Make not yourself such a promise of that life
 Which is not yours to dispose of.
Card.   Who plac'd thee here?
Bos. Her lust, as she intended.
Card.   Very well,   295
 Now you know me for your fellow murderer.
Bos. And wherefore should you lay fair marble colours
 Upon your rotten purposes to me?
 Unless you imitate some that do plot great treasons,

288–9. Too . . . whither] *so Dyce i;* . . . done, / I . . . *Q.* 289. whither]
Q2; whether *Q.* 289. *Dies*] *Q4.* 295–6. Very . . .] *so Dyce i; one line*
Q; . . . me / For . . . *Haz.*

---

282. *equal*] equitable.

287–8. '*Tis* . . . *done*] from *Arcadia,* I. iv (*Wks,* I. 24): '. . . it is weakenes
too much to remember what should have beene done'.

288–9. *I . . . whither*] Dent has shown that devotional writers often
applied this phrase to death as a journey to an unknown destination;
Webster used it in *W.D.,* v. vi. 107 (in Flamineo's parody of dying) and 249
(for Vittoria's penultimate speech), and *D.L.C.,* v. v. 10.

297–8.] i.e., like painting rotten wood to simulate marble; cf. *Arcadia,*
II. xvii (*Wks,* I. 260): 'Shall I labour to lay marble coulours over my
ruinous thoughts?'

299–301.] i.e., the cardinal has spoken fairly in order to allay suspicion
before covering his tracks by slaying Bosola; from Chapman, *Penitential*

And when they have done, go hide themselves i'th' graves
Of those were actors in't?   301

Card. No more, there is a fortune attends thee.

Bos. Shall I go sue to Fortune any longer?
'Tis the fool's pilgrimage.

Card.   I have honours in store for thee.

Bos. There are a many ways that conduct to seeming   305
Honour, and some of them very dirty ones.

Card. Throw to the devil
Thy melancholy: the fire burns well,
What need we keep a stirring of 't, and make
A greater smother? thou wilt kill Antonio?   310

Bos. Yes.

Card.   Take up that body.

Bos.   I think I shall
Shortly grow the common bier for churchyards.

Card. I will allow thee some dozen of attendants
To aid thee in the murder.

Bos.   O, by no means:
Physicians that apply horse-leeches to any rank swelling 315
use to cut off their tails, that the blood may run through
them the faster; let me have no train when I go to shed
blood, lest it make me have a greater when I ride to the
gallows.

Card. Come to me after midnight, to help to remove that
body to her own lodging: I'll give out she died o'th'   321

302.] *so this ed.; ... more, | There ... Q; ... is | A ... Dyce i.*   305–6.] *so
Q; as prose conj. Leech.*   314. O ...] *separate line Q; as prose Dyce i.*
320–2.] *so this ed.; ... body | To ... Plague; | 'Twill ... (3 lines) Q; ...
remove | That ... out | She ... enquiry | After ... Dyce i; ... me | After
body | To ... Plague; | 'Twill ... Luc i.*

Psalms, 'A Great Man', l. 62: 'Plots treason, and lies hid in th' actors
graue.'

  304. *'Tis ... pilgrimage*] Cf. the proverbs, 'Fortune favours fools', and
'God sends fortune to fools' (Tilley F600 and G220).

  305–6.] Cf. Hall, *Epistles*, I. iii: 'I care not how many thousand ways
there are to seeming honour, besides this of vertue: they all (if more) still
leade to shame.'

plague; 'twill breed the less inquiry after her death.

Bos. Where's Castruchio, her husband?

Card. He's rode to Naples to take possession

Of Antonio's citadel.   325

Bos. Believe me, you have done a very happy turn.

Card. Fail not to come:—there is the master-key

Of our lodgings; and by that you may conceive

What trust I plant in you.

Bos.   You shall find me ready.

Exit Cardinal.

O poor Antonio, though nothing be so needful   330

To thy estate as pity, yet I find

Nothing so dangerous. I must look to my footing:

In such slippery ice-pavements, men had need

To be frost-nail'd well; they may break their necks else.

The precedent's here afore me: how this man   335

Bears up in blood! seems fearless! Why, 'tis well:

Security some men call the suburbs of hell,

Only a dead wall between. Well, good Antonio,

I'll seek thee out, and all my care shall be

To put thee into safety from the reach   340

329.1.] *so Dyce i; after* you *Q* (*Exit*).

330–2. O . . . *dangerous*] from *Arcadia*, II. x (*Wks*, I. 207): 'In deede our state is such, as though nothing is so needfull unto us as pittie, yet nothing is more daungerous unto us, then to make our selves so knowne as may stirre pittie.'

333–4.] *frost-nail'd* is recorded in *O.E.D.* (1594), but not *ice-pavements* (although similar compounds were common).

336. *Bears . . . blood*] probably, 'persists, or drives forward, in shedding blood'; but the phrase is obscure. *O.E.D.* first cites *bears up* = 'to maintain one's ground' in 1656 (21c; but see, also, 19, 20 and 29 a and b), and, while *blood* commonly = 'bloodshed, manslaughter' etc., the phrase *in blood* is also a technical hunting term = 'full of life' (*O.E.D.*, 7).

337.] Cf. Hecate in *Mac.*, III. v. 32–3: 'security / Is mortals' chiefest enemy', and Tilley W152.   *security* = 'confidence that one is secure'.

suburbs of hell was a common phrase among preachers (so Dent, who quoted Adams, *Gallant's Burden* (1612), C1ᵛ: 'Securitie is the very suburbes of Hell . . .', in a passage probably used for III. ii. 323–5).

338. *dead*] unbroken, continuous (cf. *O.E.D.*, 25); the same sense is implied at v. v. 97, with a similar quibble by association with 'graves'.

Of these most cruel biters, that have got
Some of thy blood already. It may be
I'll join with thee, in a most just revenge.
The weakest arm is strong enough, that strikes
With the sword of justice:—still methinks the duchess   345
Haunts me: there, there!—
'Tis nothing but my melancholy.
O Penitence, let me truly taste thy cup,
That throws men down, only to raise them up.   *Exit.*

SCENA III.

Enter ANTONIO *and* DELIO.
[*There is an*] ECHO *from the* Duchess' *grave.*

Delio. Yon's the cardinal's window:—this fortification
          Grew from the ruins of an ancient abbey;

345.] *so Q; . . .* Justice. / Still *. . . Q4.*   duchess] *Q;* Dutchess *Starts*
[S.D.] *Q4.*   346–7.] *so this ed.; one line Q.*   346.] *The Duchess appears*
to him (*at end of line*) *conj. this ed.*

v. iii. 0.1–2.] *Samp subs.; Antonio, Delio, Eccho,* (*from . . . Graue.*) *Q.*

---

341. *biters*] blood-suckers (cf. *O.E.D., bite, v,* 3); Webster used *horse-
leech* thus in *W.D.,* v. vi. 166. Or, perhaps, short for 'sheep-biters' (cf.
v. ii. 50–1, and note).

342. *blood*] i.e., Antonio's children.

344–5. *The . . . justice*] from *Arcadia,* III. xii (*Wks,* I. 422): 'think not
lightly of never so weake an arme, which strikes with the sword of justice.'

345–7.] Perhaps a S.D. should be added to indicate that the duchess
appears to Bosola; in *W.D.,* IV. i. 102, '*Enter Isabella's Ghost*' accompanies
'. . . I'll close mine eyes, / And in a melancholic thought I'll frame / Her
figure 'fore me . . . methinks she stands afore me . . . 'Tis my melancholy . . .'
Certainly Bosola should act as if *he* actually sees her.

A melancholy person may imagine 'a thousand chimeras and visions,
which to his thinking he certainly sees, bugbears, talks with black men,
ghosts, goblins, &c.' (Burton, *Anatomy,* I. iii. I. ii.)

Bosola's *melancholy* is now a true melancholy of remorse, not the affectation of a malcontent (cf. I. i. 76, note).

348–9.] possibly influenced by Alexander, *Croesus,* v. i. 2774–6: 'Though
I haue tasted of afflictions cup, / Yet it may be, the gods for a good cause /
Haue cast me downe to raise a thousand vp'.

v. iii. 0.2. Echo . . . grave] See Intro., pp. xxxiv–xxxv and xxix.

And to yon side o'th' river, lies a wall,
Piece of a cloister, which in my opinion
Gives the best echo that you ever heard,   5
So hollow, and so dismal, and withal
So plain in the distinction of our words,
That many have suppos'd it is a spirit
That answers.

Ant.   I do love these ancient ruins:
We never tread upon them but we set   10
Our foot upon some reverend history.
And questionless, here in this open court,
Which now lies naked to the injuries
Of stormy weather, some men lie interr'd
Lov'd the church so well, and gave so largely to't,   15
They thought it should have canopy'd their bones
Till doomsday; but all things have their end:
Churches and cities, which have diseases like to men,
Must have like death that we have.

Echo.   *Like death that we have.*

Delio. Now the echo hath caught you:—

Ant.   It groan'd methought, and gave   20
A very deadly accent.

Echo.   *Deadly accent.*

Delio. I told you 'twas a pretty one: you may make it
A huntsman, or a falconer, a musician,
Or a thing of sorrow.

19. *et seq. Like . . . have, et seq.*] *italicized Q.*

9–11. *I do . . .*] from Florio, III. ix, of the ruins of ancient Rome: 'Is it
by Nature or by the errour of fantasie, that the seeing of places, wee know
to have bin frequented or inhabited by men, whose memorie is esteemed
or mencioned in stories, doeth in some sorte moove and stirre vs vp as much
or more, than the hearing of their noble deedes, or reading of their com-
positions ? . . . So great a power of admonition is in the verie place: And that
in this Citty is most infinite; for which way soeuer wee walke, wee sette our
foote upon some Historie' (from Cicero, *De Finibus,* V. 1–2).

17–19. *all . . . we have*] The idea is common and found, for example, in
Florio, II. xxiii. *diseases* is used quibblingly, for, as well as in its modern
sense, *disease* was often used = 'absence of ease, trouble, disturbance'
(*O.E.D.,* 1).

Echo.   *A thing of sorrow.*

Ant. Ay sure: that suits it best.

Echo.   *That suits it best.*   25

Ant. 'Tis very like my wife's voice.

Echo.   *Ay, wife's voice.*

Delio. Come, let's walk farther from't:—
    I would not have you go to th' cardinal's tonight:
    Do not.

Echo.   *Do not.*

Delio. Wisdom doth not more moderate wasting sorrow   30
    Than time: take time for't; be mindful of thy safety.

Echo. Be mindful of thy safety.

Ant.   Necessity compels me:
    Make scrutiny throughout the passes
    Of your own life, you'll find it impossible
    To fly your fate.

Echo.   *O, fly your fate !*   35

Delio. Hark: the dead stones seem to have pity on you
    And give you good counsel.

Ant. Echo, I will not talk with thee,
    For thou art a dead thing.

Echo.   *Thou art a dead thing.*

Ant. My duchess is asleep now,   40
    And her little ones, I hope sweetly: O heaven,
    Shall I never see her more ?

Echo.   *Never see her more.*

Ant. I mark'd not one repetition of the echo

---

27. let's] *Q4;* let's vs *Q.*   28. go] *Qᵇ;* too *Qᵃ; not in Q2.*   33. passes]
Q; passages *Q4.*   35. *Echo.*] *Q4 subs.; not in Q (speech inset).*

---

27. *let's*] This seems the better emendation on metrical grounds,
especially in view of the elided 'from 't'. Compositor A's error might be due
to an uncertainty like that which led him to print 'lets's' at v. v. 28, where
the right reading is clearly 'let's'.

33. *passes*] events (cf. *O.E.D.,* 5); however, *Q4*'s emendation gains
some support from *D.L.C.,* v. v. 67–8: 'you haue met both / In these
seuerall passages . . .'

34–5. *impossible . . . fate*] proverbial; cf. Tilley F83.

But that: and on the sudden, a clear light
Presented me a face folded in sorrow.   45

Delio. Your fancy, merely.

Ant. Come: I'll be out of this ague;
For to live thus is not indeed to live:
It is a mockery, and abuse of life—
I will not henceforth save myself by halves;   50
Lose all, or nothing.

Delio.   Your own virtue save you!
I'll fetch your eldest son, and second you:
It may be that the sight of his own blood
Spread in so sweet a figure may beget
The more compassion.

Ant.   How ever, fare you well: 55
Though in our miseries Fortune have a part,
Yet in our noble suff'rings she hath none—
Contempt of pain, that we may call our own.   *Exeunt.*

SCENA IV.

Enter Cardinal, PESCARA, MALATESTE, RODERIGO,
and GRISOLAN.

Card. You shall not watch tonight by the sick prince,

55.] *so Dyce i; . . . compassion. / How . . . Q.*   *Ant.] conj. Samp, Luc i;
not in Q, Dyce i.*

v. iv. 0.1–2.] *Dyce i; Cardinall . . . Rodorigo, Grisolan. Bosola, Ferdinand,
Antonio, Seruant Q.*

44–5. *on . . . sorrow*] See Intro., p. xxxv.
47. *ague*] Cf. v. iv. 67–9.
48–9.] Cf. Matthieu, *Inventory*, p. 1050: 'But it shall be an incomparable
miserie to bee alwayes depriued of the Kings grace and fauour, without the
which the best conditions are most lamentable, and a life of this manner
how short soeuer, is a tedious and a languishing Life, it is no Life, it is to
languish and to abuse Life.'
50.] Cf. Florio, II. xv: 'I will neither feare, nor save my selfe by halfes.'
53. *his*] i.e., the cardinal's.
56–8.] from Alexander, *A.T.*, IV. ii. 2455–7: 'For in our actions Fortune
hath a part, / But in our suffrings, all things are our owne: / Loe now I loath
the world . . .'.

His grace is very well recover'd.

Mal. Good my lord, suffer us.

Card.   O, by no means;
The noise, and change of object in his eye,
Doth more distract him: I pray, all to bed,   5
And though you hear him in his violent fit,
Do not rise, I entreat you.

Pes. So sir, we shall not—

Card.   Nay, I must have you promise
Upon your honours, for I was enjoin'd to't
By himself; and he seem'd to urge it sensibly.   10

Pes. Let our honours bind this trifle.

Card. Nor any of your followers.

Mal.   Neither.

Card. It may be to make trial of your promise
When he's asleep, myself will rise, and feign
Some of his mad tricks, and cry out for help,   15
And feign myself in danger.

Mal.   If your throat were cutting,
I'd not come at you, now I have protested against it.

Card. Why, I thank you.   [*Withdraws.*]

Gris.   'Twas a foul storm tonight.

Rod. The Lord Ferdinand's chamber shook like an osier.

Mal. 'Twas nothing but pure kindness in the devil   20
To rock his own child.   *Exeunt* [*all except the* Cardinal].

Card. The reason why I would not suffer these
About my brother, is because at midnight
I may with better privacy convey
Julia's body to her own lodging:—   25
O, my conscience!
I would pray now: but the devil takes away my heart
For having any confidence in prayer.

---

18. *Withdraws*] *Luc i subs.*   21. *all . . . Cardinal*] *Dyce i subs.*   25–6.] *so
this ed.; one line Q.*

27–8.] from *Arcadia*, III. xiii (*Wks*, I. 432), of a coward: 'Faine he
would have prayed, but he had not harte inough to have confidence in
praier.' *For* = 'from'.

About this hour I appointed Bosola
To fetch the body: when he hath serv'd my turn,   30
He dies.   *Exit.*

Enter BOSOLA.

Bos. Hah? 'twas the cardinal's voice: I heard him name
Bosola, and my death: listen, I hear one's footing.

Enter FERDINAND.

Ferd. Strangling is a very quiet death.
Bos. [*Aside*] Nay then, I see I must stand upon my guard.   35
Ferd. What say' to that? whisper, softly: do you agree to't?
So it must be done i'th' dark: the cardinal
Would not for a thousand pounds the doctor should see it.
                                                          Exit.

Bos. My death is plotted; here's the consequence of murder:
We value not desert, nor Christian breath,   40
When we know black deeds must be cur'd with death.

Enter ANTONIO and Servant.

Serv. Here stay sir, and be confident, I pray:
I'll fetch you a dark lantern.   *Exit.*
Ant. Could I take him at his prayers,
There were hope of pardon.
Bos.   Fall right my sword! [*Stabs him.*]
I'll not give thee so much leisure as to pray.   46
Ant. O, I am gone! Thou hast ended a long suit

31.1.] *so Dyce i; at ll. 0.1–2 Q.*   33.1.] *so Dyce i; at ll. 0.1–2 Q.*   34.
quiet] *Q2;* quiein *Q.*   35. *Aside*] *Dyce ii.*   then, I see] *Q 3 (subs.);* then
I see, *Q.*   36–8.] *so Q; as prose Dyce i.*   36. say'] *Q;* say *Q2;* say you
Q3.   37. So] *Q;* So; *Dyce ii.*   40–1.] *italicized Q (,,We . . .).*   41.1.]
so Q4 subs.; at ll. 0.1–2 Q.   45. S.D.] *Dyce ii.*

41. black . . . death] a rehandling of the proverb found in Seneca and, for
example, *W.D.*, II. i. 319: 'Small mischiefs are by greater made secure'
(cf. Tilley C826).

43. *dark lantern*] Cf. II. iii. 0.1 and note.

47. *suit*] (1) 'petition', and (2) 'quest, chase'; i.e., punning on 'pray' of
the previous line.

In a minute.

Bos.   What art thou?

Ant.   A most wretched thing,
That only have thy benefit in death,
To appear myself.

[*Enter* Servant *with a light.*]

Serv.   Where are you, sir?   50

Ant. Very near my home:—Bosola!

Serv.   O, misfortune!

Bos. Smother thy pity, thou art dead else:—Antonio!
The man I would have sav'd 'bove mine own life!
We are merely the stars' tennis-balls, struck and banded
Which way please them—O good Antonio,   55
I'll whisper one thing in thy dying ear
Shall make thy heart break quickly: Thy fair duchess
And two sweet children—

Ant.   Their very names
Kindle a little life in me.

Bos.   Are murder'd!

Ant. Some men have wish'd to die   60
At the hearing of sad tidings: I am glad
That I shall do't in sadness; I would not now
Wish my wounds balm'd, nor heal'd, for I have no use
To put my life to. In all our quest of greatness,
Like wanton boys whose pastime is their care,   65
We follow after bubbles, blown in th' air.

49. thy] *Q;* this *Q4.*   50. S.D.] *Q4.*   51. Bosola!] *Dyce i;* Bosola? *Q.*
61. sad] *Q;* glad *conj. Brereton (ap. Luc i).*

49. *benefit*] good deed, favour.
50. *To...myself*] i.e., he has only his mere self to show; this is a quibbling answer to Bosola's 'What art thou?' (l. 48).
54–5. *We...them*] a familiar conceit; it is found in *Arcadia* (*Wks*, I. 330 and II. 177), Florio (III. ix) and Plautus, *Captivi,* Prol. 22 (so Sykes and Lucas).   *banded* = 'bandied'.   Cf. v. v. 100–2, note.
62. *in sadness*] 'in earnest'; i.e., punning on *sad* of l. 61.
65–6.] Alexander, Parsons, and Drummond are among the moralizing authors in whose works Dent has found this idea.

  Pleasure of life, what is't ? only the good hours
  Of an ague; merely a preparative to rest,
  To endure vexation:—I do not ask
  The process of my death; only commend me   70
  To Delio.
Bos. Break heart!—
Ant.   And let my son fly the courts of princes.
                 [*Dies.*]

Bos. Thou seem'st to have lov'd Antonio ?
Serv.   I brought him hither,
  To have reconcil'd him to the cardinal.
Bos. I do not ask thee that:—   75
  Take him up, if thou tender thine own life,
  And bear him, where the Lady Julia
  Was wont to lodge.—O, my fate moves swift!
  I have this cardinal in the forge already,
  Now I'll bring him to th' hammer:—O direful misprision!
  I will not imitate things glorious,   81
  No more than base: I'll be mine own example.
  On, on: and look thou represent, for silence,
  The thing thou bear'st.   *Exeunt.*

72.1.] *Dyce i.*

 67–8. *Pleasure . . . ague*] Cf. Hall, *Epistles*, I. ii: 'All these earthly delights . . . are but as a good day betweene two agues. . .'

 68–9. *merely . . . vexation*] Cf. almost the last words of Flamineo, in *W.D.*, v. vi. 273–4: '. . . rest breeds rest, where all seek pain by pain', and *D.M.*, II. v. 59–61.

 72. *And . . . princes*] Cf. the last words of Vittoria, in *W.D.*, v. vi. 261–2: 'O happy they that never saw the court, / Nor ever knew great man but by report.'

 80. *misprision*] perhaps a quibble: (1) 'mistake', and (2) 'failure to recognize value' (cf. *O.E.D.*, *sb.*¹ and *sb.*²).

 81–2.] Cf. the words of the dying Flamineo, in *W.D.*, v. vi. 256–7: 'I do not look / Who went before, nor who shall follow me . . .' and also *W.D.*, v. i. 75–7.

SCENA V.

Enter Cardinal, *with a book.*

Card. I am puzzled in a question about hell:
        He says, in hell there's one material fire,
        And yet it shall not burn all men alike.
        Lay him by:—how tedious is a guilty conscience!
        When I look into the fish-ponds, in my garden,   5
        Methinks I see a thing, arm'd with a rake
        That seems to strike at me:—

Enter BOSOLA, *and* Servant *with* ANTONIO's *body.*

                                        Now! art thou come?
        Thou look'st ghastly:
        There sits in thy face some great determination,
        Mix'd with some fear.

---

v. v. o.1.] *Q4; Cardinall (with a Booke) Bosola, Pescara, Malateste,
Rodorigo, Ferdinand, Delio, Seruant with Antonio's body Q.   7–8.]
so Dyce ii; one line Q; . . . me: / Now . . . Har.   7. S.D.] so Dyce ii;
at l. 0.1 Q.*

---

v. v. o.1. with a book] an old stage-device for indicating melancholy or
introspection: see for example, *Spanish Tragedy*, III. xiii, *Hamlet*, II. ii,
Marston's *Antonio's Revenge*, II. iii, '*Second Maiden's Tragedy*', IV. iv, etc.

2–3.] Dent quoted two accounts, Luis de Granada (tr. 1598) and
Dialogues of S. Gregory (tr. 1608): 'The fire of hell is but one: yet doth it
not in one manner torment all sinners. . .'

4. *Lay him by*] to be echoed later, at ll. 89–90.

tedious] besides the modern senses, this could mean 'painful, troublesome' (*O.E.D.*, 2); the latter sense is found in *A.V.*, III. i. 73: 'the tedious-
ness of his importunate suit'.

5–7. *When . . . me*] The ultimate source is an account of Pertinax by
Julius Capitolanus; it was several times repeated, as in Lavater, *Of Ghosts*
(1572), Shakespeare Ass. Rep., p. 61: 'for ye space of three dayes before he
was slayne by a thrust, [he] sawe a certayne shaddowe in one of his fishe-
pondes, which with a sword ready drawen threatened to slay him, & therby
much disquieted him.' See Dent for further occurrences.

7. Enter Bosola] The timing of this entry, on the talk of striking,
accentuates its menace and the sense of Fate moving swiftly and inexorably.

8. *ghastly*] Meanings ranged from 'causing terror' to 'ghost-like' and
'full of fear'.

9–10. *There . . . fear*] Cf. *Arcadia*, I. ix (*Wks*, I. 57): 'he might see in his
countenance some great determination mixed with feare.'

Bos.   Thus it lightens into action: 10
   I am come to kill thee.
Card.   Hah ? help ! our guard !
Bos. Thou art deceiv'd:
   They are out of thy howling.
Card. Hold: and I will faithfully divide
   Revenues with thee.
Bos.   Thy prayers and proffers   15
   Are both unseasonable.
Card.   Raise the watch !
   We are betray'd !
Bos.   I have confin'd your flight:
   I'll suffer your retreat to Julia's chamber,
   But no further.
Card.   Help ! we are betray'd !

      Enter[, *above,*] PESCARA, MALATESTE, RODERIGO
                [, *and* GRISOLAN].

Mal.   Listen:—
Card. My dukedom for rescue !
Rod.   Fie upon his counterfeiting !   20
Mal. Why, 'tis not the cardinal.
Rod.   Yes, yes, 'tis he:
   But I'll see him hang'd, ere I'll go down to him.
Card. Here's a plot upon me, I am assaulted ! I am lost,
   Unless some rescue !
Gris.   He doth this pretty well:
   But it will not serve to laugh mè out of mine honour.   25
Card. The sword's at my throat:—
Rod.   You would not bawl so loud then.
Mal. Come, come:

16–17. Raise . . . betray'd] *so Luc i; one line Q.*   19. S.D.] *so Dyce i;
at l. o.1 Q; at end of line Q4.   above]* Q4.   *and Grisolan]* Dyce i.
25. serve] *Q3;* serue; *Q.*   27–8.] *so McIl; one line Q; . . .* go / To . . . *Dyce ii.*

---

   13. *howling*] For Webster *howling* often implied wailing and, even,
tears; cf. *W.D.,* v. iii. 35–7; v. iv. 65; v. vi. 156; and *D.L.C.,* v. iv. 183.

  Let's go to bed: he told us thus much aforehand.

Pes. He wish'd you should not come at him: but believe 't,

  The accent of the voice sounds not in jest.   30

  I'll down to him, howsoever, and with engines

  Force ope the doors.   [*Exit above.*]

Rod.   Let's follow him aloof,

  And note how the cardinal will laugh at him.

    [*Exeunt, above,* MALATESTE, RODERIGO, *and* GRISOLAN.]

Bos. There's for you first—   *He kills the Servant.*

  'Cause you shall not unbarricade the door   35

  To let in rescue.

Card. What cause hast thou to pursue my life?

Bos.   Look there:—

Card. Antonio!

Bos.   Slain by my hand unwittingly:—

  Pray, and be sudden; when thou kill'd'st thy sister,

  Thou took'st from Justice her most equal balance,   40

  And left her naught but her sword.

Card.   O, mercy!

Bos. Now it seems thy greatness was only outward;

  For thou fall'st faster of thyself, than calamity

  Can drive thee. I'll not waste longer time: there! [*Stabs him.*]

Card. Thou hast hurt me:—

---

32. S.D.] *Dyce i.* 33.1.] *Dyce i.* 34–6.] *so Dyce i;* . . . doore / To . . .
(*2 lines*) *Q;* . . . unbarracade / The . . . (*two lines*) *Luc i.* 34. S.D.] *so
this ed.; after l. 36 Q.* 37. What . . . life] *so Q;* . . . thou / To . . . *Luc i.*
44. S.D.] *Q4.*

---

  40. *equal*] just, impartial.

  42–4. *thy . . . thee*] from *Arcadia,* II. xxix (*Wks,* I. 332): 'For Antiphilus
that had no greatnesse but outwarde, that taken away, was readie to fall
faster than calamitie could thrust him.' Unlike Ferdinand and Bosola, the
cardinal changes in a moment to a grovelling and panicky suppliant. See
l. 13, note, above.

  Webster used similar words for the *Character,* 'An Intruder into
Favour': 'all this gay glitter shewes on him, as if the Sunne shone in a
puddle . . .: and when hee is falling, hee goes of himselfe faster then misery
can driue him.'

  When the cardinal is wounded by his brother, however, he recognizes the
demands of Justice and regains control of himself (ll. 53–5, *et seq.*).

Bos.   Again!   [*Stabs him again.*]

Card.   Shall I die like a leveret   45

    Without any resistance? help, help, help!

    I am slain!

Enter FERDINAND.

Ferd.   Th' alarum! give me a fresh horse:

    Rally the vaunt-guard, or the day is lost:

    Yield, yield! I give you the honour of arms,

    Shake my sword over you—will you yield?   50

Card. Help me, I am your brother.

Ferd.   The devil!

    My brother fight upon the adverse party?

    There flies your ransom.   *He wounds the Cardinal, and*
                              in the scuffle gives Bosola
                              his death-wound.

Card.   O Justice!

    I suffer now, for what hath former been:

    Sorrow is held the eldest child of sin.   55

Ferd. Now you're brave fellows:—Caesar's fortune was

45. S.D.] *Dyce ii.*   47. S.D.] *so Q4; at l. 0.1 Q.*   51. devil!] *Dyce i;*
diuell? Q.   53. S.D.] *so this ed.; to right of ll. 52–3 Q.*   54. been] *Q4;*
bin Q.   55.] *italicized this ed.;* "Sorrow ... *Q.*

---

45. *leveret*] young hare; Turbeville considered a *leveret* too 'feeble' to be
worth hunting (*Hunting* (1576), p. 170).

47. *give . . . horse*] Cf. *R3*, v. iv. 7 and 13: 'my kingdom for a horse';
contrast the cardinal's cry at l. 20, above.

48. *vaunt-guard*] vanguard; the obsolete form is kept in this edition
because of associations with 'vaunt', *sb.* = 'boast'.

49. *I . . . arms*] either 'I salute you as soldiers' (so Sampson), or 'I, as a
soldier, honour you as if you were dead' ('Military honours' = 'marks of
respect paid by troops at burials etc.'; see *O.E.D.*, honour, *sb.*, 5d).

53. *There . . . ransom*] Being killed, he cannot be held for ransom.

55.] Cf. Giovanni's warning to Flamineo, *W.D.*, v. iv. 21–3: 'Study your
prayers, sir, and be penitent, / . . . I have heard grief nam'd the eldest child
of sin.'

56–8. *Caesar's . . . disgrace*] from Whetstone, *Heptameron* (1582), H2:
'What difference was there between the Fortunes of Cesar and Pompey,
when their endes were both violent: saue that I hould Cesars to be the
harder: for that, he was murthered in the Armes of Prosperytie, and
Pompey, at the feete of Disgrace.'

harder than Pompey's; Caesar died in the arms of prosperity, Pompey at the feet of disgrace:—you both died in
the field. The pain's nothing: pain many times is taken
away with the apprehension of greater, as the toothache   60
with the sight of a barber that comes to pull it out—
there's philosophy for you.

Bos. Now my revenge is perfect: *He kills Ferdinand.*
                                   sink, thou main cause
Of my undoing!—The last part of my life
Hath done me best service.   65

Ferd. Give me some wet hay, I am broken-winded—
I do account this world but a dog-kennel:
I will vault credit, and affect high pleasures,
Beyond death.

Bos.   He seems to come to himself,
Now he's so near the bottom.   70

Ferd. My sister! O! my sister! there's the cause on't:
Whether we fall by ambition, blood, or lust,
Like diamonds, we are cut with our own dust.   [*Dies.*]

Card. Thou hast thy payment too.

Bos. Yes, I hold my weary soul in my teeth,   75

---

63. S.D.] *so this ed.; to right of l. 65 Q; after* cause *Dyce i.*   69–70. He
. . .] *so Dyce i; one line Q.*   71. O!] *Q;* O *Dyce i.*   my sister!] *Q3;* my
sister, *Q.*   72–3.] *italicized this ed.;* "Whether . . . / "Like . . . *Q.*
73. Dies] *Dyce i.*

---

63. S.D.] Compositor B probably placed this direction as he did because
there was most space to the right of the text at that point; he clearly misplaced IV. ii. 237 S.D. for such a reason.

66.] Markham recommended 'Grass in Summer, and Hay sprinkled
with water in Winter' for a horse that was broken-winded (quoted by Lucas
from *Masterpiece Revived*, ed. 1688, p. 72).

68. *vault credit*] overleap expectation, or belief.

72–3.] Cf. Nashe, *Christ's Tears* (1593), Dedic.: 'An easie matter is it
for anie man to cutte me (like a Diamond) with mine own dust'; the
phrase was probably proverbial, a variant of 'Diamonds cut diamonds'
(Tilley D323).

Ferdinand seems to imply that each man is his own worst enemy; but (as
Dent suggested) he might mean that his sister was his *own dust.*

75. *hold* . . .] Cf. Florio, II. xxxv: 'The soule must be held fast with ones
teeth, since the lawe to liue in honest men, is not to liue as long as they

'Tis ready to part from me:—I do glory
That thou, which stood'st like a huge pyramid
Begun upon a large and ample base,
Shalt end in a little point, a kind of nothing.

[*Enter* PESCARA, MALATESTE, RODERIGO, *and* GRISOLAN.]

Pes. How now, my lord?
Mal.   O, sad disaster!
Rod.   How comes this?   80
Bos. Revenge, for the Duchess of Malfi, murdered
By th' Arragonian brethren; for Antonio,
Slain by this hand; for lustful Julia,
Poison'd by this man; and lastly, for myself,
That was an actor in the main of all   85
Much 'gainst mine own good nature, yet i'th' end
Neglected.
Pes.   How now, my lord?
Card.   Look to my brother:
He gave us these large wounds, as we were struggling
Here i'th' rushes:—and now, I pray, let me
Be laid by, and never thought of.   [*Dies.*] 90
Pes. How fatally, it seems, he did withstand
His own rescue.
Mal.   Thou wretched thing of blood,
How came Antonio by his death?
Bos. In a mist: I know not how—
Such a mistake as I have often seen   95
In a play:—O, I am gone!—
We are only like dead walls, or vaulted graves,

79.1.] *Q4 subs.*   83. this] *Q4;* his *Q.*   90. *Dies*] *Q4.*

---

please, but so long as they ought'; this is based on Seneca, *Epist.*, civ. 3.
  77–9. *thou . . . nothing*] See Intro., pp. xxvi–xxvii, for the origin of this passage.
  89. *rushes*] Green rushes were commonly strewed on the floors of apartments and on the stages of public theatres.
  94. *mist*] Cf. IV. ii. 188, and note.
  97. *dead*] continuous, unbroken; see V. ii. 338, and note.

That ruin'd, yields no echo:—Fare you well—
It may be pain, but no harm to me to die
In so good a quarrel. O, this gloomy world!   100
In what a shadow, or deep pit of darkness,
Doth womanish and fearful mankind live!
Let worthy minds ne'er stagger in distrust
To suffer death, or shame for what is just—
Mine is another voyage.   [*Dies.*] 105
Pes. The noble Delio, as I came to th' palace,
Told me of Antonio's being here, and show'd me
A pretty gentleman, his son and heir.

Enter DELIO [*with* Antonio's Son].

Mal. O sir, you come too late!
Delio.   I heard so, and
Was arm'd for't ere I came. Let us make noble use   110
Of this great ruin; and join all our force
To establish this young, hopeful gentleman
In's mother's right. These wretched eminent things
Leave no more fame behind 'em than should one
Fall in a frost, and leave his print in snow;   115
As soon as the sun shines, it ever melts,
Both form, and matter:—I have ever thought
Nature doth nothing so great, for great men,
As when she's pleas'd to make them lords of truth:

---

98. yields] Q (yieldes); yield *Dyce i.*   105. Dies] *Q4.*   108.1.] so *Q4;*
at *l. o.1* Q.   with . . . Son] *Dyce i subs.*

99–100. *It . . . quarrel*] probably proverbial (so Dent): cf. *Arcadia,* III. ix
(*Wks,* I. 400): 'thinking it wrong, but no harme to him that shoulde die in
so good a cause.'

100–2. *O . . .*] from *Arcadia,* V (*Wks,* II. 177): 'in such a shadowe, or
rather pit of darkenes, the wormish mankinde lives, that neither they knowe
how to foresee, nor what to feare: and are but like tenisballs, tossed by the
racket of hyer powers.'

118–19.] from *Arcadia,* II. vii (*Wks,* I. 190): 'Nature having done so
much for them in nothing, as that it made them Lords of truth, whereon all
the other goods were builded.'

Integrity of life is fame's best friend,   120
Which nobly, beyond death, shall crown the end.   *Exeunt.*

FINIS.

120–1.] *italicized Q* ("*Integrity . . .*).

121.] Cf. the proverb, 'The end crowns (or tries) all' (Tilley E116).

APPENDIX I

The Source of *The Duchess of Malfi*,
from William Painter's *The Palace of Pleasure*,
Volume ii (1567)

Editorial Note

The first edition of Painter is here reprinted from the copy in the Folger Library. A very few changes in punctuation and capitalization and some minor corrections have been introduced; abbreviations have been expanded.

Footnotes indicate passages verbally echoed in *The Duchess*. A collation follows, recording all 'substantive' editorial changes, usually in favour of the second quarto of 1575 (?); it also lists a selection of further readings from the second quarto which significantly modify or clarify the sense. A = first quarto; B = second quarto.

Modern editions of the complete *Palace of Pleasure*, by J. Haslewood (1813), J. Jacobs (1890), and H. Miles (1929), follow the second edition, which was 'corrected and augmented' by Painter. But the original text may be preferred as a less 'varnished' tale; Painter's changes on almost every page aimed at elegance and clarity, and so a direct phrase was often replaced with one more studied or decorous, and sometimes strictures upon the duchess' behaviour were toned down.

If an editor's taste did not encourage him to choose the first quarto, the need to provide students of Webster with a version of the source of *The Duchess* which has not been reprinted since the sixteenth century will dictate its adoption in the present context. Not only is the tone different but, at times, characterization as well: so Bosola was an 'assured manqueller' before becoming a 'pestilent' one, and Delio had 'small acquaintance' with Antonio before the second edition said he had none. We cannot be sure that we have read Webster's main source until both editions have been studied. And if we could have one only, it should probably be the first: while in emphasis or idea *The Duchess* once seems closer to the first and once to the second edition (III. ii. 276–9 and III. iii. 60–1; see footnotes, p. 195), on one occasion Webster seems to echo the words of the first and not of the second (III. i. 24–7; see footnote, p. 186).

THE DUCHESSE OF MALFI

The Infortunate mariage of a Gentleman, called *ANTONIO
BOLOGNA*, with the Duchesse of *MALFI*, and the pitifull death
of them bothe.

The xxiij. Nouel.

The greater Honor and authoritie men haue in this world, and the
greater their estimation is, the more sensible and notorious are the
faultes by them committed, and the greater is their slander. In lyke
manner more difficult it is for that man to tolerate and sustaine
Fortune, which all the dayes of his life hathe liued at his ease, if by
chaunce hee fall into any great necessitie, than for hym which neuer
felt but woe, mishappe, and aduersitie. *Dyonisius* the Tyrant of
Sicilia, felte greater payne when hee was expelled his kingdome, than
Milo did, being banished from *Rome*. For so muche as the one was a
Soueraigne Lord, the sonne of a King, a Justiciarie on earth, and the
other but a simple Citizen of a Citie, wherein the people had Lawes,
and the lawes of Magistrates had in reuerence. So likewyse the fall of
a high and loftie Tree, maketh a greater noyse, than that whiche is
lowe and little. Highe Towers and stately Palaces of Princes be seene
further off, than the poore Cabans and homely shephierds Sheepe-
cotes. The Walles of loftie Cities salute the viewers of the same
farther of, than the simple caues, which the poore doe dig belowe the
Mountaine rocks. Wherefore it behoueth the Noble, and such as haue
charge of Common wealth, to liue an honest lyfe, and beare their port
vpryght, that none haue cause to take ill example vpon dyscourse of
their deedes and naughtie life. * And aboue all, that modestie ought
to be kept by women, whome as their race, Noble birth, authoritie
and name, maketh them more famous, euen so their vertue, honestie,
chastitie, and continencie more praiseworthy. And behouefull it is,
that like as they wishe to be honoured aboue all other, so their life do
make them worthy of that honour, without disgracing their name by
deede or woorde, or blemishing that brightnesse which may com-
mende the same. I greatly feare that all the Princely factes, the ex-
ploits and conquests done by the *Babylonian* Queene *Semyramis*,
neuer was recommended with such praise, as hir vice had shame in
records by those which left remembrance of ancient acts. Thus I say,
bicause a woman being as it were the Image of sweetenesse, curtesie
and shamefastnesse, so soone as she steppeth out of the right tracte,
and leaueth the smel of hir duetie and modestie, bisides the deni-
gration of hir honor, thrusteth hir self into infinite troubles and

* Wherefore . . . : I. i. 11–15.

causeth the ruine of such which should be honored and praised, if womens allurement solicited them not to follie. I wil not here indeuor my self to seeke for examples of *Samson, Salomon* or other, which suffred themselues fondly to be abused by women: and who by meane of them be tumbled into great faults, and haue incurred greater perils. Contenting my self to recite a right pitifull Historie done almost in our time, when the French vnder the leading of that notable captaine *Gaston de Foix*, vanquished the force of *Spaine* and *Naples* at the iourney of *Rauenna* in the time of the French king called *Levves* the twelfth, * who married the Lady *Marie*, daughter to king *Henry* the seuenth, and sister to the victorious Prince of worthy memory king *Henry* the eight, wife (after the death of the sayd *Levves*) to the puissant Gentleman *Charles*, late Duke of *Suffolke*.

In that very time then liued a Gentleman of *Naples*, called *Antonio Bologna*, who hauing bene Master of houshold to *Fredericke* of *Aragon*, sometime King of *Naples*, after the French had expelled those of *Aragon* out of that Citie, the sayde *Bologna* retired into *Fraunce*, and thereby recouered the goods, which hee possessed in his countrey. The Gentleman bisides that he was valient of his persone, a good man of warre, and wel estemed amongs the best, had a passing numbre of good graces, which made him to be beloued and cherished of euery wight: and for riding and managing of great horse, he had not his fellow in *Italy*: ** he could also play exceeding well and trim vpon the Lute, whose faining voyce so well agreed therunto, that the most melancholike persons wold forget their heauinesse, vpon hearing of his heauenly noise: and besides these qualities, hee was of personage comely, and of good proportion. To be short, Nature hauing trauailed and dispoyled hir Treasure house for inriching of him, he had by Arte gotten that, which made him most happy and worthy of praise, which was, the knowledge of good letters, wherin hee was so well trained, as by talke and dispute thereof, he made those to blush that were of that state and profession. *Antonio Bologna* hauing left *Fredericke* of *Aragon* in *Fraunce*, who expulsed out of *Naples* was retired to king *Levves*, went home to his house to liue at rest and to auoyd trouble, forgetting the delicates of Courtes and houses of great men, to be the only husband of his owne reuenue. But what? It is impossible to eschue that which the heauens haue determined vpon us: and lesse the vnhappe, whych seemeth to follow vs, as it were naturally proceeding from our mothers wombe: In such wise as many times, he which seemeth the wisest man, guided by misfortune, hasteth himself wyth stouping head to fall headlong into his deathe and ruine. Euen so it chaunced to this *Neapolitane* Gentleman: for in the very same place where he attained his aduancement,

* when . . . : I. i. 73-4.   ** for . . . : I. i. 140.

he receiued also his diminution and decay, and by that house which
preferred hym to what he had, he was depriued, both of his estate and
life: the discourse whereof you shall vnderstand. I haue tolde you
already, that this Gentleman was Maister of the King of *Naples*
houshold, and being a gentle person, a good Courtier, wel trained
vp, and wise for gouernment of himself in the Court and in the service
of Princes, the Duchesse of *Malfi* thought to intreat him that hee
would serue hir, in that office which he serued the king. This Duchesse was of the house of *Aragon*, and sister to the Cardinal of *Aragon*
which then was a rich and puissant personage. Being thus resolued,
was wel assured that she was not deceiued: for so much as she was
persuaded, that *Bologna* was deuoutly affected to the house of *Aragon*,
as one brought vp there from a child. Wherfore sending for him home
to his house, she vsed vnto him these, or like words: "Master
Bologna, sith your ill fortune, nay rather the vnhap of our whole
house is such, as your good Lord and master hath forgon his state and
dignitie, and that you therwithall haue lost a good Master, wythout
other recompence but the praise which euery man giueth you for your
good seruice, I haue thought good to intreat you to do me the honor,
as to take charge of the gouernment of my house, and to vse the same,
as you did that of the king your master. I know well that the office is
to vnworthy for your calling: notwithstanding you be not ignoraunt
what I am, and how neere to him in bloud, to whom you be so faithfull
and louing a seruaunt: and albeit that I am no Queene, endued with
great reuenue, yet with that little I haue, I bear a Princely heart: and
such as you by experience do knowe what I haue done, and daily do
to those which depart my seruice, recompensing them according to
their paine and trauaile: magnificence is obserued as well in the
Courts of poore Princes, as in the stately Palaces of great Kings and
monarches. I do remembre that I haue red of a certain noble gentleman, a *Persian* borne, called *Ariobarzanes*, who vsed great examples
of curtesie and stoutnes towards king *Artaxerxes*, wherwith the king
wondred at his magnificence, and confessed himself to be vanquished: you shall take aduise of this request, and I in the mean time
do think you will not refuse the same, as well for that my demaund is
iust, as also being assured, that our house and race is so well imprinted in your heart, as it is impossible that the memory therof can
be defaced." The gentleman hearing the courteous demaund of the
Duchesse, knowing himself how deepely bound he was to the name
of *Aragon*, and led by some vnknowen prouocation to his great yll
luck, answered hir in this wise: "I wold to god madame, that with so
good reason and equitie I were able to make denial of your commaundement, as iustly you require the same: wherfore for the boun-
den duety which I owe to the name and memorie of the house of

Aragon, I make promise that I shall not only sustain the trauail, but also the daunger of my life, daily ready to be offred for your seruice: but I feele in minde I know not what, which commaundeth me to withdraw my self to liue alone at home at my house, and to be content with the little I haue, forgoing the sumptuouse charge of Princes houses, which life would be wel liked of my self, were it not for the feare that you madame shold be discontented with my refusal, and that you shold conceiue, that I disdained your offred charge, or contempne your Court for respect of the great Office I bare in the Court of the Kyng, my Lord and Master. For I cannot receiue more honor, than to serue hir, which is of that stock and royall race. Therefore at all aduentures I am resolued to obey your wil, and humbly to satisfy the duty of the charge wherin it pleaseth you to imploy me, more to pleasure you for auoiding of displeasure: then for desire I haue to liue an honorable life in the greatest princes house of the world, sith I am discharged from him in whose name resteth my comfort and only stay, thinking to have liued a solitary life, and to passe my yeres in rest, except it were in the pore abilitie of my seruice to the house, wherunto I am bound continually to be a faithful seruaunt. Thus Madame, you see me to be the rediest man of the world, to fulfill the request, and accomplish such other seruice wherin it shall please you to imploy me." The Duchesse thanked him very heartily, and gaue him charge of all hir householde traine, commaunding eche person to do him such reuerence as to hir self, and to obey him as the chief of all hir familie. This Lady was a widow, but a passing faire Gentlewoman, fine and very yong, hauing a yong sonne vnder hir guard and keping, left by the deceased Duke hir husband, togither with the Duchie, the inheritaunce of hir childe. Now consider hir personage being such, hir easy life and delicate bringing vp, and daily seeing the youthely trade and maner of Courtiers life, whether she felt hir self prickt with any desire, which burned hir heart the more incessantly, as the flames were hidden and couert: from the outward shew whereof she stayd hir self so well as she could. But she following best aduise, rather esteemed the proofe of mariage, than to burne with so little fire, or to incurre the exchange of louers, as many vnshamefast strumpets do, which be rather giuen ouer, than satisfied with pleasure of loue. And to say the truthe, they be not guided by wisdomes lore, which suffer a maiden ripe for mariage to be long vnwedded, or yong wife long to liue in widdowes state, what assurance so euer they make of their chaste and stayed life. For bookes be so full of such enterprises, and houses stored with examples of such stolne and secrete practises, as there neede no further proofe for assurance of our cause, the same of it self being so plaine and manifest. And a great follie it is to build the fantasies of chastitie, amid the follies of worldly pleasures.

I will not goe about to make those matters impossible, ne yet wil iudge at large, but that there be some maidens and wiues, which wisely can conteine themselues amongs the troupe of amorous sutors. But what ? the experience is very hard, and the proofe no lesse daungerous, and perchaunce in a moment the minde of some peruerted, whych all their liuing dayes haue closed their eares from the wordes of those that haue made offer of louing seruice, we neede not run to forayne Histories, ne yet to seeke records that be auncient, sith we may see the daily effects of the like, practized in Noble houses, and Courtes of Kings and Princes. That this is true, example of this fair Duchesse, who was moued with that desire which pricketh others that be of Flesh and bone. ⋆ This Lady waxed very weary of lying alone, and grieued hir heart to be without a match, specially in the night, when the secrete silence and darknesse of the same presented before the eies of hir minde, the Image of the pleasure which she felt in the life time of hir deceased Lord and husband, ⋆⋆ whereof now feeling hir selfe despoiled, she felt a continuall combat, and durst not attempte that which she desired most, but eschued the thing wherof hir minde liked best. "Alas (said she) is it possible after the taste of the value of honest obedience which the wife oweth vnto hir husband, that I should desire to suffer the heat which burneth and altereth the martired minds of those that subdue them selues to loue ? Can such attempt pierce the heart of me to become amorous by forgetting and straying from the limittes of honest life ? But what desire is this ? I haue a certaine vnacquainted lust, and yet very well know not what it is that moueth me, and to whome I shall vow the spoile thereof. I am truely more fonde and foolish than euer *Narcissus* was, for there is neither shadow nor voyce vpon which I can well stay my sight, nor yet simple Imagination of any worldly man, whereupon I can arrest the conceipt of my vnstayed heart, and the desires which prouoke my mind. *Pygmalion* loued once a Marble piller, and I haue but one desire, the coloure wherof is more pale than death. ⋆⋆⋆ There is nothyng which can giue the same so much as one spot of vermilion rud. If I do discouer these appetites to any wight, perhaps they will mock me for my labor, and for all the beautie and Noble birth that is in me, they wil make no conscience to deeme me for their iesting stock, and to solace themselues with rehersall of my fond conceits. But sith there is no enimie in the field, and that but simple suspition doth assaile vs, we must breake of the same, and deface the entier remembrance of the lightnesse of my braine. It apperteineth vnto me to shew my self, as issued forth of the Noble house of *Aragon*. To me it doeth belong to take heede how I erre or degenerate from the royall bloud wherof

⋆ moued . . . : I. i. 453.   ⋆⋆ when . . . : IV. i. 12–15.
⋆⋆⋆ *Pygmalion* . . . : I. i. 454–5.

I came." In this sort that fair widow and yong Princesse fantasied in the nyght vpon the discourse of hir appetites. But when the day was come, seeing the great multitude of the *Neapolitan* Lords and gentlemen which marched vp and downe the Citie, eying and beholding their best beloued, or vsing talk of mirth with them whose seruaunts they were, al that which she thought vpon in the night, vanished so sone as the flame of burned straw, or the pouder of the Canon shot, and purposed for any respect to liue no longer in that sort, but promised the conquest of some friend that was lustie and discreete. But the difficultie rested in that she knew not vpon whom to fixe hir loue, fearing to be slaundered, and also that the light disposition and maner of most part of youth wer to be suspected, in such wise as giuing ouer all them whych vauted vpon their Gennets, Turkey Palfreis, and other Coursers along the Citie of *Naples*, she purposed to take repast of other Venison, than of that fond and wanton troupe. So hir mishap began already to spin the threede which choked the aire and breath of hir vnhappie life. Ye haue heard before that M. *Bologna* was one of the wisest and most perfect gentlemen that the land of *Naples* that tyme brought forth, and for his beautie, proportion, galantnesse, valiance, and good grace, without comparison. His fauor was so sweete and pleasant, as they which kept him companie, had somwhat to do to abstain their affection. Who then could blame this faire Princesse, if (pressed with desire of matche, to remoue the ticklish instigations of hir wanton flesh, and hauing in hir presence a man so wise) she did set hir minde on him, or fantasie to mary him ? wold not that partie for calming of his thirst and hunger, being set at the table before sundry sorts of delicate viands, ease his hunger ? Me think the person doth greatly forget himself, which hauing handfast vpon occasion, suffreth the same to vanish and flie away, sith it is wel knowne that she being bald behinde, hath no place to sease vpon, when desire moueth vs to lay hold vpon hir. Which was the cause that the Duchesse becam extremely in loue with the master of hir house. In such wise as before al men, she spared not to praise the great perfections wherwith he was enriched, whom she desired to be altogether hirs. And so she was inamored, that it was as possible to see the night to be void of darknesse, as the Duchesse without the presence of hir *Bologna*, or else by talk of words to set forth his praise, the continual remembrance of whome (for that she loued him as hir self) was hir only minds repast. The gentleman that was ful wise, and had at other times felt the great force of the passion which procedeth from extreme loue, immediatly did mark the countenance of the Duchesse, and perceiued the same so nere, as vnfainedly he knew that very ardently the Ladie was in loue with him: and albeit he saw the inequality and difference betwene them both, she being sorted out of the royal bloud, yet knowing loue to haue no respect to state or dignity, determined to folow his fortune, and to serue hir which so louingly shewed hir self to him. Then sodainly reprouing his fonde conceit, hee sayd vnto himself: "What follie is that I enterprise, to the great preiudice and perill of mine honor and life? Ought the wisdom of a Gentleman to straie and wandre through the assaults of an appetite rising of sensuality, and that reason giue place to that which doeth participate with brute beastes depriued of all reason by subduing the mynde to the affections of the body? No no, a vertuous man ought to let shine in him self the force of the generositie of his mynde. This is not to liue according to the spirite, when pleasure shall make vs forget our duetie and sauegard of our Conscience. The reputation of a wise Gentleman resteth not onely to be valiant, and skilfull in feates of armes, or in seruice of the Noble: But nedefull it is for him by discretion to make himselfe prayse worthy, and by vanquishing of him self to open the gate to fame, whereby he may euerlastingly make himselfe glorious to all posteritie. Loue pricketh and prouoketh the spirit to do wel, I do confesse, but that affection ought to be addressed to some vertuous end, tending to mariage, for otherwise that vertuous image shall be soyled with the villanie of beastly pleasure. Alas (said he,) how easie it is to dispute, when the thing is absent, which can bothe force and violently assaile the bulwarks of most constant hearts. I full well doe see the trothe, and doe feele the thing that is good, and know what behoueth me to follow: but when I view that diuine beautie of my Ladie, hir graces, wisdome, behauior and curtesie, when I see hir to cast so louing an eie vpon me, that she vseth so great familiaritie, that she forgetteth the greatnesse of hir house to abase hir self for my respect: how is it possible that I should be so foolish to dispise a duetie so rare and precious, and to set light by that which the Noblest would pursue with all reuerence and indeuor? Shall I be so much voide of wisedome to suffer the yong Princesse to see hir self contempned of me, to conuert hir loue to teares, by setting hir mynde vpon an other, to seeke mine ouerthrow? Who knoweth not the furie of a woman? specially of the Noble dame, by seeing hir self despised? No, no, she loueth me, and I will be hir seruaunt, and vse the fortune proffred. Shal I be the first simple Gentleman that hath married or loued a Princesse? Is it not more honourable for me to settle my minde vpon a place so highe, than vpon some simple wenche by whome I shall neither attaine profit, or aduauncement? *Baldouine* of *Flaunders*, did not hee a Noble enterprise when he caried away *Iudith* the daughter of the *French* King, as she was passing vpon the seas into England, to be married to the king of that Countrey? I am neither Pirat nor aduenturer, for that the Ladie loueth me. What wrong doe I then to any person by yelding loue againe? Is not she at

libertie ? To whome ought she to make accompt of hir dedes and do-
ings, but to God alone and to hir owne conscience ? I will loue hir,
and cary like affection for the loue which I know and see that she
beareth vnto me, being assured that the same is directed to good end,
and that a woman so wise as she is, will not commit a fault so filthy, as
to blemish and spot hir honor." Thus *Bologna* framed the plot to inter-
taine the Duchesse (albeit hir loue alredy was fully bent vpon him)
and fortified him self against all mishap and perillous chaunce that
might succeede, as ordinarily you see that louers conceiue all things
for their aduauntage, and fantasie dreames agreable to that which
they most desire, resembling the mad and Bedlem persons, which
haue before their eies, the figured fansies which cause the conceit of
their furie, and stay themselues vpon the vision of that, which most
troubleth their offended brain. On the other side, the Duchesse was
in no lesse care of hir louer, the wil of whom was hid and secrete,
which more did vexe and torment hir, than the fire of loue that burned
hir so feruently. She could not tell what way to hold, to do him understand hir heart and affection. She feared to discouer the same vnto
him, doubting either of some fond and rigorous answer, or of reueling
of hir mind to him, whose presence pleased hir more than all the men
of the world. "Alas (said she,) am I happed into so strange misery,
that with mine own mouth I must make request to him, which with al
humilitie ought to offer me his seruice ? Shall a Ladie of such bloud
as I am, be constrained to sue, wher all other be required by impor-
tunat instance of their suters ? * Ah loue, loue, what so euer he was
that clothed thee with such puissance, I dare say he was the cruel
enimie of mans fredom. It is impossible that thou hadst thy being in
heauen, sith the clemencie and courteous influence of the same in-
uesteth man with better benefits, than to suffer hir nourse children to
be intreated with such rigor. He lieth which sayth that *Venus* is thy
mother, for the sweetenesse and good grace that resteth in that pitifull
Goddesse, who taketh no pleasure to see louers perced with so egre
trauails as that which afflicteth my heart. It was some fierce cogitation
of *Saturne* that brought thee forth, and sent thee into the world to
breake the ease of them which liue at rest without any passion or grief.
Pardon me Loue, if I blaspheme thy maiestie, for the stresse and end-
lesse grief wherein I am plunged, maketh me thus to roue at large,
and the doubts which I conceiue, do take away the health and soundnesse of my mind, the little experience in thy schole causeth this
amaze in me, to be solicited with desire that countersayeth the duetie,
honor, and reputation of my state: the partie whome I loue, is a
Gentleman, vertuous, valiant, sage, and of good grace. In this there
is no cause to blame Loue of blindnesse, for all the inequalitie of our

* Alas . . . : I. i. 441–2.

houses, apparant vpon the first sight and shew of the same. But from whence issue the Monarches, Princes and greater Lords, but from the naturall and common masse of earth, whereof other men doe come? what maketh these differences betwene those that loue eche other, if not the sottish opinion which we conceiue of greatnesse, and preheminence: as though naturall affections be like to that ordained by the fantasie of men in their lawes extreme. * And what greater right haue Princes to ioyn with a simple gentlewoman, than the Princesse to mary a Gentleman, and such as *Anthonio Bologna* is, in whome heauen and nature haue forgotten nothing to make him equall with them which marche amongs the greatest. I thinke we be the daily slaues of the fond and cruell fantasie of those Tyraunts, which say they haue puissance ouer vs: and that straining our will to their tirannie, we be still bound to the chaine like the galley slaue. ** No no, *Bologna* shall be my husband, for of a friend I purpose to make him my loyall and lawfull husband, meaning therby not to offend God and men togither, and pretend to liue without offense of conscience, whereby my soule shall not be hindred for anything I do, by marying him whom I so straungely loue. I am sure not to be deceiued in Loue. He loueth me so much or more as I do him, but he dareth not disclose the same, fearing to be refused and cast off with shame. Thus two united wils, and two hearts tied togither with equal knot cannot choose but bring forth fruites worthie of such societie. *** Let men say what they list, I will do none otherwise than my head and mind haue already framed. Semblably I neede not make accompt to any persone for my fact, my body, and reputation being in full libertie and freedome. The bond of mariage made, shall couer the fault which men would deeme, and leauing mine estate, I shall do no wrong but to the greatnesse of my house, which maketh me amongs men right honorable. But these honors be nothing worth, where the minde is voide of contentation, and where the heart prickt forward by desire leaueth the body and mind restlesse without quiet." Thus the Duchesse founded hir enterprise, determining to mary hir housholde Maister, seeking for occasion and time, meete for disclosing of the same, and albeit that a certaine naturall shamefastnesse, which of custome accompanieth Ladies, did close hir mouth, and made hir to deferre for a certaine time the effect of hir resolued minde, yet in the end vanquished with loue and impacience, she was forced to breake of silence, and to assure hir self in him, reiecting feare conceiued of shame, to make hir waie to pleasure, which she lusted more than marriage, the same seruing hir, but for a Maske and couerture to hide her follies and shamelesse lusts, for which she did the penance that hir follie

* But . . . : II. i. 101-4.   ** we . . . : IV. ii. 27-8.
*** Thus . . . : I. i. 480 and 487.

deserued. For no colorable dede or deceitful trompery can serue the
excuse of any notable wickednesse. She then throughly persuaded in
hir intent, dreamyng and thinking of nought else, but vpon the im-
bracement of hir *Bologna*, ended and determined hir conceits and
pretended follies: and vpon a time sent for him vp into hir chamber,
as commonly she did for the affaires and matters of hir house, and
taking him aside vnto a window, hauing prospect into a garden, she
knew not how to begin hir talk: (for the heart being seased, the minde
troubled, and the wittes out of course, the tongue failed to doe his
office,) in such wise, as of long time she was vnable to speake one
onely woord. Hee surprised with like affection, was more astonned by
seeing the alteration of his Ladie. So the two Louers stoode still like
Images beholding one another, without any mouing at all, vntil the
Ladie the hardiest of them bothe, as feeling the most vehement and
greatest grief, tooke *Bologna* by the hand, and dissembling what she
thought, vsed this or such like language: "If any other besides your
self, Gentleman, should vnderstand the secretes which now I purpose
to disclose, I doubt what speeche were necessary to colour my
woords: But being assured of your discretion and wisdom, and with
what perfection nature hath indued you, and Arte, hauing accomplished that in you which nature did begin to work, as one bred and
brought vp in the royall Court of the second *Alphonse*, of *Ferdinando*
and *Frederick* of *Aragon* my cousins, I wil make no doubt at all to
manifest to you the hidden secretes of my heart, being well persuaded
that when you shall both heare and sauor my reasons, and tast the
light which I bring forthe for me, easily you may iudge that mine
aduise cannot be other, than iust and reasonable. But if your conceits
shall straye from that which I shal speak, and deeme not good of that
which I determine, I shall be forced to thinke and say that they which
esteeme you wise and sage, and to be a man of good and ready wit, be
maruelously deceiued. Notwithstanding my heart foretelleth that it
is impossible for maister *Bologna* to wandre so farre from equitie, but
that by and by he wil enter the lystes, and discerne the white from
black, and the wrong from that which is iust and right. For so much
as hitherto I neuer saw thing done by you, which preposterated or
peruerted the good iudgement that all the world esteemeth to shine
in you, the same well manifested and declared by your tongue, the
right iudge of the mind: you know and see how I am a widow through
the death of that noble Gentleman of good remembrance, the Duke
my Lord and husband: you be not ignoraunt also, that I haue liued
and gouerned my self in such wise in my widow state, as there is no
man so hard and seuere of iudgement, that can blason reproche of me
in that which apperteineth to the honesty and reputation of such a
Ladie as I am, bearing my port so right, as my conscience yeldeth no

remorse, supposing that no man hath wherewith to bite and accuse me. Touching the order of the goods of the Duke my sonne, I have vsed them with such diligence and discretion, as bisides the dettes which I haue discharged sithens the death of my Lord, I haue purchased a goodly Manor in *Calabria*, and haue annexed the same to the Dukedom of his heire: and at this day doe not owe one pennie to any creditor that lent mony to the Duke, which he toke vp to furnish the charges in the warres, which he sustained in the seruice of the Kings our soueraine Lords in the late warres for the kingdome of *Naples*. I haue as I suppose by this meanes stopped the slaunderous mouth, and giuen cause vnto my sonne, during his life to accompt himself bound vnto his mother. Now hauing till this time liued for other, and made my self subiect more than Nature could beare, I am entended to chaunge both my life and condition. I haue till thys time run, trauailed, and remoued to the Castels and Lordships of the Dukedome, to *Naples* and other places, being in mind to tary as I am a widow. But what? new affaires and new councel hath possest my mind. I haue trauailed and pained my self inough, I haue too long abidden a widowes life, I am determined therefore to prouide a husband, * who by louing me, shal honor and cherish me, according to the loue which I shal bear to him, and my desert. For to loue a man without mariage, God defend my heart should euer think, and shall rather die a hundred thousand deathes, than a desire so wicked shold soile my conscience, knowing well that a woman which setteth hir honor to sale, is lesse than nothing, and deserueth not that the common aire shold breathe vpon hir, for all the reuerence that men do beare or make them. I accuse no person, albeit that many noble women haue their forheds marked, with the blame of dishonest life, and being honored of some, be neuerthelesse the common fable of the people. ** To the intent then that such mishap happen not to me, and perceiuing my self vnable stil thus to liue, being yong as I am, and (God be thanked) neither deformed nor yet painted, I had rather be the louing wife of a simple feere, than the Concubine of a king or great Prince. And what? is the mightie Monarche able to wash away the fault of his wife which hath abandoned him contrary to the duty and honesty which the vndefiled bed requireth? no les then Princesses that whilom trespassed with those which wer of baser stuffe than themselues. *Mesalina* with her imperial robe could not so wel couer hir faultes, but that the Historians do defame hir with the name and title of a common woman. *Faustina* the wife of the sage Monarch *Marcus Aurelius*, gained lyke report by rendring hir self to others pleasure, bisides hir lawful spouse. To mary my self to one that is mine equall, it is impossible, for so much as there is no Lord in all

* I . . . : I. i. 387.   ** many . . . : III. i. 24–7.

this Countrey meete for my degree, but is to olde of age, the rest
being dead in these later warres. To mary a husband that yet is but a
child, is follie extreeme, for the inconueniences which daily chaunce
thereby, and the euil intreatie that Ladies do receiue when they come
to age, and their nature waxe cold, by reason whereof, imbracements
be not so fauorable, and their husbands glutted with ordinary meat
vse to run in exchange. Wherefore I am resolued without respite or
delay, to choose some wel qualitied and renoumed Gentleman, that
hath more vertue than richesse, of good Fame and brute, to the intent
I may make him my Lord, espouse and husband. For I cannot imploy
my loue vpon treasure, which may be taken away, where richesse of
the minde do faile, and shall be better content to see an honest
Gentleman with little reuenue to be praised and commended of euery
man for his good deedes, than a rich carle curssed and detested of all
the world. Thus much I say, and it is the summe of all my secretes,
wherein I pray your Councell and aduise. I know that some wil be
offended wyth my choise, and the Lords my brothers, specially the
Cardinall will think it straunge, and receiue the same with ill diges-
ture, that muche a do shall I haue to be agreed with them and to
remoue the grief which they shall conceiue against me for this mine
enterprise: wherefore I would the same should secretely be kept,
vntil without perill and daunger either of my self or of him, whome
I pretende to mary, I may publish and manifest, not my loue but the
mariage which I hope in God shall soon be consummate and accomplished with one, whome I doe loue better than my self, and who as
I full well do know, doeth loue me better than his owne proper life."
Maister *Bologna*, which till then harkned to the Oration of the
Duchesse without mouing, feeling himself touched so neere, and
hearing that his Ladie had made hir approche for mariage, stode stil
astonned, his tongue not able to frame one word, * only fantasied a
thousand *Chimeraes* in the aire, and formed like numbre of imagina-
tions in his minde, not able to coniecture what hee was, to whome the
Duchesse had vowed hir loue, and the possession of hir beauty. He
could not thinke that this ioy was prepared for himself for that his
Ladie spake no woord of him, and he lesse durst open his mouth, and
yet was wel assured that she loued him beyond measure. Notwithstanding knowing the ficklenesse and vnstable heart of women, he
sayd vnto himself that she would chaunge hir minde, for seing him
to be so great a Cowarde, as not to offer hys service to a Ladie by
whome he saw himself so manie times bothe wantonly looked vpon,
and intertained with some secresie more than familiar. ** The Duchesse which was a fine and subtile dame, seeing hir friend rapt with
the passion, and standing stil vnmoueable through feare, pale and

---

* Maister . . . : I. i. 450–5. ** he sayd . . . : I. i. 425–6.

amazed, as if hee had bene accused and condempned to die, knew
by that countenaunce and astonishment of *Bologna*, that she was perfectly beloued of him: and so meaning not to suffer hym any longer
to continue in that amaze, ne yet to further fear him, wyth hir dissembled and fained mariage of any other but with him, she toke him
by the hand, and beholding him with a wanton and luring eye, (in
such sort as the curious Philosophers themselues would awake, * if
such a Lampe and torch did shine within their studies), she sayde
thus vnto hym: "Seignor *Anthonio*, I pray you be of good cheere, and
torment not your self for any thing that I haue said: I know well, and
of long time haue perceyued what good and faithfull loue you beare
me, and with what affection you haue serued me, sithens first you
vsed my companie. Thinke me not to be so ignorant, but that I know
ful wel by outward signes, what secretes be hid in the inner heart: and
that coniectures many times doe giue me true and certaine knowledge of concealed things. And am not so foolish to thinke you to be
so vndiscrete, but that you haue marked my countenaunce and
maner, and therby haue knowen that I haue bene more affectioned
to you, than to any other. For that cause (sayd she, straining him by
the hand very louingly, and with cherefull coloure in hir face) I swear
vnto you, and doe promise that if you so thinke meete, it shall be none
other but your self whom I wil haue, and desire to take to husband
and lawfull spouse, assuring my self so much of you, as the loue which
so long time hath ben hidden and couered in our hearts, shal appeare
by so euident proofe, as only death shal end and vndoe the same."
The gentleman hearing such sodain talk, and the assurance of that
which he most wished for, albeit he saw the daunger extreme wherunto he launched himself by espousing this great Ladie, and the enimies he shold get by entring such aliance: notwithstanding building
vpon vaine hope, and thinking at length that the choler of the
Aragon brothers would passe away if they understoode the mariage,
determined to pursue the purpose, and not to refuse that great preferment, being so prodigally offred, for which cause he answered his
Lady in this maner. "If it were in my power madame, to bring to
passe that, which I desire for your seruice by acknowledging of the
benifits and fauors which you depart vnto me, as my mind presenteth
thanks for the same, I wold think my self the happiest Gentleman
that lyueth, and you the best serued Princesse of the world. For one
better beloued (I dare presume to say, and so long as I liue wil
affirm) is not to be found. If til this time I delayed to open that which
now I discouer vnto you, I beseeche you Madame to impute it to the
greatnesse of your estate, and to the duetie of my calling and office in
your house, being not seemely for a seruant to talk of such secretes

* in . . .: III. ii. 40–2.

with his Ladie and mistresse. And truely the pain which I haue indured to holde my peace, and to hide my griefe, hath bene more noysome to me than one hundred thousand like sorowes together, although it had ben lawfull to haue reuealed them to some trusty friend: I do not deny madame, but of long time you did perceiue my follie and presumption, by addressing my minde so high, as to the *Aragon* bloud, and to such a Princesse as you be. And who can beguile the eye of a Louer, specially of hir, whose Paragon for good minde, wisedom and gentlenesse is not? And I confesse to you bisides, that I haue most euidently perceiued how certain loue hath lodged in your gracious heart, wherwith you bare me greater affection than you did to any other within the compasse of your familie. But what? Great Ladies hearts be fraught with secretes and conceits of other effects than the minds of simple women, which caused me to hope for none other guerdon of my loyal and faithfull affection, than death, and the same very short, sith that litle hope accompanied with great, nay rather extreme passion, is not able to giue sufficient force, both to suffer and to stablish my heart with constancie. Now for so much as of your motion, grace, curtesie and liberalitie the same is offred, and that it pleaseth you to accept me for yours, I humbly beseche you to dispose of me not as husband, but of one which is, and shalbe your seruaunt for euer, and such as is more ready to obey, than you to commaund. It resteth now Madame, to consider how, and in what wise our affairs are to be directed, that things being in assurance, you may so liue without peril and brute of slaunderous tongues, as your good fame and honest report may continue without spot or blemish."

Beholde the first Acte of the Tragedie, and the prouision of the fare which afterwardes sent them bothe to their graue, who immediately gaue their mutuall Faith: and the houre was assigned the next day, that the fair Princesse shold be in hir chamber alone, attended vpon with one only Gentlewoman which had ben brought vp with the Duchesse from hir cradle, and was made priuie to the heauy mariage of those two louers which was consummate in hir presence. And for the present time they passed the same in words, for ratification wherof they went to bed togither. But the pain in the end was greater than the pleasure, and had ben better for them bothe, yea and also for the third, that they had shewed them selues so wyse in the deede, as discrete in keping silence of that which was done. For albeit their mariage was secrete, and therby politikely gouerned them selues in their stelthes and robberies of loue, and that *Bologna* more oft held the state of the steward of the house by day, than of Lord of the same, and by night supplied that place, * yet in the end, the thing was per-ceiued which they desired to be closely kept. And as it is impossible

* *Bologna* . . .: III. ii. 7–8.

to till and culture a fertile ground, but that the same must yelde some
frute, euen so the Duchesse after many pleasures (being ripe and
plentiful) became with child, which at the first astonned the maried
couple: neuerthelesse the same so well was prouided for, as the first
childbedde was kept secrete, and none did know thereof. The childe
was nourced in the towne, and the father desired to haue him named
Frederick, for remembraunce of the parents of his wife. Now fortune
which lieth in daily waite and ambushment, and liketh not that men
shold long loiter in pleasure and passetime, being enuious of such
prosperity, cramped so the legges of our two louers, as they must
needes change their game, and learne some other practise: for so
much as the Duchesse being great with childe again, and deliuered
of a girle, the businesse of the same was not so secretely done, but
that it was discouered. And it suffised not that the brute was noised
through *Naples*, but that the sound flew further off. As eche man doth
know that rumor hath many mouthes, who with the multitude of his
tongues and Trumps, proclaimeth in diuers and sundry places, the
things which chaunce in al the regions of the earth, euen so that
babling foole caried the newes of that second childbed to the eares
of the Cardinall of *Aragon* the Duchesse brother, being then at *Rome*.
Think what ioy and pleasure the *Aragon* brothers had, by hearing the
report of their sisters facte. I dare presume to say, that albeit they
were extremely wroth with this happened slaunder, and with the dishonest fame whych the Duchesse had gotten throughout *Italie*, yet
farre greater was their sorrow and grief, for that they did not know
what hee was that so courteously was allied to their house, and in their
loue had increased their ligneage. And therfore swelling wyth despite, and rapt with furie to see themselues so defamed by one of their
bloud, they purposed by all meanes whatsoever it cost them, to know
the lucky louer that had so wel tilled the Duchesse their sisters field. *
Thus desirous to remoue that shame from before their eyes, and to
be reuenged of a wrong so notable, they sent espials round about, and
scoutes to *Naples*, to view and spy the behauior and talk of the
Duchesse, to settle some certaine iudgement of him, whych steal-
ingly was become their brother in law. The Duchesse Court being in
thys trouble, shee dyd continually perceiue in hir house, hir brothers
men to mark hir countenance, and to note those that came thither to
visite hir, and to whom she vsed greatest familiaritie, ** bicause it is
impossible but that the fire, although it be raked vnder the ashes,
must give some heat. And albeit the two louers vsed eche others companie, without shewing any signe of their affection, yet they purposed
to chaunge their estate for a time, by yelding truce to their pleasures.
Yea, and although *Bologna* was a wise and prouident personage, fear-

* tilled . . .: II. v. 19.   ** mark . . .: I. i. 252–5.

ing to be surprised vpon the fact, or that the Gentlewoman of the Chamber corrupted with Money, or forced by feare, shold pronounce any matter to his hinderance or disauantage, determined to absent himself from *Naples*, yet not so sodainly but that hee made the Duchesse his faithfull Ladie and companion priuie of his intent. And as they were secretely in their chamber togither, hee vsed these or such like woords: "Madame, albeit the right good intent and vn-stained conscience, is free from fault, yet the iudgement of men hath further relation to the exterior apparance, than to vertues force and innocencie it self, as ignorant of the secrets of the thought: and so in things that be wel done, we must of necessitie fall into the sentence of those, whom beastly affection rauisheth more, than ruled reason. You see the solempne watch and garde which the seruaunts of the Lords your brothers do within your house, and the suspicion which they haue conceiued by reason of your second childbed, and by what meanes they labor truely to know how your affaires proceede, and things do passe. I feare not death where your seruice may be ad-uaunced, but if herein the maiden of your chamber be not secrete, if she be corrupted, and if she kepe not close that which she ought to do, it is not ignorant to you that it is the losse of my life, and shall die sus-pected to be a whoremonger and varlet, even I, (I say) shall incurre that perill, which am your true and lawfull husband. Thys separation chaunceth not by Iustice or desert, sith the cause is too righteous for vs: but rather your brethren will procure my death, when I shall thinke the same in greatest assurance. If I had to do but with one or two, I wold not change the place, ne march one step from *Naples*, but be assured, that a great band, and the same wel armed will set vpon me. I pray you madame suffer me to retire for a time, for I am assured that when I am absent, they will neuer soile their hands, or imbrue their sweards in your bloud. If I doubted any thing at al of perill touching your owne person, I had rather a hundred hundred times die in your companie, than liue to see you no more. But out of doubt I am, that if the things were discouered, and they knew you to be be-gotten with childe by me, you should be safe, where I shold sustaine the penaunce of the fact, committed without fault or sinne. And ther-fore I am determined to goe from *Naples*, to order mine affaires, and to cause my Reuenue to be brought to the place of mine abode, and from thence to *Ancona*, vntil it pleaseth God to mitigate the rage of your brethren, and recouer their good wils to consent to our mariage. But I meane not to doe or conclude any thing without your aduise. And if this intent doe not like you, giue me councell Madame, what I were best to doe, that both in life and death you may knowe your faithfull seruaunt and louing husband is ready to obey and please you."

This good Ladie hearing hir husbands discourse, vncertain what to doe, wept bitterly, as wel for grief to lose his presence, as for that she felt hir self with child the third time. The sighes and teares, the sobbes and heauie lookes, which she threwe forth vpon hir sorowfull husband, gaue sufficient witnesse of hir paine and grief. And if none had heard hir, I thinke hir playntes woulde haue well expressed hir inwarde smarte of minde. But like a wise Ladie, seeing the alleaged reasons of hir husband, licensed him, although against hir minde, not without vtterance of these few words, before hee went out of hir Chamber: "Deare husband, if I were so well assured of the affection of my brethren, as I am of my maides fidelitie, I would entreat you not to leaue me alone: specially in the case I am, being with childe. But knowing that to be iust and true which you haue sayd, I am content to force my wil for a certaine time, that hereafter we may liue at rest together, ioyning our selues in the companie of our children and familie, voide of those troubles, which great Courts ordinarily beare within the compasse of their Palaces. Of one thing I must intreat you, that so often as you can by trustie messenger, you send me woord and intelligence of your health and state, bicause the same shal bryng vnto me greater pleasure and contentation, than the welfare of mine owne: and bicause also, vpon such occurrentes as shall chaunce, I may prouyde for mine owne affaires, the suretie of my self, and of our children." In saying so, she embraced him very amorously, and he kissed hir wyth so great sorrow and grief of heart, as the soule thought in that extasie out of his body to take hir flight, sorowful beyond mesure so to leue hir whome he loued, * for the great curtesies and honor which he had receiued at hir hands. In the end, fearing that the *Aragon* espials wold come and perceiue them in those priuities, *Bologna* tooke his leaue, and bad hys Ladie and spouse Farewell.

And this was the second Acte of this Tragicall Historie, to see a fugitife husband secretely to mary, especially hir, vpon whom he ought not so much as to loke but with feare and reuerence. Beholde here (O ye foolish louers) a Glasse of your lightnesse, and ye women, the course of your fonde behauior. It behoueth not the wise sodainly to execute their first motions and desires of their heart, for so much as they may be assured that pleasure is pursued so neare with a repentance so sharp to be suffred, and hard to be digested, as their voluptuousnesse shall vtterly discontent them. True it is, that mariages be done in Heauen, and performed in earth, but that saying may not be applied to fooles, which gouerne themselues by carnall desires, whose scope is but pleasure, and the reward many times equal to their follie. Shall I be of opinion that a housholde seruaunt ought to sollicite, nay rather suborne the daughter his Lord without punishment, or that a

* kissed . . . : III. v. 88–90.

vile and abiect person dare to mount vpon a Princes bed? No no, pollicie requireth order in all, and eche wight ought to be matched according to their qualitie, without making a pastime of it to couer our follies, and know not of what force loue and desteny be, except the same be resisted. A goodly thing it is to loue, but where reason loseth his place, loue is without his effect, and the sequele rage and madnesse. Leaue we the discourse of those which beleue that they be constrained to folowe the force of their minde, and may easily subdue themselues to the lawes of vertue and honesty, like one that thrusteth his head into a sack, and thinks he can not get out, such people do please themselues in their losse, and think all well that is noisom to their health, daily folowing their contrarie. Come we again then to sir *Bologna*, who after he had left his wife in hir Castell, went to *Naples*, and hauing sessed a rent vpon hir landes, and leuied a good summe of money, he repaired to *Ancona*, a Citie of the patrimonie of the *Romane* Church, whither he caried his two children, which he had of the Duchesse, causing the same to be brought vp with such diligence and care, as is to be thought a father wel affectioned to his wife would doe, and who delighted to see a braunche of the tree, that to him was the best beloued fruit of the world. There he hired a house for his train, and for those that waited vpon his wife, who in the meane time was in great care, and could not tell of what woode to make hir arowes, perceiuing that hir belly began to swell, and grow to the time of hir deliuerie, seeing that from day to day, hir brothers seruaunts were at hir back, voide of councel and aduise, if one euening she had not spoken to the Gentlewoman of hir chamber, touching the douts and peril wherin she was, not knowing how she might be deliuered from the same. That maiden was gentle and of a good minde and stomake, and loued hir mistresse very derely, and seeing hir so amazed and tormenting hir self to death, minding to fray hir no further, ne to reproue hir of hir fault, which could not be amended, but rather to prouide for the daunger whereunto she had hedlong cast hir self, gaue hir this aduise: "How now Madame (said she,) is that wisdom which from your childhode hath bene so familiar in you, dislodged from your brest in time, when it ought chiefly to rest for incountring of those mishaps that are comming vpon vs? Thinke you to auoid the dangers, by thus tormenting your self, except you set your hands to the work, thereby to giue the repulse to aduerse fortune? I haue heard you many times speake of the constancie and force of minde, which ought to shine in the dedes of Princesses, more clerely than amongs those dames of baser house, and which ought to make them appere like the sunne amid the little starres. And yet I see you now astonned, as though you had neuer forseene that aduersitie chaunceth so wel to catch the great within his clouches, as the base and simple sort. Is it but now, that you haue called to remembraunce, that which might insue your mariage with sir *Bologna*? Did hys only presence assure you against the waits of fortune, and is it the thought of paines, feares and frights, which now turmoileth your dolorous mind? Ought you thus to vexe your self, when néde it is to think how to saue both your honor, and the frute within your intrailes? If your sorow be so great ouer sir *Bologna*, and if you feare your childbed wil be descried, why seeke you not meanes to attempt some voyage, for couering of the fact, to beguile the eyes of them which so diligently do watch you? Doth your heart faile you in that matter? Whereof do you dreame? Why sweat and freat you before you make me answer?" "Ah sweete heart (answered the Duchesse,) if thou feltest the paine which I do suffer, thy tongue wold not be so much at will, as thou shewest it now to be for reprofe of my smal constancie. I do sorow specially for the causes which thou alleagest, and aboue all, for that I know wel, that if my brethren had neuer so litle intelligence of my being with child, I were vndone and my life at an end, ★ and per-aduenture poore wench, thou shouldest beare the penaunce for my sinne. But what way can I take, that stil these candles may not giue light, and I may be voided of the traine which ought to wayt vpon my brethren? I thinke if I should descend into Hel, they would know, whither any shadowe there were in loue with me. Now gesse if I should trauaile the Realme, or retire to any other place, whither they wold leaue me at peace? Nothing lesse, sith they would sodainly sus-pect that the cause of my departure proceeded of desire to liue at libertie, to dallie wyth him, whome they suspect to be other than my lawfull husbande. And it may be as they be wicked and suspicious, and will doubt of my greatnesse, so shall I be farre more infortunate by trauailyng than here in miserie amidde myne anguishe: and you the rest that be keepers of my Councell, shall fal into greater daunger, vpon whome no doubt they wil be reuenged, and flesh themselues for your vnhappy waiting and attendance vpon vs." "Madame (said the bolde maiden,) be not afraide, and follow mine aduise. For I hope that it shall be the meanes both to see your spouse, and to rid those troublesome verlets out of your house, and in like manner safely to deliuer you into good assuraunce." "Say your minde (sayd the Ladie,) for it may be that I will gouerne my self according to the same." "Mine aduise is then, (sayd the Gentlewoman,) to let your houshold vnderstand, that you haue made a vow to visite the holy Temple of our Lady of *Loretto*, (a famous place of Pilgrimage in *Italie*) and that you commaund your traine to make themselues ready to waite vpon you for accomplishment of your deuotion, and from thence you shall take your iourney to soiorne at *Ancona*, whither be-

★ I . . . : III. ii. 111 and 164.

fore you depart, you shall send your moueables and plate, with such
money as you shall think necessarie. And afterwardes God will performe the rest, and through his holy mercy will guide and direct all
your affaires." The Duchesse hearing the mayden speake those
woords, and amazed of hir sodaine inuention, could not forbeare to
embrace and kisse hir, blessing the houre wherin she was borne, and
that euer she chaunced into hir companie, to whome afterwardes she
sayd: "My wench, I had well determined to giue ouer mine estate
and noble porte, ioyfully to liue like a simple Gentlewoman with my
deare and welbeloued husband, but I could not deuise how I should
conueniently departe this Countrey wythout suspition of some follie:
and sith that thou hast so well instructed me for bringing the same
to passe, I promise thee that so diligently thy councel shal be performed, as I see the same to be right good and necessarie. For rather
had I see my husband, being alone without title of Duchesse or great
Lady, than to liue without him beautified with the graces and foolish
names of honor and preheminence."* This deuised plot was no
soner grounded, but she gaue such order for execution of the same,
and brought it to passe wyth such dexteritie, as the Ladie in lesse than
viij. dayes had conueyed and sent the most part of hir moueables, and
specially the chiefest and best to *Ancona,* taking in the meane time hir
way towards *Loretto* after she had bruted hir solempne vow made for
that Pilgrimage. It was not sufficient for this foolish woman to take
a husband, more to glut hir libidinous appetite, than for other occasion, except she added to hir sinne, an other execrable impietie,
making holy places and dueties of deuotion, to be as it were the ministers of hir follie. ** But let vs consider the force of Louers rage,
which so soone as it hath seased vpon the minds of men, we see how
maruellous be the effects thereof, and with what straint and puis-
saunce that madnesse subdueth the wise and strongest worldlings.
Who wold think that a great Ladie wold haue abandoned hir estate,
hir goods and childe, would haue misprised hir honor and reputation,
to folow like a vagabond, a pore and simple Gentleman, *** and him
bisides that was the houshold seruaunt of hir Court ? And yet you see
this great and mightie Duchesse trot and run after the male, like a
female Wolfe or Lionesse (when they goe to sault,) and forget the
Noble bloud of *Aragon* **** wherof she was descended, to couple
hir self almost with the simplest person of all the trimmest Gentlemen
of *Naples.* But turne we not the example of follies, to be a matter of
consequence: for if one or two become bankrupt of their honor, it
foloweth not good Ladies, that their facte should serue for a matche

* rather . . .: III. ii. 276–9.
** added . . .: III. ii. 317–18 and III. iii. 60–1.
*** Who . . .: III. iv. 24–6.   **** Noble . . .: II. v. 21–3.

to your deserts, and much lesse a patron for you to folow. * These
Histories be not written to train and trap you, to pursue the thousand
thousand slippery sleightes of Loues gallantise, but rather carefully
to warn you to behold the semblable faultes, and to serue for a drugge
to discharge the poyson which gnaweth and fretteth the integritie and
soundnesse of the soule. The wise and skilfull Apothecary or compositor of drugges, dresseth Vipers flesh to purge the patient from
hote corrupted bloude, which conceiueth and engendreth Leprosie
within his body. In like manner, the fonde loue, and wicked ribauld-
rie of *Semiramis, Pasiphae, Messalina, Faustina* and *Romida* is
shewed in wryt, that euery of you should feare to be numbred and
recorded amongst such common and dishonorable women. You
Princes and great Lordes read the follies of *Paris,* the adulteries of
Hercules, the daintie and effeminate life of *Sardanapalus,* the tirannie
of *Phalaris, Busiris* or *Dionysius* of *Scicile,* and see the History of
Tiberius, Nero, Caligula, Domitian and *Heliogabalus,* and spare not to
numbre them amongs our wanton youthes which soile themselues
with such villanies more filthily than the swine do in the durt. Al this
intendeth it an instruction for your youth to follow the infection and
whoredome of those monsters ? Better it were all those bokes were
drenched in bottomlesse depth of seas, than christian life by their
meanes shold be corrupted : but the example of the wicked is induced
for to eschue and auoid them as the life of the good and honest is
remembred to frame and addresse our behauior in this world to be
praise worthy and commended. Otherwise the holinesse of sacred
writ shold serue for an argument to the vnthrifty and luxurious to
confirm and approue their beastly and licencious wickednesse. Come
we again then to our purpose: the good Pilgrime of *Loretto* went
forth hir voyage to atchieue hir deuotions, and to visite the Saint for
whose Reliques she was departed the Countrey of the Duke hir
sonne. When she had done hir suffrages at *Loretto,* hir people thought
that the voyage was at an end, and that she wold haue returned again
into hir Countrey. But she said vnto them, that sith she was so neere
Ancona, being but xv. miles off, she would not returne before she had
seen the auncient and goodly city, which diuers Histories do greatly
recommend, as wel for the antiquitie, as for the pleasant seat therof.
All were of hir aduise, and went to see the antiquities of *Ancona,* and
she to renue the pleasures which she had before begon with hir
Bologna, who was aduertised of all hir determination, resting now
like a God, possessed with the iewels and richesse of the Duchesse,
and had taken a faire palace in the great streat of the Citie, by the gate
wherof the train of his Ladie must passe. The Harbinger of the
Duchesse posted before to take vp lodging for the traine: but

* it . . . : III. ii. 286–8.

Bologna offred vnto him his Palace for the Lady. So *Bologna* which was already welbeloued in *Ancona*, and entred new amitie and great acquaintance with the Gentlemen of the Citie, with a goodly troupe of them, went forth to meete his wife, to whome he presented his house, and besought hir that she and hir traine would vouchsafe to lodge with him. She receiued the same very thankfully, and withdrew hir self vnto his house, who conducted hir thither, not as a Husband, but like hym that was hir humble and affectionate seruaunt. But what needeth much discourse of woordes ? The Duchesse knowing that it was impossible but eche man must be priuie to hir facte, and know what secretes hath passed betweene hir and hir Husband, to the ende that no other opinion of hir Childebed should be conceyued, but that which was good and honest, and done since the accomplishment of the mariage, the morrowe after hir arriuall to *Ancona*, assembled all hir traine in the Hall, of purpose no longer to keepe secrete that syr *Bologna* was hir Husbande, and that already she had had two Children by him, and againe was great with childe. And when they were come together after dinner, in the presence of hir husband, she spake vnto them these words: "Gentlemen, and al ye my trusty and louing seruants, highe time it is to manifest to euery of you, the thing which hath ben done before the face, and in the presence of him who knoweth the most obscure and hydden secrets of our thoughts. And needefull it is not to kepe silent that which is neither euill done ne hurtfull to any person. If things could be kept secrete and still remaine vnknown, except they were declared by the doers of them, yet would not I commit the wrong in concealing that, which to discouer vnto you doth greatly delite me, and deliuereth my mind from exceeding grief, in such wise as if the flames of my desire could breake out with such violence, as the fire hath taken heat within my mind, ye shold see the smoke mount vp with greater smoulder than that which the mount *Gibel* doeth vomit forth at certaine seasons of the yeare. And to the intent I may not keepe you long in this suspect, this secrete fire within my heart, and that which I will cause to flame in open aire, is a certain opinion which I conceiue for a mariage by me made certaine yeares past, at what time I chose and wedded a husband to my fantasie and liking, desirous no longer to liue in widow state, and vnwilling to doe the thing that should preiudice and hurt my conscience. The same is done, and yet in one thing I haue offended, which is by long keeping secrete the performed mariage: for the wicked brute dispearsed through the realme by reason of my childbed, one yere past, hath displeased some, howbeit my conscience receiueth comfort, for that the same is free from fault or blot. Now know ye therfore what he is, whome I acknowledge for my Lord and spouse, and who it is that lawfully hath me espoused in the presence of this Gentlewoman whom you see, which is the witnesse of our Nuptials and accorde of mariage. This gentleman here present *Antonio Bologna*, is he to whom I haue sworn and giuen my faith, and hee againe to me hath ingaged his owne. He it is whom I accompt for my spouse and husband, and with whome henceforth I meane to rest and continue. In consideration wherof, if there be any heere amongs you all, that shall mislike of my choise, and is willing to wait vpon my sonne the Duke, I meane not to let them of their intent, praying them faithfully to serue him and to be carefull of his person, and to be vnto him so honest and loyall, as they haue bene to me so long as I was their mistresse. But if any of you desire stil to make your abode with me, and to be partakers of my wealth and woe, I wil so entertain him, as hee shall haue good cause to be contented, if not, depart ye hence to *Malfi*, and the steward shall prouide for either of you according to your degree: for touching my self I do minde no more to be termed an infamous Duchesse: rather had I be honored with the title of a simple Gentlewoman, or with that estate which she can haue that hath an honest husband, and with whom she holdeth faithfull and loyall companie, than reuerenced with the glory of a Princesse, sub-iect to the despite of slaunderous tongues. Ye know (said she to *Bologna*) what hath passed betwene vs, and God is the witnesse of the integritie of my Conscience, wherefore I pray you bring forth our children, that each man may beholde the fruites raised of our alliance." Hauing spoken those words, and the children brought forth into the hall, all the companie stode stil so astonned with that new success and tale, as though hornes sodainely had started forth their heads, and rested vnmoueable and amazed, like the great marble piller of *Rome* called *Pasquile*, for so much as they neuer thought, ne coniectured that *Bologna* was the successor of the Duke of *Malfi* in his mariage bed.

This was the preparatiue of the *Catastrophe* and bloudie end of this Tragedie. For of all the Duchesse seruaunts, there was not one that was willing to continue with their auncient mistresse, who with the faithful maiden of hir chamber remained at *Ancona*, enioying the ioyful embracements of hir husband, in al such pleasure and delights as they doe, which hauing liued in feare, be set at liberty, and out of al suspition, plunged in a sea of ioy, and fleting in the quiet calme of al passetime, where *Bologna* had none other care, but how to please his best beloued, and she studied nothing else but how to loue and obey him, as the wife ought to do hir husband. But this faire weather lasted not long, for although the ioyes of men do not long endure, and wast in litle time, yet delights of louers be lesse firme and stedfast, and passe away almost in one moment of an hour. Now the seruaunts of the Duchesse which were retired, and durst tary no longer with hir, fearing the fury of the Cardinal of *Aragon* brother to the Ladie, the very day they departed from *Ancona*, deuised amongs themselues that one of them shold ride in post to *Rome*, to aduertise the Cardinal of the Ladies mariage, to the intent that the *Aragon* brethren shold conceiue no cause to accuse them of felonie and treason. That determination spedily was accomplished, one posting towards *Rome*, and the rest galloping to the Countrey and Castels of the Duke. These newes reported to the Cardinal and his brother, it may be coniectured how grieuously they toke the same, and for that they were not able to digest them with modestie, the yongest of the brethren, yelled forth a thousand cursses and despites, against the simple sexe of womankind. * "Ha (said the Prince, transported with choler, ** and driuen in to deadly furie,) what law is able to punish or restrain the foolish indiscretion of a woman, that yeldeth hir self to hir own desires? What shame is able to bridle and withdrawe hir from hir minde and madnesse? Or with what feare is it possible to snaffle them from execution of their filthinesse? There is no beast be he neuer so wilde, but man sometime may tame, and bring to his lure and order. The force and diligence of man is able to make milde the strong and proud, and to ouertake the swiftest beast and foule, or otherwise to attaine the highest and deepest things of the world: but this incarnate diuelish beast the woman, no force can surmount hir, no swiftnesse can approche hir mobilitie, no good mind can preuent hir sleights and deceites, they seeme to be procreated and borne against all order of nature, and to liue without law, which gouerneth all other things indued wyth some reason and vnderstanding. But what a great abhomination is this, that a Gentlewoman of such a house as ours is, hath forgotten hir estate, and the greatnesse of hir aliance, besides the nobilitie of hir deceased husband, with the hope of the towarde youth of the Duke hir sonne and our Nephew. Ah false and vile bitch, I sweare by the almightie God and by his blessed wounds, that if I can catch thee, and that wicked knaue thy chosen mate, I will pipe ye both such a galiarde, as ye neuer felt the lyke ioy and mirthe. I will make ye daunce such a bloudy bargenet, as your whorish heate for euer shall be cooled. What abuse haue they committed vnder title of mariage, which was so secretely done, as their Children do witnesse their filthy embracements, but their promise of faith was made in open aire, and serueth for a cloke and visarde for their most filthy whoredome. *** And what if mariage was concluded, be we of so little respect, as the carion beast would not vouchsafe to aduertise vs of hir entent? Or is *Bologna* a man worthy to be allied or mingled with the royall bloud of *Aragon* and *Castille*? **** No no, be hee neuer so

* yelled . . .: II. v. 31–6.   ** transported . . .: II. v. 12–13.

*** serueth . . .: III. iii. 60–1.   **** royall . . .: II. v. 21–3.

good a Gentleman, his race agreeth not with kingly state. But I make
to God a vowe, that neuer will I take one sound and restfull sleepe, *
vntill I haue dispatched that infamous fact from our bloud, and that
the caitife whoremonger be vsed according to his desert." The Cardinall also was out of quiet, grinding his teeth togither, chattering
forthe Jacke and Apes *Pater noster*, promising no better vsage to their
Bologna than his yonger brother did. And the better to intrap them
both (without further sturre for that time) they sent to the Lord
Gismondo Gonsago, the Cardinal of *Mantua*, then Legate for Pope
Iulius the second at *Ancona*, at whose hands they enioyed such
friendship, as *Bologna* and all his familie were commaunded spedily
to auoide the Citie. But for al that the Legate was able to do, of long
time he could not preuaile. *Bologna* had so great intelligence within
Ancona. Neuerthelesse whiles he differred his departure, hee caused
the most part of his train, his children and goods to be conueyed to
Siena, an auncient Citie of *Thoscane*, which for the state and liberties,
had long time bene at warres with the *Florentines*, in such wise as the
very same day that newes came to *Bologna* that he shold departe the
Citie within xv. dayes, hee was ready, and mounted on horseback to
take his flight to *Siena*, which brake for sorrow the hearts of the
Aragon brethren, seeing that they were deceiued and frustrate of
their intent, bicause they purposed by the way to apprehend *Bologna*,
and to cut him in pieces. But what ? the time of his hard luck was not
yet expired, and so the marche from *Ancona* serued not for the
Theatre of those two infortunate louers ouerthrow, who certain
moneths liued in peace in *Thoscane*. The Cardinal night nor day did
sleepe, and his brother stil did wayt to performe his othe of reuenge.
And seeing their enimie out of feare, they dispatched a post to
Alfonso Castruccio, the Cardinal of *Siena*, that he might entreat the
Lord *Borghese*, chief of the seignorie there, that their sister and
Bologna should be banished the Countrey and limits of that Citie,
which with small sute was brought to passe. These two infortunate,
husband and wife, were chased from al places, and so vnlucky as
whilom *Acasta* was, or *Oedipus*, after his fathers death and incestuous
mariage with his mother, vncertain to what Saint to vow themselues,
and to what place to take their flight. In the end they determined to
goe to *Venice*, and to take their flight to *Ramagna*, there to imbarke
themselues for to retire to the sauegarde of the Citie, enuironned with
the sea *Adriaticum*, the richest in *Europa*. But the poore soules
made their reconing there without their hoste, failing half the price
of their banket. For being vpon the territorie of *Forly*, one of the
train a farre off, did see a troupe of horsemen galloping towardes
their company, which by their countenaunce shewed no signe of

---

* But . . . : II. v. 76–9 and IV. i. 23–4.

peace or amitie at all, which made them consider that it was some ambush * of their enimies. The *Neapolitan* Gentleman seeing the onset bending vpon them, began to fear death, not for that he cared at all for his mishap and ruine, but his heart began to cleaue for heauinesse to see his wife and litle children ready to be murdered, and serue for the passetime of the *Aragon* brethrens eyes, for whose sakes he knew himself already predestinate to die, and that for despite of him, and to accelerate his death by the ouerthrow of his, he was assured that they wold kil his children before his face and presence. But what is there to be done, where counsell and meanes to escape do faile ? Ful of teares therfore, astonishment and fear, he expected death so cruel as man could deuise, and was alredy determined to suffer the same with good corage, for any thing that the Duchesse could say vnto him. He might well haue saued himself and his eldest sonne by flight, being both wel mounted vpon two good Turkey horsses, which ran so fast, as the quarrel discharged forth of a crosbow. But he loued too much his wife and children, and wold keepe them companie both in life and death. In the end the good Ladie sayd vnto him: "Sir for all the ioyes and pleasures which you can doe me, for Gods sake saue your self and the little infant next you, who can wel indure the galloping of the horse. For sure I am, that you being out of our companie, we shal not need to fear any hurt. But if you do tary, you wil be the cause of the ruine and ouerthrow of vs all, and receiue therby no profit or aduantage: take this purse therfore, and saue your self, attending better Fortune in time to come." The poore gentleman *Bologna* knowing that his wife had pronounced reason, and perceiuing that it was impossible from that time forth that she or hir traine could escape their hands, taking leaue of hir, and kissing his children not forgetting the money which she offred vnto him, willed his seruants to saue themselues by such meanes as they thought best. So giuing spurrs vnto his horse, he began to flee amaine, and his eldest sonne seeing his father gone, began to followe in like sorte. And so for that time they two were saued by breaking of the intended yll luck like to light vpon them. And in a place to rescue himself at *Venice*, hee turned another way, and in great iourneys arriued at *Millan*. In the meane time the horsemen were approched neere the Duchesse, who seeing that *Bologna* had saued himself, very courteously began to speake vnto the Ladie, were it that the *Aragon* brethren had giuen them that charge, or feared that the Ladie wold trouble them with hir importunate cries and lamentations. One therfore amongs them sayd vnto hir: "Madame, we be commaunded by the Lordes your brethren, to conducte you home vnto your house, that you may receiue again the gouernment of the Duchie, and the

* consider . . . : III. v. 56.

order of the Duke your sonne, and doe maruell very much at your folly, for giuing your self thus to wander the Countrey after a man of so small reputation as *Bologna* is, who when he hath glutted his lusting lecherous mind with the comelinesse of your Noble personage, wil despoil you of your goods and honor, and then take his legs into some strange countrey." The simple Ladie, albeit grieuous it was vnto hir to heare such speech of hir husband, yet held hir peace and dissembled what she thought, glad and well contented with the curtesy done vnto hir, fearing before that they came to kill hir, and thought hir self already discharged, hoping vpon their courteous dealings, that she and hir Children from that time forth should liue in good assuraunce. But she was greatly deceyued, and knew within shorte space after, the good will hir brethren bare vnto hir. For so soone as these gallants had conducted hir into the kingdome of *Naples*, to one of the Castels of hir sonne, she was committed to prison with hir children, and she also that was the secretarie of hir infortunate mariage. Till this time Fortune was contented to proceede with indifferent quiet against those Louers, but henceforth ye shall heare the issue of their little prosperous loue, and how pleasure hauing blinded them, neuer forsoke them vntill it had giuen them the ouerthrow.

It booteth not heere to recite fables or histories, contenting my self that ladies do read without too many weeping teares, the pitiful end of that miserable princesse, who seeing hir self a prisoner in the companie of hir litle children and welbeloued Maiden, paciently liued in hope to see hir brethren appaised, comforting hir self for the escape of hir husband out of the hands of his mortal foes. But hir assurance was changed into an horrible feare, and hir hope to no expectation of suretie, when certain dayes after hir imprisonment, hir Gaoler came in, and sayd vnto hir: "Madame I do aduise you henceforth to consider vpon your conscience, for so much as I suppose that euen this very day your life shall be taken from you." I leaue for you to thinke what horrour and traunce assailed the feeble heart of this pore Lady, and with what eares she receiued those cruell newes, but hir cries and mones together with hir sighes and lamentations, declared with what cheere she receiued that aduertisement. "Alas (sayd she) is it possible that my brethren should so farre forget themselues, as for a fact nothing preiudiciall vnto them, cruelly to put to death their innocent sister, and to imbrue the memory of their fact, in the bloud of one which neuer did offend them? Must I against all right and equitie be put to death before the Iudge or Magistrate haue made trial of my life, and known the vnrighteousnesse of my cause? Ah God most righteous, and bountiful father, beholde the malice of my brethren, and the tyrannous crueltie of those which wrongfully doe seeke my

bloud. Is it a sinne to mary ? * Is it a fault to flie and auoide the sinne
of whoredome ? What lawes be these, where mariage bed and ioyned
matrimony is pursued with like seueritie as murder, theft and
aduoutrie ? And what Christianitie in a Cardinall, to shed the bloud
which he ought to defend ? What profession is this, to assaile the innocent by the hie way side and to reue them of lyfe, in place to punish
theeues and murderers ? O Lord God thou art iust, and dost al things
righteousty, I see well that I haue trespassed against thy Maiestie in
some other notorious crime than by mariage : I most humbly therfore
beseeche thee to haue compassion vpon me, and to pardon mine
offences, accepting the confession and repentance of me thine humble
seruaunt for satisfaction of my sinnes, which it pleased thee to wash
away in the precious bloud of thy sonne our Sauior, that being so
purified, I might appere at the holy banket in thy glorious kingdome."
When she had thus finished hir prayer, two or three of the ministers
which had taken hir bisides *Forly*, came in, and sayd vnto hir : "Now
Madame make ready your self to goe to God, for beholde your houre
is come." "Praised be that God (sayd she) for the wealth and woe
which it pleaseth him to send vs. But I beseeche you my friendes to
haue pitie vpon these lyttle children and innocent creatures. ** Let
them not feele the smarte which I am assured my brethren beare
against their poore vnhappie father." "Well well Madame (sayd
they,) we will conuey them to such a place, as they shal not want."
"I also recommend vnto you (quod she) this poore maiden, and entreat hir wel, in consideration of hir good seruice done to the infortunate Duchesse of *Malfi*." As she had ended those woords, the two
Ruffians did put a corde *** about hir neck, and strangled hir. The
mayden seeing the piteous tragedie commensed vpon hir mistresse,
cried out amain, and cursed the cruell malice of those tormenters,
and besought God to be witnesse of the same, and crying out vpon
his diuine Maiestie, she besought him to bend his iudgement against
them which causelesse (being no Magistrates,) **** hadde killed such
innocent creatures. "Reason it is (said one of the tyrants) that thou
be partaker of the ioy of thy mistresse innocencie, sith thou hast bene
so faithfull a minister, and messanger of hir follies." And sodainly
caught hir by the hair of the head, and in stead of a carcanet *****
placed a roape about hir necke. "How now (quod she,) is this the
promised faith which you made vnto my Ladie ?" But those woords
flew into the air with hir soule, in companie of the miserable
Duchesse.

But hearken now the most sorowfull scene of all the tragedie. The

* Is . . . : III. ii. 109–11.   ** I . . . : IV. ii. 203–5.
*** corde: IV. ii. 165.1.   **** causelesse . . . : IV. ii. 298–304.
***** in . . . : IV. ii. 249.

litle children which had seen all the furious game done vpon their mother and hir maide, as nature prouoked them, or as some presage of their mishap led them therunto, kneled vpon their knees before those tyrants, and embracing their legs, wailed in such wise, as I think that any other, except a pitilesse heart spoiled of all humanitie, wold haue had compassion. And impossible it was for them to vnfold the embracements of those innocent creatures, which seemed to fore-think their death by the wilde lokes and countenance of those roi-sters. Wherby I think that needes it must be confessed that nature hath in hir self, and vpon vs imprinted some signe of diuination, and specially at the hour and time of death, in such wise as the very beasts feele some conceits, although they see neither sword nor staffe, and indeuor to auoyde the cruell passage of a thing so fearful, as the separation of two things so neerely vnited, euen the body and soule, which for the motion that chaunceth at the very instant, sheweth how nature is constrained in that monstruous separation, and more than horrible ouerthrow. But who can appease a heart determined to do euil, and hath sworn the death of another forced therunto by some special commaundement? The *Aragon* brethren ment hereby noth-ing else, but to roote out the whole name and race of *Bologna*. And therfore the two ministers of iniquitie did like murder and slaughter vpon those two tender babes, as they committed vpon their mother, not without some motion of horror, for doing of an act so detestable. Behold here how far the crueltie of man extendeth, when it coueteth nothing else but vengeance, and marke what excessiue choler the minde of them produceth, which suffer themselues to be forced and ouerwhelmed with furie. Leaue we apart the crueltie of *Euchrates*, the sonne of the king of *Bactria*, and of *Phraates* the sonne of the *Persian* Prince, of *Timon* of *Athens*, and of an infinite numbre of those which were rulers and gouerners of the Empire of *Rome*: and let vs match with these *Aragon* brethren, one *Vitoldus*, Duke of *Lituania*, the crueltie of whom, constrained his own subiects to hang themselues, for fear least they shold fall into his furious and bloudy hands. We may confesse also these brutal brethren to be more butcherly than euer *Otho* erle of *Monferrato*, and prince of *Vrbin*, was, who caused a yeoman of his chamber to be wrapped in a sheete poudred with sulpher and brimston, and afterwards kindled with a candle, was scalded and consumed to death, * bicause only he waked not at an hour by him apointed. Let vs not excuse them also from some affinity with *Manfredus* the sonne of *Henry* the second Emperor, who smoldered his own father, being an old man, betwene ij. couerleds. These former furies might haue some excuse to couer their crueltie, but these had no other cause but a certain beastly madnesse which

* wrapped . . . : II. v. 66–70.

moued them to kil those litle children their neuews, who by no
meanes could preiudice or anoy the Duke of *Malfi* or his title, in the
succession of his Duchie, the mother hauing withdrawn hir goods,
and was assigned hir dowry: but a wicked hart must needes bring
forth semblable works according to his malice. In the time of these
murders, the infortunate Louer kept himself at *Millan* wyth his
sonne *Frederick*, and vowed himself to the Lord *Siluio Sauello*, who
that time besieged the Castell of *Millan*, in the behalf of *Maximilian
Sforcia*, which in the end he conquered and recouered by composition with the French within. But that charge being atchieued, the
generall *Sauello* marched from thence to *Cremona* with his campe,
whither *Bologna* durst not folow, but repaired to the Marquize of
Bitonte, in which time the *Aragon* brethren so wrought, as his goods
were confiscate at *Naples*, and he driuen to his shifts to vse the golden
Duckates which the Duchesse gaue him to relieue him self at *Millan*,
whose Death althoughe it was aduertised by many, yet hee coulde not
be persuaded to beleue the same, for that diuers which went about to
betray him, and feared he should flie from *Millan*, kept his beake in
the water, (as the Prouerbe is,) and assured him both of the life and
welfare of his spouse, and that shortly his brethren in law wold be
reconciled, bicause that many Noble men fauored him well, and
desired his returne home to his Countrey. * Fed and filled with that
vaine hope, he remained more than a yeare at *Millan*, frequenting the
companie, and well entertained of the richest Marchants and
Gentlemen of the Citie: and aboue all other, he had familiar accesse
to the house of the Ladie *Hippolita Bentiuoglia*, where vpon a day
after dinner, taking his Lute in hand, wheron he could exceedingly
wel play, he began to sing a certain Sonnet, which he had composed
vpon the discourse of his misfortune, the tenor whereof is this.

The song of Antonio Bologna,
the husband of the Duchesse of Malfi.

If loue, the death, or tract of time, haue measured my distresse,
  Or if my beating sórrowes may my languor well expresse:
Then loue come sone to visit me, which most my heart desires,
  And so my dolor findes some ease, through flames of fansies fires.
The time runnes out his rolling course, for to prolong mine ease,
  To thend I shall enjoy my loue, and heart himself appease.
A cruell Darte brings happy death, my soule then rest shall finde:
  And sleping body vnder tombe, shall dreame time out of minde.
And yet the Loue, the time, nor Death, lokes not how I decrease:
  Nor giueth eare to any thing of this my wofull peace.

* diuers . . . : v. i. 1–5 and 71–2.

Full farre I am from my good happe, or halfe the ioy I craue,
　　Wherby I change my state with teares, and draw full nere my graue.
The courteous Gods that giues me life, nowe moues the Planets all:
　　For to arrest my groning ghost, and hence my sprite to call.
Yet from them still I am separd, by things vnequall here,
　　Not ment the Gods may be vniust, that bredes my changing chere.
For they prouide by their foresight, that none shall doe me harme:
　　But she whose blasing beuty bright, hath brought me in a charm
My mistresse hath the powre alone, to rid me from this woe:
　　Whose thrall I am, for whome I die, to whome my sprite shall goe.
Away my soule, go from the griefs, that thee oppresseth still,
　　And let thy dolor witnesse beare, how much I want my will.
For since that loue and death himself, delights in guiltlesse bloud,
　　Let time transport my troubled sprite, where dest'ny semeth good.

His song ended, the poore Gentleman could not forbeare from
pouring forth his luke warme teares, which aboundantly ran downe
his heauie face, and his panting sighes truely discouered the alteration of his mind, which moued eche wight of that assembly to pitie
his mournefull state: and one specially of small acquaintaunce, and
yet knew the deuises which the *Aragon* brethren had trained and con-
spired against him: that unacquainted Gentleman his name was
Delio, one very well learned and of trimme inuention, and very excellently hath endited in the *Italian* vulgar tongue. Who knowing the
Gentleman to be husbande to the deceased Duchesse of *Malfi* came
vnto him, and taking him aside, sayd: "Sir, albeit I haue no great
acquaintance with you, this being the first time that euer I saw you,
to my remembrance, so it is, that vertue hath such force, and maketh
gentle mindes so amorous of their like, as when they doe beholde eche
other, they feele themselues coupled as it were in a bande of minds,
that impossible it is to diuide the same. Now knowing what you be,
and the good and commendable qualities in you, I compte it my
duetie to reueale that which may chaunce to breede you damage.
Know you then, that I of late was in companie with a Noble man of
Naples, which is in this Citie, banded with a certaine companie of
horsemen, who tolde me that hee had a speciall charge to kill you, and
therfore prayed me (as he seemed) to require you not to come in his
sight, to the intent hee might not be constrained to doe that, which
should offende his Conscience, and grieue the same all the dayes of
his life. Moreouer I haue worse tidings to tell you, which are, that the
Duchesse your wife is deade by violent hand in prison, and the moste
parte of them that were in hir companie. Besides this assure your
self, that if you doe not take heede to that which this *Neapolitane* captaine hathe differed, other will doe and execute the same. This much

I haue thought good to tell you, bicause it would verie much grieue me, that a Gentleman so excellent as you be, should be murdered in that miserable wise, and would deeme my selfe vnworthy of life, if knowing these practises I should dissemble the same." Wherunto *Bologna* answered: "Syr *Delio* I am greatly bounde vnto you, and giue you heartie thankes for the good will you beare me. But of the conspiracie of the brethren of *Aragon*, and the death of my Ladie, you be deceyued, and somme haue giuen you wrong intelligence. For within these two dayes I receiued letters from *Naples*, wherein I am aduertised, that the right honorable and reuerende Cardinall and his brother be almost appeased, and that my goodes shall be rendred againe, and my deare wife restored." "Ah syr (sayd *Delio*,) how you be beguiled and fedde with follies, and nourished with sleights of Courte. Assure your self that they which wryte these trifles, make such shamefull sale of you, as the Butcher doeth of his flesh in the shambles, and so wickedly betray you, as impossible it is to inuent a Treason more detestable: but bethinke you well thereof." When he had sayde so, hee tooke his leaue, and ioyned himself in companie of fine and pregnant wittes, there assembled togither. In the meane tyme, the cruell spryte of the *Aragon* brethren were not yet appeased with the former murders, but needes must finish the last acte of *Bologna* his Tragedie by losse of his life, to keepe his wife and Children companie, so well in an other worlde, * as hee was vnited with them in Loue in this fraile and transitorie passage. The *Neapolitan* gentleman before spoken of by *Delio*, which had taken an enterprise to satisfie the barbarous Cardinal, to berieue his Countreyman of life, hauing changed his minde, and differing from day to day to sorte the same to effect, which hee had taken in hande, it chaunced that a *Lombarde* of larger conscience than the other, inuegled with Couetousnesse, and hired for readie money, practised the death of the Duchesse pore husband. This bloudy beast was called *Daniel de Bozola* that had charge of a certaine bande of footemen in *Millan*. This newe *Iudas* and assured manqueller, within certaine dayes after, knowing that *Bologna* oftentimes repaired to heare seruice at the Church ** and couent of *S. Fraunces*, secretly conueyed himself in ambush, hard bisides the church of *S. Iames* whether he came, (being accompanied with a certaine troupe of souldioures) to assaile the infortunate *Bologna*, who was sooner slaine than hee was able to thinke vpon defense, and whose mishap was such, that he which killed him had good leisure to saue himself by reason of the little pursuite made after him. Beholde heere the Noble facte of a Cardinall, and what sauer it hath of Christian puritie, to commit a slaughter for a facte

* keepe . . . : III. v. 71–2 and IV. ii. 18–19 and 211–12.
** knowing . . . : V. ii. 132–5.

done many yeares past vpon a poore Gentleman which neuer thought him hurte. Is this the sweete obseruation of the Apostles, of whom they vaunt themselues to be the successors and folowers ? And yet we cannot finde nor reade, that the Apostles, or those that stept in their trace, hired Ruffians and Murderers to cut the throtes of them which did them hurt. But what ? It was in the time of *Iulius* the second, who was more marshall than christian, and loued better to shed bloud than giue blessing to the people. Such ende had the infortunate mariage of him, which ought to haue contented himself with that degree and honor that hee had acquired by his deedes and glory of his vertues, so much by eche wight recommended. We ought neuer to clime higher than our force permitteth, ne yet surmount the bounds of duety, and lesse suffer our selues to be haled fondly forth with desire of brutal sensualitie. The sinne being of such nature, that hee neuer giueth ouer the partie whome he mastereth, vntil he hath brought him to the shame of some Notable follie. You see the miserable discourse of a Princesse loue, that was not very wise, and of a gentleman that had forgotten his estate, which ought to serue for a loking glasse to them which be ouer hardie in making of enterprises, and doe not measure their abilitie with the greatnesse of their attemptes: where they ought to maintaine themselues in reputation, and beare the title of wel aduised: foreseeing their ruine to be example to all posteritie, as may be seene by the death of *Bologna*, and of all them which sprang of him, and of his infortunate spouse his Ladie and mistresse.

But we haue discoursed inoughe hereof, sith diuersitie of other Histories doe call vs to bring the same in place, which were not much more happie than those, whose Historie ye haue already tasted.

Collation

p. 178, l. 14. she vsed] *A;* and vpon hys repaire vsed *B.*
p. 179, l. 11. is of that stock] *A;* is the paragon of . . . *B.*
p. 182, ll. 19–20. vertuous image] *A;* vnspotted Image *B.*
p. 182, ll. 24–5. diuine beautie] *A;* pereles beauty *B.*
p. 184, l. 3. masse of earth] *B;* mosse of . . . *A.*
p. 186, ll. 29–30. fable of the people] *A;* Fable of the Worlde *B.*
p. 188, l. 31. *Aragon* brothers would] *B; Aragon* brother would *A.*
p. 189, l. 26. honest report] *B;* honest port *A.*
p. 190, l. 32. espials round about] *B;* espial round . . . *A.*
p. 191, l. 33. the things were discouered] *A;* our affaires were . . . *B.*
p. 192, l. 30. And this was] *B;* And thus was *A.*
p. 193, l. 14. rent vpon hir landes] *B;* . . . his landes *A.*
p. 194, l. 3. is it the thought] *B;* was it . . . *A.*
p. 194, l. 28. doubt of my greatnesse] *A;* . . . my beynge wyth Chylde *B.*
p. 195, ll. 16–17. foolish names of honor] *A;* Names . . . *B.*

p. 195, ll. 26–7. ministers of hir follie] *A;* shadowes of . . . *B.*

p. 199, ll. 8–9. coniectured how grieuously] *B;* considered how . . . *A.*

p. 199, ll. 10–11. yelled forth] *A;* yalped forth *B.*

p. 199, l. 21. deepest things] *B;* deepest thing *A.*

p. 199, l. 37. filthy embracements] *A;* Lecherous loue *B.*

p. 201, l. 34. in a place to rescue] *A;* where he thought to . . . *B.*

p. 203, l. 6. and to reue them of lyfe] *B; not in A.*

p. 206, l. 19. small acquaintaunce] *A;* no acquaintance *B.*

p. 207, l. 33. assured manqueller] *A;* pestilent manqueller *B.*

APPENDIX II

'O, let us howl, some heavy note'
(IV. ii. 61–72)

Commentary and Transcription by
David Greer

The music for this song survives in three seventeenth-century manuscripts:

- A. New York Public Library, Drexel MS. 4175, No. 42 (c. 1620–30; with lute accompaniment).[1]
- B. British Museum, Add. MS. 29481, ff. 5ᵛ–6 (c. 1630; vocal part only, with elaborate embellishments).
- C. New York Public Library, Drexel MS. 4041, Pt II, No. 26 (c. 1650; with thorough-bass accompaniment).

In sources A and B it is unattributed, but in C Robert Johnson (c. 1582 ?–1633) is cited as the composer; this is almost certainly correct. The three sources present numerous variants in the music, but A and B are in substantial agreement, whereas C seems to be a later version, in which (amongst other revisions) the chromatic inflections on 'howl' have been eliminated. The lute part of A is rather unsatisfactory in that, besides containing several obvious scribal errors, it is extremely scanty in places. Nevertheless, because of its date, and because its vocal line is in general agreement with B, this version has been chosen for transcription here, as presenting the music as it was probably performed in the first productions of the play.[2]

In this transcription an E♭ has been added to the key-signature, the note-values have been halved, and slurs and regular barring inserted.

[1] According to the table of contents this manuscript originally contained another setting of 'O, let us howl' (No. 4), but this is now missing. See John P. Cutts, ' "Songs vnto the Violl and Lute"—Drexel MS. 4175', *Musica Disciplina*, xvi (1962), pp. 73–92.

[2] For other transcriptions see John P. Cutts, *La Musique de Scène de la Troupe de Shakespeare*, Paris, 1959, pp. 40–5 (versions *A*, *B*, & *C*), and Ian Spink, *Robert Johnson: Ayres, Songs and Dialogues* (*The English Lute-Songs*, 2nd Series, xvii), London, 1961, pp. 32–3 (version *C*).

Some notes have been added to the original accompaniment to fill out the texture; such additions are indicated by small notation. All other alterations and corrections are listed below. The text of this Revels Plays edition is used here; the following variants occur in the three manuscripts:

> throat] throats *A*.   Of beasts, and] Of beasts or *C*.   fowl] fowls *A*.   bill] bell *A, B*.   have cloy'd your] hath cloy'd our *A, B, C*.   your hearts] our hearts *A, B, C*.   love] peace *A, B*.

Stylistically, 'O, let us howl, some heavy note' is an example of the declamatory type of song which developed in England in the second decade of the seventeenth century. Apart from the sinister inflections on 'howl' noted above, other features appropriate to a 'mad song' may be observed, such as the wayward harmonic twist in bars 5–6 and the wide leaps in bars 7–9.

O, let us howl ————, some hea-vy note, Some deadly dogged howl-,

Sounding as from the threat-'ning throat Of beasts, and fat - al

fowl! As ra-vens, screech-owls, bulls, and bears, We'll bill and bawl

our parts, Till · irk-some noise have cloy'd your

EMENDATIONS TO *A*

The first number refers to the bar; V = voice, Au = accompaniment
(upper stave), Al = accompaniment (lower stave); the second number indicates the note or chord within the bar, excluding rests and
editorial additions. As in the transcription, note-values are halved.

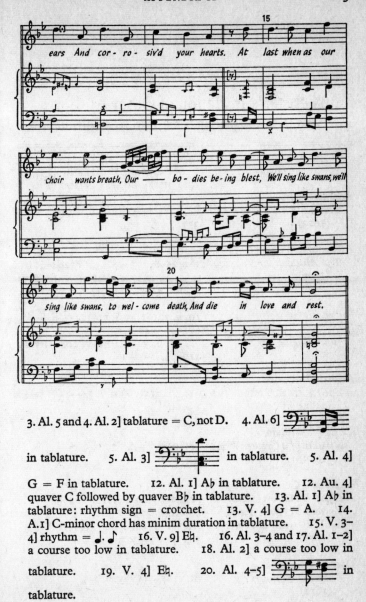

3. Al. 5 and 4. Al. 2] tablature = C, not D.   4. Al. 6]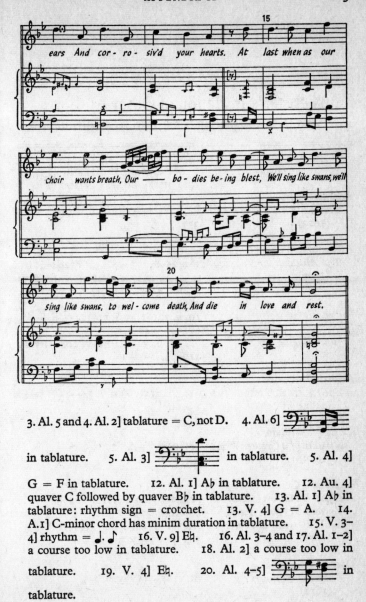

in tablature.   5. Al. 3] in tablature.   5. Al. 4]

G = F in tablature.   12. Al. 1] A♭ in tablature.   12. Au. 4]
quaver C followed by quaver B♭ in tablature.   13. Al. 1] A♭ in
tablature: rhythm sign = crotchet.   13. V. 4] G = A.   14.
A.1] C-minor chord has minim duration in tablature.   15. V. 3–
4] rhythm = ♩. ♪   16. V. 9] E♮.   16. Al. 3–4 and 17. Al. 1–2]
a course too low in tablature.   18. Al. 2] a course too low in
tablature.   19. V. 4] E♮.   20. Al. 4–5] in

tablature.

Webster's Imitation of Other Authors;
an index to passages cited in this edition

AUTHOR	CORRESPONDING PASSAGES IN 'THE DUCHESS OF MALFI'
Adams, Thomas	
The Gallant's Burden (1612)	(?) I. i. 49–52; III. ii. 323–5; V. ii. 327.
Alexander, William	
The Alexandrean Tragedy (1607)	I. i. 25–8, 173–7, 209, (?) 264–6; III. i. 52–4; III. iv. 44; III. v. 50–1, 96–7; IV. ii. 144–5, 225; (?) V. i. 23; V. iii. 56–8.
Croesus (1604)	III. ii. 321–2; IV. i. 11–12; IV. ii. 8–10; (?) V. ii. 348–9.
Julius Caesar (1607)	(?) III. ii. 34–42; III. v. 108–9; V. ii. 119–20.
Ariosto, Ludovico	
Satires, tr. R. Tofte (1608)	(?) I. i. 313; (?) II. i. 34–7; (?) IV. ii. 13–14.
Camden, William	
Remains of a Greater Work (1605)	(?) III. v. 35–6.
Chapman, George	
Bussy D'Ambois (1604)	(?) I. i. 158–9; (?) IV. i. 102–3.
Byron's Tragedy (1608)	(?) III. ii. 323–5.
Seven Penitential Psalms (1612)	I. i. 181–2; III. iii. 62–4; (?) IV. i. 102–3; V. ii. 299–301.
Donne, John	
The First Anniversary (1611)	III. v. 82–3; (?) V. ii. 111.

Ignatius his Conclave (1611)   (?) II. iv. 16–19; III. i. 31–5; III. v. 39–40.

Progress of the Soul (1612)   (?) I. i. 201–3; III. v. 105–6; (?) IV. ii. 39–43.

Elyot, Sir Thomas
   The Image of Governance (1541)   (?) I. i. 5–15, 398–403.

Goulart, Simon
   Admirable Histories, tr. E. Grimeston (1607)   v. ii. 5–19, 90–4.

Guazzo, Stefano
   Civil Conversation, tr. G. Pettie (1581)   I. i. 190–205; (?) III. ii. 137–9.

Guevara, Antonio de
   The Dial of Princes, tr. T. North (1557)   (?) IV. ii. 306–7.

Hall, Joseph
   Characters (1608)   I. i. (?) 163–6, (?) 171–2, 184–5, (?) 416, 438–40, (?) 451–2; (?) II. v. 37–8; (?) IV. i. 32–3.

   Epistles (1611)   I. i. (?) 37–8, (?) 242–3, (?) 438–40; III. v. 120–1; IV. ii. 261; V. ii. 305–6; V. iv. 67–8.

Jonson, Benjamin
   The Masque of Queens (1609)   III. ii. 254.

   Sejanus (1605)   III. v. 97–8.

Marston, John
   The Dutch Courtezan (1605)   (?) IV. ii. 18–19.

Matthieu, Pierre
   Henry IV, tr. E. Grimeston (1612)   III. ii. 122–33, 238–40; III. iii. 41–7; III. v. 12–17.

   Louis XI, tr. E. Grimeston (1614)   (?) II. v. 32–3.

Matthieu, Pierre (*cont.*)

'Supplement', Jean de   IV. i. 16–17, 36–8; IV. ii. 27–30; V. iii.
  Serres, *General Inven-*   48–9.
  tory, tr. E. Grimeston
  (1607)

Montaigne, Michel de
  Essays, tr. J. Florio (1603)   I. i. (?) 31–2, 42–4, (?) 59–60; II. i.
    (?) 26–8, 78–81, 89–90, (?) 99–101,
    101–7, (?) 118–19, (?) 144–5; II. ii.
    23–4, (?) 75–9; III. iv. 40–2; (?) IV. ii.
    118–20; V. i. (?) 43–6, (?) 74; V. iii.
    9–11, 50; V. v. 75.

Nashe, Thomas
  Christ's Tears (1593)   V. v. 72–3.
  The Unfortunate Traveller   II. ii. 36–48; (?) IV. ii. 262–3.
    (1594)

Overbury, Thomas
  The Wife and   Ded., 13–14; (?) I. i. 339–40; (?) V. ii.
    Characters (1614)   228.

Painter, William
  The Palace of Pleasure   I. i. 16–22, (?) 93–104; (?) III. v. 7–9.
    (1567)   [See also echoes noted in footnotes to
     App. I.]

Sidney, Sir Philip
  Arcadia (1590)   III. ii. 61–2, 70–1, 72–5, 77–81, 84–5,
     255, 259–60, (?) 262–5, 270–3; III.
     v. (?) 18–19, (?) 71–2, (?) 78–81,
     111–13; IV. i. 3–8, 12–15, 84–90,
     92–4; IV. ii. 31–2, (?) 35–6, 329–33,
     363–4; V. ii. 30–1, (?) 133–4, 167–8,
     170–2, 174–5, 175–7, 193–6, 218–21,
     235–41, (?) 263–4, 287–8, (?) 297–8,
     330–2, 344–5; V. iv. 27–8; V. v. 9–10,
     42–4, (?) 99–100, 100–2, 118–19.
  Astrophel and Stella (1591)   III. v. 76–7.

Whetstone, George
  An Heptameron of Civil   I. i. 56–7, (?) 298–9; III. ii. 24–32;
    Discourses (1582)   (?) IV. i. 77–9; V. v. 56–8.

Glossarial Index to the Annotations

An asterisk indicates that the annotation referred to contains information as to sense or usage not provided by *The Oxford English Dictionary*. When a gloss is repeated in the annotations, only the first occurrence is indexed.

Adamant, *sb.*, III. v. 54, v. ii. 261
adventure, III. v. 98
affect, *vb*, I. i. 395
anatomy, V. ii. 78–80
angel, I. i. 263–4
answer, *vb*, Commendatory Verses, 27
apparently, II. i. 150
apparition, III. ii. 142
arm, *vb*, V. ii. 166
arras, III. ii. 60
ascendant, lord of the, II. i. 96
atheist, I. i. 162
atonement, IV. ii. 353
attainted, II. v. 23

Balsamum, II. v. 24
band, *sb.*, II. i. 5
basilisk, III. ii. 86–7
*bear up, V. ii. 336
bell, *vb*, IV. ii. 66
benefit, V. iv. 49
bill, *sb.*, III. ii. 172–3
*bill, *vb*, IV. ii. 66
biter, V. ii. 341
blanch, III. v. 24
blood, I. i. 297, V. ii. 336, 342
book, by the, III. iii. 21
bottom, *sb.*, III. v. 59–60
bring, I. i. 223
broker, IV. ii. 57
brook, *vb*, III. ii. 183
bullet, III. ii. 115
bunting, III. v. 5

Cabinet, II. ii. 54

calling, V. i. 73
candy, *vb*, I. i. 275–6
cap and knee, with, III. ii. 5
caroche, I. i. 223
carry coals, II. v. 45
case, *vb*, I. i. 207
cassia, II. iv. 64
catarrh, IV. ii. 208
caterpillar, I. i. 49–52
censure, *vb*, III. i. 27
chargeable, I. i. 333
cheat, in, V. i. 6
chipping, III. ii. 224
chirurgeon, I. i. 111–12
choler, II. v. 12–13
circumference, I. i. 469
civil, V. ii. 60
clear, *adj.*, Dedication, 11–12
coal-pit, II. v. 67
cod-piece, II. ii. 36–48
colour, II. i. 168
combust, II. iii. 56–64
come to one's answer, IV. ii. 245
compass, out of, I. i. 137
competent, IV. ii. 183
complimental, I. i. 277
conceit, I. i. 494, II. iii. 34
conduct, *sb.*, Dedication, 9
consort, *sb.*, IV. ii. 1
cords of life, IV. ii. 354
corrosive, *sb.*, IV. ii. 94
corrosive, *vb*, IV. ii. 68
costive, IV. ii. 113
coulter, III. i. 56–7
couple, *sb.*, I. i. 389
course, *sb.*, III. iv. 20

217

court-gall, I. i. 23
cousin-german, II. i. 97
credit, *sb.*, V. v. 68
crow, *sb.*, I. i. 49–52
cullis, II. iv. 66
cupping-glass, II. v. 25
curious, III. ii. 293, IV. i. 112–14

Dagger, IV. i. 90
*dainty, *sb.*, II. i. 142–3
*dark lantern, II. iii. 0.1
dead, V. ii. 338
dejection, IV. ii. 375
determine of, III. iv. 29
directly, III. i. 25, IV. i. 58
discourse, *sb.*, III. ii. 255
disease, V. iii. 17–19
disembogue, II. i. 31–2
*dish, feed in a lord's, I. i. 283
dismal, III. v. 108–9
dispose, IV. ii. 371
dog-days, I. i. 39
dog-fish, III. v. 126
draw a weapon, I. i. 112–14

Eaves of night, I. i. 318
effect, *sb.*, IV. ii. 163
engine, I. i. 314, III. ii. 293
enginous, III. ii. 176–7
envious, I. i. 27
equal, V. ii. 282, V. v. 40
estate, IV. ii. 363–4
execute, I. i. 323

Familiar, *sb.*, I. i. 259
fantastical, IV. ii. 126
fetch a frisk, V. ii. 73
fig, Spanish, II. iii. 31
fighting, I. i. 105
figure, *sb.*, II. ii. 86
fin, II. i. 65
*flash, *sb.*, I. i. 156
footcloth, II. i. 42
footstep, I. i. 343
force, *vb.*, I. i. 488
forfeit a bond, III. ii. 168–70
*form, *sb.*, I. i. 156
formal, I. i. 3
**freeze, II. iii. 6, V. ii. 143

frenzy, V. i. 59
friend, III. ii. 29
frisk, V. ii. 73
frost-nailed, V. ii. 333–4

Gall, I. i. 23
galliard, I. i. 196
general, II. v. 79
general, in, I. i. 13
geometry, to hang by, I. i. 61
ghastly, V. v. 8
glass, IV. ii. 98
glass-house, II. ii. 7
gossip, *sb.*, III. ii. 68
grain, IV. ii. 55
guarded, III. iii. 33–4

Habit, I. i. 3
hand to, set, II. iii. 41
happily, II. v. 42
haunt, *vb.*, I. i. 29
high, I. i. 297
*hilts, loose in the, II. v. 3
honey-dew, I. i. 307
*honour of arms, V. v. 49
horse-leech, I. i. 53
how ever, V. i. 75
howling, V. v. 13
humorous, I. i. 499
husband, I. i. 366

*Ice-pavement, V. ii. 333–4
imposthume, IV. ii. 39–43
information, I. i. 173–7
ingenious, I. i. 355
intelligencer, I. i. 162

Jealous, I. i. 159
jealously, II. iv. 25
jennet, I. i. 116

Kissing-comfits, V. ii. 162
knave in grain, IV. ii. 55

Lamprey, I. i. 336
lay, IV. ii. 93
lay out, IV. ii. 236–7
leaguer, I. i. 221
lenitive, III. i. 75

let, *vb*, III. ii. 183
leveret, V. v. 45
lift up one's nose, III. iii. 52–3
liver, I. i. 298
*look up, Dedication, 13
*loose in the hilts, II. v. 3
luxurious, I. i. 297

Main, *sb.*, II. i. 2
mandragora, IV. ii. 235
mandrake, II. v. 1–2
measle, II. i. 53–4
melancholy, *sb.*, I. i. 76
misprision, V. iv. 80
mis-rule, lord of, III. ii. 7
mist, IV. ii. 188
model, *sb.*, III. iii. 21
morphewed, II. i. 31–2
mortification, IV. ii. 177
mother, II. i. 117
motion, I. i. 303, III. ii. 40
mummy, IV. ii. 125

Near, *adj.*, V. ii. 24
neat, I. i. 339–40
next, *adj.*, I. i. 244–6
nice, V. ii. 170–2
**night-cap, II. i. 4, 20
night-walker, II. iii. 25
noise, IV. ii. 1

*Open both ways, IV. ii. 221–2
overseer, I. i. 383
owe, IV. i. 50
owl-light, IV. ii. 334–5

Painted, III. ii. 279
palsy, II. v. 55
parcel, II. iii. 67
pare someone's nails, IV. ii. 107
parts, I. i. 473
pass, *sb.*, III. ii. 183, V. iii. 33
pay, *vb*, I. i. 438–40
perspective, IV. ii. 74, 358
perspicuous, Dedication, 28
physical, II. iv. 65
pie, I. i. 49–52
pill, II. i. 115
pistol, II. ii. 40

placket, IV. ii. 103
plastic, II. i. 32–3
play the wirè-drawer, I. i. 206
plot, *sb.*, III. iii. 7
posset, IV. ii. 111
post, *adv.*, I. i. 250
postilion, Dedication, 9
pot-gun, III. iii. 30
pour in bosom, III. i. 52
prattling, *ppl. adj.*, I. i. 423
precise, II. iii. 65
prefer, III. ii. 329
presence, I. i. 83
present, *adj.*, V. ii. 65–6
presently, II. ii. 29
progress, *vb*, I. i. 437
protest against, III. ii. 172–3
prove, III. v. 75
purchase, *sb.*, III. i. 28
purchase, *vb*, II. v. 37–8
put up, I. i. 112–14

Quaint, I. i. 260
quality, IV. i. 112–14
quicken, I. i. 482–4
quietus, I. i. 464
quit of, V. ii. 230

*Radical, II. iii. 22
reel, *vb*, I. i. 120
remove, *sb.*, III. iii. 33–4
reward, *sb.*, I. i. 59
right, III. v. 9
ring, *sb.*, I. i. 88
roaring boys, II. i. 15
rough-cast, II. i. 32–3
roundly, I. i. 330
ruin, *sb.*, II. iii. 37
run on wheels, III. ii. 176–7

Sadness, V. iv. 62
sake, for your, I. i. 369
salvatory, IV. ii. 124
scorpion, II. v. 78
scuttle, *sb.*, III. ii. 247
secretary, V. ii. 232
secular, IV. ii. 45
security, V. ii. 337
seed, IV. ii. 124

seminary, III. ii. 282
serve a turn, II. v. 9
service, II. v. 11, III. iii. 18
set hand to, II. iii. 41
settle, v. ii. 271
shape, sb., IV. i. 3–8
sheep-biter, v. ii. 50–1
shrewd turn, I. i. 181–2
silly, III. v. 102
sledge, quoit the, II. v. 43
smelt, III. v. 132
soap-boiler, IV. ii. 113
sort, sb., III. ii. 237
Spanish fig, II. iii. 31
speculative, III. iii. 47
springal, II. i. 151
stain, vb, I. i. 209
stamp, vb, v. ii. 77–8
stand engaged, III. ii. 168–70
standing, ppl. adj., I. i. 49–52
state, sb., I. i. 5
still, adv., I. i. 482–4
stop your mouth, III. ii. 20
style, vb, v. ii. 126–7
suit, v. iv. 47
sumpter-cloth, III. iii. 33–4
swing, sb., I. i. 64
Switzer, II. ii. 36–48
swoon, II. i. 116

Taffeta, III. iii. 25
take in a blood, IV. ii. 323
take up, III. ii. 168–70
tan, vb, IV. ii. 27–30
tedious, II. i. 114, v. v. 4
tent, sb., I. i. 110

*tetchiness, II. ii. 1
tetter, II. i. 78–81
throughly, v. ii. 83
throw one's cap, IV. ii. 112
tilt, sb., I. i. 120
to-year, II. i. 131
transportation, IV. ii. 56
traverse, sb., IV. i. 55.1
triumph, sb., I. i. 365

Unequal, II. v. 32–3
unjust, III. ii. 158
unkindly, III. v. 74
unvalued, III. ii. 248
use, vb, III. ii. 183

Vapour, IV. i. 91
vaunt-guard, v. v. 48
voluntary, adj., III. iii. 12

Watch, vb, II. iv. 31–2
wheel, IV. i. 81
*whispering-room, I. i. 334
whistler, IV. ii. 179
whole man, II. ii. 79
wild-fire, III. ii. 116
wilful, III. ii. 116–18
will, sb., I. i. 391
wink, vb, I. i. 349
wire-drawer, I. i. 206
woodcock, IV. ii. 88–90
wood-yard, II. ii. 63
words and matter, Commendatory
    Verses, 35–6
worm-seed, IV. ii. 124